HOW & TO COOK IT

JANE HORNBY

A recipe is a bit like a story, with a beginning, middle and, I hope, a happy ending. Whatever has spurred your interest in cooking—perhaps you're leaving home, or simply want to increase your repertoire of home-made nutritious meals—this book will guide you through these first forays into food, and show you how simple it can be to feed your family and friends, create supper from scratch, or bake a cake to be proud of. Within these pages I will show you how to cook your favorite dishes so that they work every time. This is the food that everyone loves to eat, with clear color photographs for each and every step. Every story illustrated, to show you how easy it can be.

Most of us love eating, and will happily reel off a long list of our favorite food. Or, we know what we're in the mood for: Perhaps something with a little spice, some comfort food, or a devilishly chocolaty dessert. But often the inspiration stops there. If you've ever stood aimlessly in the supermarket on a Tuesday evening after work, or wondered what on earth to feed the in-laws on Sunday, you're in good company. These recipes have been inspired by your dilemma of what to put on the table, from quick meals for the weeknight, to smart celebrations. We're taking good food back to basics with 100 delicious dishes that anyone can cook.

Occasions, rather than food groups, define how most of us eat, so that's how this book is structured. With six chapters covering everything from breakfasts to simple dinners to sharing plates, weekend meals, and more, you'll find recipes for friends to share, classic Sunday dinners for the family, indulgent meals for two, easy cakes

and baking, and stunning desserts to wow after dinner. If you're looking for a full menu, there are suggestions at the back (see page 406) and many recipes can be doubled or halved, if those quantities suit you better. Many of the recipes also have variations to try once you've mastered the basics.

I've spent most of my career encouraging people to cook at home, leaving the tricky stuff to someone else. "I'll show you, it's easy!" I often I hear myself saying to friends and family when they ask how to make a smooth white sauce, or why their cake hasn't risen. The best way to learn is by being shown, and then doing it for yourself. With that in mind, every step of every recipe comes with its own color picture, to give you a clear idea of what your food should look like at that stage. Everything has been carefully thought out to make the steps as straightforward as possible, and to replace guessing with knowing, including the details that most cookbooks leave out—that is, the look and feel of what's going on in the dish. How do you know when it's ready? What should you look for? How should it smell? And what happens if it goes wrong? I hope that when you cook from this book, you'll feel as though I'm there with you, pointing you in the right direction. There's nothing tricky to trip you up here, and you won't need any special equipment.

If you feel you don't have time to cook, I hope this book will convince you otherwise, as each recipe has been written in the most time-efficient way. All the preparation, such as chopping vegetables, happens within the recipe method at the most logical point, rather than being hidden in the ingredients list. This is cooking in real time. Crushing the garlic while you soften the onions, for example, makes more sense than preparing everything before you start. It is hard to resist doing all the chopping first, I know. But this is the way experienced cooks do it, because it saves time.

Each recipe begins with a clear photograph of every ingredient in the form you will use it in the kitchen. The quantities in the pictures are the real deal so you know we're both starting from the same point. For the photographs we cooked the recipes exactly as you would at home, using ordinary kitchen equipment. On the subject of shopping, don't worry, I won't assume you'll be at the farmers' market every day. The recipes can be created entirely from the store or supermarket, or by visiting a farmers' market whenever you can. The additional effort and attention that goes into producing good-quality ingredients really shows in the end result. Once you've stocked a basic pantry (see page 14), you'll find that cooking from scratch is not only far more tasty, but also more economical than buying store-bought. There are certain shortcut products that make life easier in a modern kitchen, such as ready-made pastry, but in most cases you'll be making your own.

People often ask what I like to cook at home, usually expecting an outlandish reply. But my answer is always the same: when I'm cooking for friends and family, I like to make something I know everyone will love, that won't stress me out, and that I can be sure will work. That's why I've tested the recipes again and again: the brownies, to get the right ooze and crust; the lasagne, to make sure it has the right richness; and the chicken pot pie, to

make sure it can be pulled straight from the refrigerator when you want to cook it. And, of course, to make sure that the recipes will work every time. I'm not only showing you what to cook and how to cook it, but also the sheer pleasure of sharing the food that you have created.

How to Make the Recipes Work for You

1

Read the recipe from start to finish before you start cooking. This will familiarize you with what's about to happen, and what to look for.

2

Unless you're a confident cook, don't change the ingredients in a recipe—you can always make it again once you're familiar with the basics. If you do have to make substitutions, make sure you swap like for like. Use white sugar for brown sugar, not honey or sweetener, for example. Baking recipes, in particular, have a careful balance of ingredients that shouldn't be scaled up or down.

3

Weigh and measure everything carefully, especially when baking. All spoons are level, unless stated otherwise.

4

Timings and knowing if something is ready are two of the biggest challenges facing new cooks. The preparation time at the start of the recipe will tell you how long you can expect to spend weighing and chopping ingredients, and includes any preliminary cooking, such as preparing a sauce or browning meat for a stew. The cooking time refers to the final stage of cooking. In some cases you'll be at the stove the whole time, such as when making a quick soup. For the recipes with longer cooking times, you'll be able to leave the food to cook and go and do something else. Remember also that ovens and stovetop burners do vary. I use my nose, eyes and ears to tell me what's going on, but I still set a timer in case my mind wanders. As you cook, ask yourself, is it golden? Does it smell good? Is it bubbling in the middle?

5

Always preheat the oven, then keep the door closed; peeking every few minutes will lower the oven temperature and affect the cooking time. It's a good idea to use an oven thermometer to check that your oven is correctly calibrated.

6

Take note of the instructions alongside each ingredient. Softened butter should be very soft, almost like mayonnaise. Red meat should be allowed to come up to room temperature before it is cooked, or your cooking times won't tally with mine. Eggs should also be at room temperature before being used.

7

Where possible, I've tried to minimize the amount of chopping required by simply slicing instead. There are photographs at the back of the book (see page 410) that illustrate exactly what "finely chopped" and all of those other terms really mean.

8

Taste as you go. Good cooks are constantly tasting their food and are aware of what's happening in their saucepans. It's the only way you'll know if the sauce is seasoned enough, or reduced enough, or spicy enough.

9

Warm your plates in the oven when serving hot food, especially something with sauce or gravy.

10

Unless otherwise specified, all herbs are fresh; all pepper is freshly ground black pepper; all salt is flaky sea salt; eggs and vegetables are medium-size (medium eggs weigh about 2¾ oz); and milk is reduced fat (2 percent).

Kitchen Equipment

This is the essential kitchen equipment you'll need for the recipes in this book.

Cutting boards

You'll need two boards: one for raw food and one for cooked. Plastic boards are hard-wearing and easier to clean. If you prefer wooden boards, choose a good-quality wood. Don't leave it soaking in water, or the wood may split. Wooden boards hold odors more readily, so I keep one side for smelly food and one for non-smelly. To stop it slipping, dampen some paper towels and put them under the board.

Knives

You'll only need a few knives for the recipes here. First, a chef's knife with a blade of about 8 inches, but this will depend on your own size—ask in a kitchen store for advice. Choose one that feels comfortable in your hand, not too light or heavy, and that can be rocked on its blade to allow you to chop in one swift movement. Next, a knife with a blade about 4 inches long is useful for smaller jobs. A small serrated knife will be handy when chopping soft fruit or trimming pastry. Finally, a bread knife, and a palette knife or frosting spatula, which is good for getting underneath cookies and other delicate things without damaging them. Blunt knives are dangerous because they're more likely to slip, so keep knives sharp using a steel or a sharpening tool.

A set of bowls

One large, medium, and small bowl for mixing. Pyrex bowls are good because they can withstand heat and their depth prevents splashes.

Pans

You'll need small, medium, and large saucepans. The large one should be deep enough for boiling plenty of water for pasta or potatoes. Also, a large frying pan, ideally about 9½ inches across, and a ridged broiler pan if you like the chargrilled look. If you're new to cooking, go for nonstick pans, but remember that quality really counts, as you're going to be using them every day. Look for pans with a thick base, which will conduct heat evenly. Choose pans with heatproof handles and lids so that you can put them under the broiler or in the oven. Glass lids are great, as you can see what's happening inside without losing heat.

Stovetop-to-oven pan

Perhaps the most useful pan of all is a large casserole that can go on the stovetop and into the oven. Make sure the handles are ovenproof. A nonstick interior is helpful but not essential. Take extra care with cast-iron pans, as the metal conducts heat very quickly and stays hot for a long time.

Roasting pans

Choose the sturdiest roasting pans you can find, as thin pans can warp when used directly on the stovetop or in the oven at high temperatures. You'll need a large one with fairly tall sides. A small one is also useful for smaller pieces of meat, as the juices will evaporate less.

Baking trays, sheets & pans

A large baking tray with a lip of about 1¼ inches is useful, as is a baking sheet with a lip along one edge only. For these recipes I have also used a standard 2-pound loaf pan measuring 8 × 4 inches; a fluted 9-inch tart pan; a 12-hole muffin pan; 11 × 7-inch baking pan; two shallow 8-inch loose-bottomed cake pans; and a 9-inch pie pan.

Baking dishes

A couple of good quality, ceramic baking dishes (also known sometimes as oven-to-tableware) will come in extremely useful, either for cooking recipes such as lasagne, or to use as serving dishes for sides and salads. Go for dishes with handles, if you can.

Measuring cups & spoons

Two-cup and four-cup measuring cups, ideally in heatproof glass, are useful for measuring liquids. If you have to choose just one, the two-cup one is more useful for measuring small quantities, and you can always refill it. For measuring non-liquid ingredients, metal or plastic spoons and cups are fine. I always take mine off the string they come on to avoid washing the whole set when I've only used one. Some spoons are too large to fit into the necks of small jars, so buy a set of narrow spoons if you can find them.

Food processor

A food processor will save a lot of time, as it can chop, grind, and mix much more quickly than even the fastest cook. They are particularly good for making pastry, as the blades keep dough cool and won't overwork the flour, guaranteeing you a tender crust. Choose a straightforward processor with a good-sized bowl. Don't worry about buying one with lots of attachments; you'll hardly ever use them.

Hand-held electric beaters

These are a must-have for baking. They add air and lightness to cake mixes, whip cream quickly, and can beat out lumps. You may prefer to use a stand mixer instead, although these are much more expensive.

Other useful equipment

a box grater with coarse and fine sides (or invest in a microplane grater, which is ideal for grating citrus fruit zest)
a pastry brush
a rolling pin
a lemon juicer
a ladle
a potato masher or ricer
some wooden spoons
a rubber spatula
a vegetable peeler
pie weights
a wire cooling rack
a balloon whisk
a sieve
a colander
a spatula/turner
some baking parchment paper

Ovens

Familiarize yourself with your oven. Does it have conventional heat, in other words a heating element at the top and bottom of the oven, or is it a fan-assisted convection oven?

Conventional electric ovens

These are hotter at the top and bottom, closer to the elements, so it's best to bake cakes and roast large cuts of meat in the middle to make sure you don't burn the tops. Put things that you want to brown or crisp up a little more, such as roast potatoes, in the top third.

Fan-assisted convection ovens

The oven temperatures in this book are for conventional ovens. In most cases, you should set the temperature of a convection oven 25 degrees lower than that of a conventional oven, but the cooking time is the same. This is because convection ovens cook food more quickly, as the hot air circulates around the food. However, do check your oven's instructions, as models vary and some temperature displays do the adjustment automatically for you. The heat from a convection oven is even, so it doesn't matter where you put the food. Convection ovens tend to need less time to preheat.

Gas ovens

These have roughly three zones of heat, the bottom being the coolest, and the top the hottest. Cook anything that needs to be browned in the top third of the oven, cakes and roasts in the middle, and anything that needs gentle cooking at the bottom.

Ingredients & Shopping

All the ingredients in this book are available from major grocery stores, but it's a good idea to try your local markets and retailers and find out what's in season. Your local butcher and fish supplier are there to help, so don't be daunted. Tell them you're new to cooking and they'll relish the opportunity to share their knowledge, hints, and tips. Spend whatever you can afford on meat and eggs—you'll notice the difference.

Meat

Your butcher will trim and roll meat for you, and often give tips about how to cook it, as well as giving you the bones for making stock, if you'd like to try it. Choose meat that comes from a traceable source and has been reared to high standards of health and welfare, and free-range or organically produced meat and poultry if you can—you'll be rewarded with meat of far superior flavor and texture. Look for red meat that's well marbled with fat, has a natural-looking color (not grey and not an unnaturally bright red), and a slight sheen, but not slimy. Bones should be white tinged with blueish-pink. Poultry should look as fresh as possible, without any discoloration on the skin or any bad smell. Again, choose the best you can afford.

Fish

Fish suppliers will scale, fillet and clean any fish, and should have a good range of seafood, either fresh or frozen, depending on where you live and the season. I know it can be hard to remember which fish is or isn't from endangered stocks. The best advice is to pick fish that is labeled as sustainably caught, and be prepared to try a new fish at your fish supplier's recommendation. Look for bright-eyed whole fish, with shiny scales, gills that are very red inside, and no fishy smell. Buying fillets can be trickier because

the key indicators of freshness (the eyes and gills) have been removed. Look for firmness, shiny scales, and sparkling, smooth flesh. Reject anything that looks dull, feels soft, or smells overly fishy.

It's harder to detect freshness with seafood such as mussels and clams, but again use your nose as a guide; it'll soon tell you what to avoid. Sometimes frozen fish and seafood can be fresher than that labeled as fresh. This is because it is frozen at sea and has had less time to deteriorate.

Eggs

Choose free-range eggs, or organic if you can afford it; the flavor is superior to that of factory and barn eggs, and the hens will have led happier lives.

Fruit & vegetables

Shopping at the farmers' market allows you to shop "greener," reducing the number of food miles the food has traveled. Often there's a chance to try interesting varieties of fruit and vegetables that you just won't find in the supermarket, because they aren't grown in the quantities that the big chains demand. I always choose fruit or vegetables that feel heavy for their size.

Wash all fruit and vegetables well before using them, since even if they look clean they can harbor small bits of grit or agricultural residues. Trim away any tough outer leaves, and peel potatoes, carrots, and other root vegetables if you like. Many vitamins and nutrients lie just beneath the skin of fruit and veg, so don't peel down too far (or leave the skins on and scrub them with a good stiff brush if you'd prefer).

Storage

Meat and poultry should be kept chilled for no more than 3 days, and stored at the bottom of the refrigerator so as to avoid any drips contaminating food below. If you want to freeze meat, poultry, or fish for later, wrap it well and freeze on the day of purchase. It's best to use it within a month. Frozen meat and fish should be defrosted in the refrigerator overnight, on a tray or large plate to catch any juices. Unless using frozen, try and buy fish and seafood on the day you want to cook it.

Eggs also need to be kept in the refrigerator, and will last for up to three weeks. Keep them away from strong-smelling foods, as they absorb odors easily.

Fresh herbs should be chilled. A great way to preserve them for up to a week is to wrap bunches in a damp paper towel, then seal in a food bag or container.

Salad leaves will keep for a couple of days if you're lucky—make sure you use the crisper drawers at the bottom of the refrigerator, and buy only the amount you need rather than buying in bulk.

Keep fruit and vegetables in the refrigerator, unless they need to ripen. A couple of exceptions to the rule are bananas, tomatoes (unless you're not planning to eat them for a few days), and avocados. Take fruit out of the refrigerator at least an hour before you want to eat it, as the cold will affect the flavor and texture. I also think that citrus fruit are easier to squeeze from room temperature.

Dairy products should be stored with care. It's best to check the label, but generally, milk, yogurts, soft cheeses, and cream will keep for about a week. If you're going to eat them as a separate course, most cheeses are much better served at room temperature.

Sell-by & use-by dates
The manufacturer's use-by date is the one to take notice of. The sell-by date is for the retailer—the food is usually fine to eat until the use-by date expires.

The Basic Pantry

A well-stocked pantry is the foundation of good cooking. By building up a collection, you'll gradually reduce the amount of shopping you'll need to do, eventually only shopping for fresh ingredients.

Oils & butter
Keep a bottle of light olive oil for general cooking, extra-virgin olive oil for dressing and finishing a dish, and sunflower or vegetable oil. The latter have little flavor and a high burning point, which makes them excellent for frying. Unsalted butter is best for cooking, as you can then determine the level of salt in your dish according to your taste.

Canned food
Legumes or vegetables from a can will often form the base of a healthy, economical meal. Start with lima beans, red kidney beans, and chopped plum tomatoes.

Pasta, noodles, lentils & dried beans
All of these will last almost indefinitely. For pasta, start out with one long shape, such as spaghetti, and one short, such as penne. Most pasta shapes can be substituted for one another.

Flours
Use corn starch for thickening, all-purpose flour for pastry (and countless other uses), and self-rising flour for baking.

Ground or whole spices
Ground or whole cumin seeds, coriander, turmeric, chili, paprika (both smoked and ordinary), cinnamon, nutmeg, and ginger are all regulars in this book. Try to buy spices in small quantities, as they lose their potency after a couple of months, and store them in a cool, dark place.

Dried herbs

When fresh herbs aren't available, some dried herbs are useful. I use oregano, thyme, and dried mixed herbs most often. Use one teaspoon dried herbs to every small bunch of fresh where they can reasonably be substituted, such as in long, slow cooking. Dried rosemary instead of fresh would be fine in a casserole, but dried parsley wouldn't be right for a Greek salad.

Sugars & honey

Choose unrefined sugars for the best flavor. Fine granulated sugar can be used for most recipes. The most useful honey is the runny, clear type that can be measured from a squeeze bottle.

Dried fruit, nuts & seeds

Look for plump dried fruit. Good-quality brands of raisins tend to have fewer of the little crunchy stalks. Nuts, especially ground nuts, can turn rancid within months, so don't stock up too much.

Mustards

Wholegrain mustard and Dijon are the most useful for cooking and have a gentle, rounded flavor. English mustard is more fiery.

Garlic

Choose garlic with tight, papery, and unblemished skin. I always go for bulbs with larger cloves.

Cheese

A block of Parmesan or other hard cheese is useful for emergencies.

Anchovies & capers

I prefer anchovies in oil and capers in brine, as they don't need to be rinsed before use, unlike those packed in salt.

Flavored oils

Sesame oil adds a hint of nutty flavor to stir-fries and steamed greens, and walnut oil gives a wonderful edge to salad dressings.

Salt & pepper

I like to use kosher salt, and to grind my own black pepper when I need it, to get as much heat and flavor as possible.

Dried chili flakes

These are quicker to use than chopping a whole chile (when that fresh flavor isn't so important) and can be sprinkled over food after cooking.

Vinegars

Choose a bottle of good-quality white- or red-wine vinegar—it will last for months and give your salad dressings and sauces a wonderful piquancy.

Bouillon cubes

The better the stock or broth, the better the end result for your dish. That said, broth made by dissolving a bouillon cube or powder in hot water is perfectly fine for adding to most recipes. Concentrated liquid stocks will give a better result, but if you can, use good quality ready-made liquid stock (or even homemade) for meat gravies. This kind of stock will give your gravy great texture and flavor, as it will contain some of the natural gelatin from the bones from which it was made. If you choose to buy organic meat, then choose organic stock, too.

Others

Worcestershire sauce, tomato puree, and vanilla extract are very useful too, along with harissa or chili paste.

Time-saving ingredients

If you like, do use store-bought pastry for your pecan pie, or buy your bread crumbs ready crumbled. Use a squirt of chili paste instead of chopping one fresh, if you'd prefer. The important thing is that you're cooking!

Berry Smoothie

Preparation time: 5 minutes
Serves 2

Quick, filling and healthy, smoothies make a delicious change from cereal or toast for breakfast. Frozen berries are very convenient—if you only want to use a handful, the rest won't need eating up quickly. To make it with seasonal fresh fruit, try a mix of raspberries and blackberries.

1 ripe medium banana
scant ½ cup frozen summer
    berries, defrosted in the
    refrigerator overnight
⅔ cup plain yogurt
1¼ cups milk
2 tbsp honey

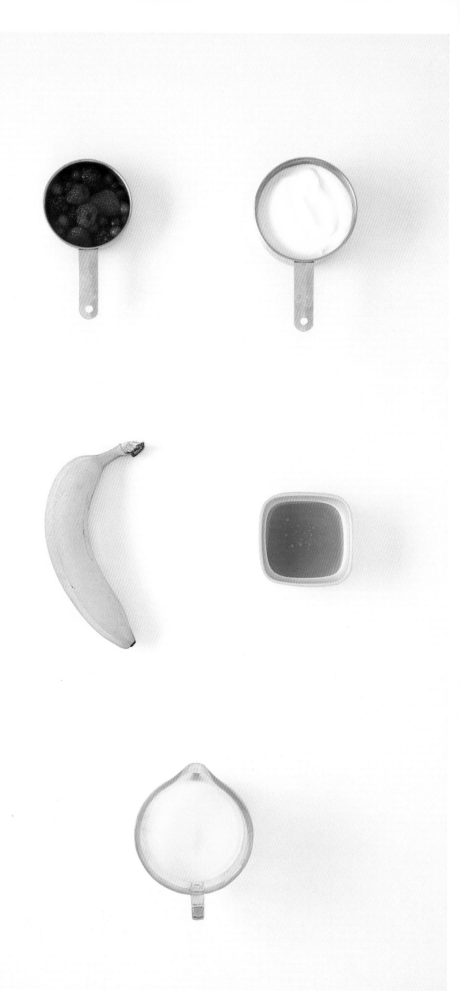

1
Put all of the ingredients into
a blender.

2
Pulse for about 1 minute, until you
have a thick, smooth mixture.

3
Pour into 2 tall glasses and enjoy
immediately.

WHAT KIND OF YOGURT?
Choose a mild, Greek-style yogurt
rather than a plain yogurt, as this
can be a bit sharp in flavor, and can
overpower the fruit.

VARIATION
For a more filling smoothie, try
adding 2 tablespoons steel-cut oats
to the mixture before you blend it.

Cinnamon Rolls

Preparation time: 30 minutes,
plus 1½ hours for rising
Cooking time: 25 minutes
Makes 12

Here's something really worth
getting out of bed for. As with most
dough-based recipes, these sticky
rolls take a little while to put together,
but this recipe cuts out any lengthy
kneading. The rolls are best eaten
warm, so if you want to make
them the night before, follow the tip
on page 22.

scant 4¼ cups all-purpose flour,
    plus extra for shaping the dough
1 tsp kosher salt
¼ cup fine sugar
1 (¼-oz) packet fast-rising yeast
1¼ sticks (⅔ cup) very soft unsalted
    butter, plus extra for the pan
½ cup milk, plus 2 tbsp
    for the icing
2 large eggs
½ tsp vegetable oil
⅓ cup light brown sugar
1 tsp ground cinnamon
⅔ cup raisins, golden raisins,
    or a mixture of both
½ cup pecans
1¼ cups confectioners' sugar

1
Put the flour, salt, fine sugar, and yeast into a large bowl. Melt 4 tablespoons of the butter in a small pan. Take the pan off the heat, then use a fork to beat in the ½ cup milk, and then the eggs.

2
Quickly mix the wet ingredients into the dry, until you have a rough, sticky dough. Cover with plastic wrap, then set it aside for 10 minutes.

3
Sprinkle a little of the flour over your work surface, then scrape the dough out of the bowl onto it.

4
Dust the top of the dough with a little flour. With dry, floured hands, knead the dough into a smooth, springy ball. This should only take 30 seconds or so.

HOW TO KNEAD
Hold the left edge of the dough down with one hand, then grab the farthest edge and push it away from you. Fold the stretched dough back on top of itself, press it down with your palm, give the dough a quarter turn, then repeat. After a few turns the dough will be smooth and elastic. Sprinkle with more flour if the dough sticks.

5
Rub a little oil around the inside of a large bowl, then put the dough into it. Lightly oil a sheet of plastic wrap and cover the bowl. Put the bowl in a warm (not hot) place. After 1 hour, the dough will have doubled in size.

6
Flour the work surface and your hands, then turn the dough out onto it. Press the dough out to a rectangle about 16 × 12 inches using your knuckles and palms.

7

For the filling, spread the remaining soft butter over the dough, then sprinkle with the brown sugar, cinnamon, and raisins. Chop the pecans, and scatter over.

8

Take hold of one of the long sides, then roll the dough around the filling, as though you're rolling up a carpet.

9

Using a sharp knife dipped in a little flour, cut off the very ends of the roll and discard them, then cut the rest of the roll into 12 equal slices.

10

Use a little butter to grease the inside of a baking or roasting pan measuring around 10 × 9 inches. Put the rolls in the pan, cut-sides up, spaced apart.

11

Rub a little vegetable oil over a sheet of plastic wrap, then loosely drape it over the rolls. Leave in a warm place for 30 minutes, or until the dough looks puffy and they have grown together. Preheat the oven to 350°F.

12

Bake the rolls for 25 minutes, until risen and golden. Cool in the pan for 15 minutes, then turn out of the pan and put them onto a cooling rack. Sift the confectioners' sugar into a bowl, then mix with 2 tablespoons milk to make a smooth, runny icing. Spoon it over the rolls while they're still warm.

GETTING AHEAD

Make the dough the day before, then put the rolls into the refrigerator at the end of step 10. They will rise, but at a slower rate. Next day, take them and leave at room temperature for an hour or so or until they have grown together, as in step 11. Bake as before.

Eggs Benedict

Preparation time: 15 minutes
Cooking time: 15 minutes
Serves 2

Start the weekend in style with this classic brunch dish. Hollandaise sauce has a reputation for being difficult, but follow this method and you'll have a rich, smooth sauce without any stress. Look for the carton of eggs with the longest sell-by date: The fresher the egg, the more the white and yolk will cling together as it poaches.

¾ stick (6 tbsp) unsalted butter, plus
    extra for spreading
6 very fresh large eggs
½ tsp plus 1 tbsp white-wine vinegar
½ lemon
1 tsp kosher salt
1 pinch cayenne pepper, plus
    extra to serve
2 English muffins
2 slices cooked ham
salt and pepper

1
First make the hollandaise. Melt the butter in a small saucepan, then keep it bubbling very gently over the lowest heat possible. Meanwhile, bring a pan of water to a gentle simmer.

2
Separate 2 of the eggs (see page 243), putting the yolks into a medium heatproof mixing bowl with ½ teaspoon vinegar. Set the bowl on top of the pan of simmering water, making sure the base of the bowl does not touch the water.

3
Using a hand-held electric mixer, whisk the yolks for about 3 minutes, or until they have thickened and have turned very pale in color. Make sure that the water in the pan is just simmering below, not boiling.

4
Keep whisking, then pour in the warm butter in about 6 batches, whisking well after each addition. Remove the pan from the heat as soon as all the butter has been added. If the sauce splits and turns runny, don't worry: Scrape it into a cold bowl and whisk in a tablespoon of cold water until it comes back together. If that doesn't work, try whisking the split mixture into another egg yolk in a clean bowl.

5
Squeeze the lemon, then stir 1 teaspoon of the juice into the sauce with the cayenne pepper. Season with a little salt and more lemon, if you like. The sauce should have a good balance of richness and tanginess. If it seems too thick, add 2 teaspoons hot water. Cover the surface of the sauce with plastic wrap to prevent a skin forming on the top. It will stay warm over the pan while you poach the eggs.

6

To poach the eggs, half-fill a pan with hot water. Bring to a boil, add 1 teaspoon salt and 1 tablespoon vinegar, then turn the heat down to a very gentle simmer, with a bubble rising to the surface every now and then. Crack 1 egg into a cup. Fill a bowl with hot water and set to one side for later. Using a slotted spoon, stir the water in the pan into a whirlpool.

7

Gently slide the egg from the cup into the middle of the swirling water. Don't worry if it looks messy to begin with—it will become a neater, rounder shape as it spins and cooks.

8

Keep the water at a gentle simmer for 3 minutes, until the white is set and the yolk is still soft. Don't disturb the egg as it cooks. Now use the slotted spoon to carefully lift the egg from the pan and into the bowl of hot water. Poach the remaining eggs and set them aside in the hot water as each one is cooked.

9

Cut the muffins in two, then toast them in the toaster. Put onto plates, then spread with butter. Fold half a piece of ham onto each piece of muffin. Lift an egg out of the water using a slotted spoon, holding a paper towel under the spoon for a few seconds to absorb any drops of water (these could make the muffins soggy). Ease one egg on top of the ham, then repeat with the rest of the eggs.

10

Spoon on plenty of the hollandaise sauce and enjoy immediately. Sprinkle with a little more cayenne, if you like.

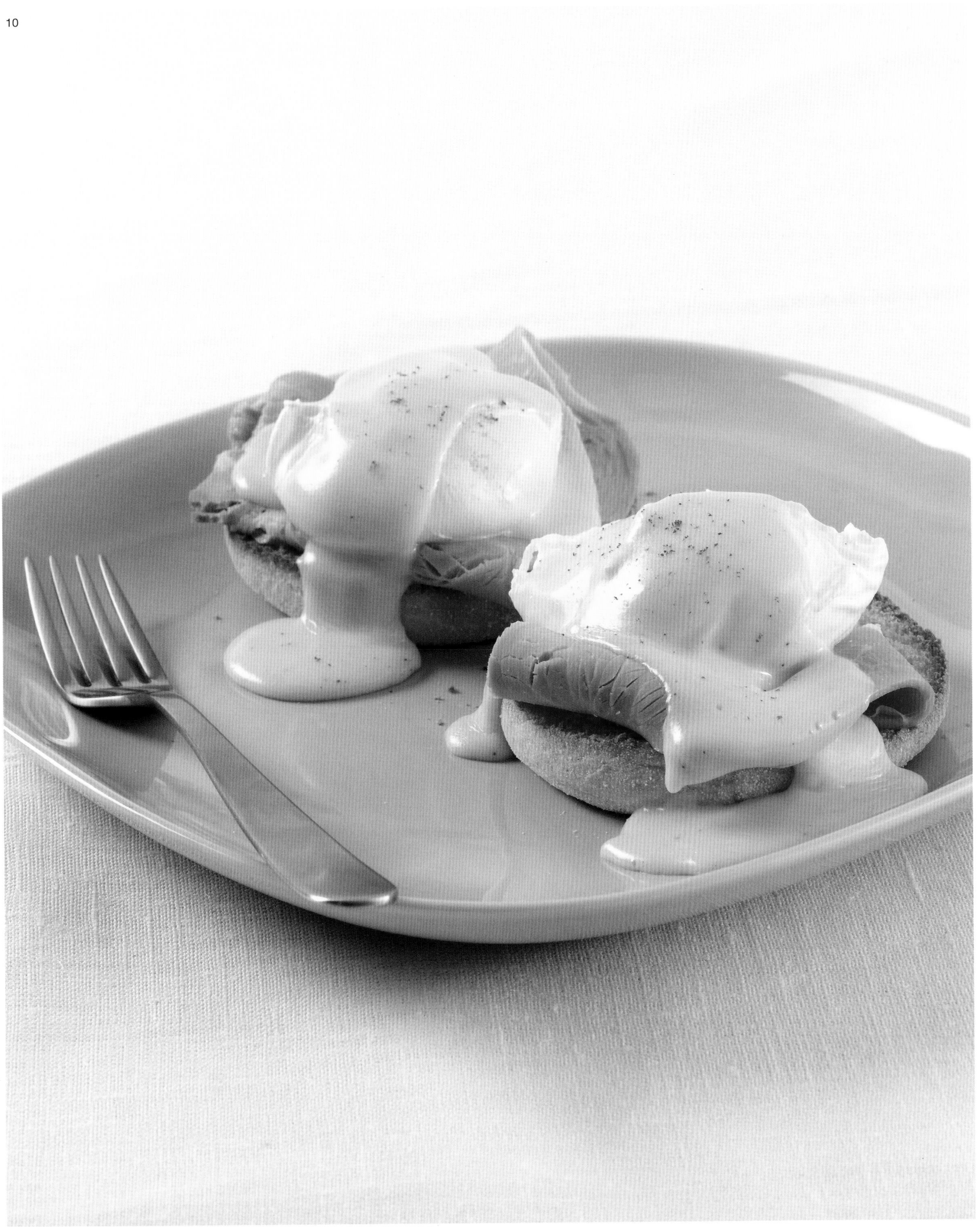

Scrambled Egg
& Smoked Salmon Bagels

Preparation time: 5 minutes
Cooking time: 2 minutes
Serves 2 (easily doubled)

Add a little style to your breakfast
with creamy scrambled eggs and
a few ruffles of delicate smoked
salmon. Smoked salmon comes in
slices or as trimmings, and either
will work for this recipe.

2 poppy seed or plain bagels

4 large eggs

2 tbsp milk or light cream

2 tbsp butter

3½ oz smoked salmon

1 handful fresh chives (or choose
   chervil or dill if you prefer)

salt and pepper

1
Preheat the oven to 275°F and put 2 large plates in it to warm. Halve the bagels, then toast them in the toaster or under the broiler. Keep them warm in the oven while you scramble the eggs.

2
Put the eggs and milk or cream in a bowl or measuring cup, beat with a fork, then season with salt and pepper.

3
Heat a small frying pan over medium heat. After about 30 seconds, add half of the butter and leave it until it foams.

4

Pour in the eggs, leave them for a few seconds, then stir with a wooden spoon. Make sure you stir around the edge of the pan, as this is where it is hottest, and where the eggs will cook the most quickly.

5

Cook for 1 minute only, then take the pan off the heat and snip in most of the chives using a pair of scissors. The eggs won't look ready yet, but the heat left in the pan will continue cooking them while you butter the bagels.

6

Spread the remaining butter over the bagels, then put them onto the warmed plates. Spoon the eggs over the bagels, then top with the slices of smoked salmon. Sprinkle with the final few chives and a little black pepper, and serve immediately.

French Toast with Poached Plums

Preparation time: 20 minutes
Cooking time: 10 minutes
Serves 4

French toast is a wonderful
breakfast that needs surprisingly
few ingredients: just stale bread,
milk, sugar, and eggs. A little cooked
seasonal fruit transforms it into
a café-style brunch that's easy to
create at home.

---

6 ripe plums

5 tbsp sugar

4 large eggs

scant 1 cup whole milk

1 tsp vanilla extract

8 slices white bread (day old
   is perfect)

2 tbsp butter, or more if needed

1 pinch ground cinnamon

4 tbsp Greek yogurt, to serve

1
Cut the plums in half, then carefully ease out the pits with your fingers or the tip of the knife. Put the plums into a medium saucepan, sprinkle with 3 tablespoons of the sugar, then add 5 tablespoons water.

2
Cover the pan and cook the plums over low-to-medium heat for 15 minutes, stirring once or twice until soft and surrounded with lots of pink syrup. If your plums are over or under-ripe, they will take a little less, or more, time to cook down. Set aside to cool.

3
Preheat the oven to 350°F and have ready some paper towels and a large baking sheet. In a large bowl, beat together the eggs, milk, 1 tablespoon sugar, and the vanilla extract using a fork. Submerge one slice of bread in the egg mixture, then let it soak for 30 seconds. Transfer to a plate, then repeat with a couple more pieces.

4

Put a large nonstick frying pan over medium heat. After 30 seconds, add 1 tablespoon of butter. Once it's foaming, carefully add 3 of the soaked slices, or more if you can fit them in the frying pan. Fry the bread for 2 minutes, until golden brown underneath. Flip each slice with a spatula, then cook for another 2 minutes, or until the second side is golden and the bread is springy to the touch in the middle. Soak a few more slices while you wait, and mix the remaining sugar and cinnamon.

5

Eat the first batch immediately, sprinkled with some of the cinnamon sugar, or transfer to the baking sheet lined with paper towels and put in the oven to keep warm.

6

Wipe what's left of the butter out of the pan with paper towels, then add the remaining butter. When it is foaming, fry the remaining slices. When ready, sprinkle these with cinnamon sugar too.

7

Serve the French toast with the plums and spoonfuls of Greek yogurt.

GETTING AHEAD
You can cook the plums several days ahead, then warm them in a pan shortly before serving. If you can't find plums, try apricots, or simply serve with prepared fruit compote from a jar.

Full English Breakfast

Preparation time: 10 minutes
Cooking time: about 30 minutes
Serves 2 (easily doubled)

This multi-ingredient breakfast is a national institution in England, and it's perfect for a weekend treat. The only challenge is keeping it all hot— that's why I cook everything in the oven (except the eggs) instead of using several pans. Roasting the breakfast is also a much healthier option than frying. As broilers can vary so much, this method is more reliable than using a broiler when it comes to timings.

---

4 good-quality pork sausages

2–3 tbsp sunflower or vegetable oil

2 ripe tomatoes

2 large-cap mushrooms
   (portobello are a good choice)

2 slices bread (white or whole wheat)

6 strips bacon, dry-cured if you can
   find it

2 very fresh large eggs

salt and pepper

1

2

3

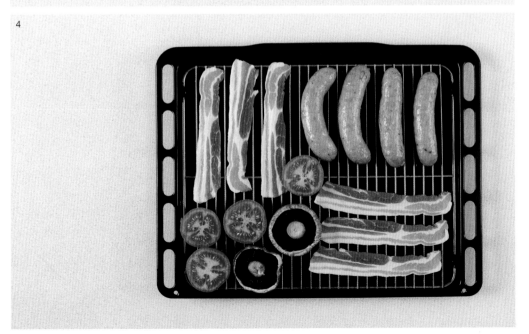

4

1
Preheat the oven to 425°F. Put the sausages onto the rack of a broiler pan. Don't prick them. Brush with a little of the oil.

2
Roast the sausages in the oven for 10 minutes. Meanwhile, cut the tomatoes in half through the middle (rather than through the green stalk) and trim the stems of the mushrooms. Brush the cut sides of the tomatoes and the gill sides of the mushrooms with more oil. Season with salt and pepper.

3
Lightly brush a little oil over both sides of the bread, then cut into triangles.

4
Remove the broiler pan from the oven, then turn the sausages over. Put the tomatoes, mushrooms, and bacon onto the rack. Space everything out as much as possible.

WHY DRY-CURED BACON?
Dry-cured bacon is the best choice for an English breakfast. As the name suggests, the bacon is processed without adding extra water to the pork. This means that it will release much less liquid, therefore shrinking less and crisping up more than other bacon. The thickness of bacon varies dramatically, so keep an eye on it as it cooks. If yours cooks more quickly, simply put it onto a plate, cover with foil and keep warm.

5

Return the pan to the oven for 15 minutes, adding the bread to the pan when there are 5 minutes of cooking time left. Everything will have shrunk a little as it cooks, so there will be room; just shuffle everything around to make space, if you need to. Breakfast is ready when the bacon fat is golden and crisp at the edges, the tomatoes are softened, and the mushrooms look dark and juicy. Turn off the oven and put 2 plates in to warm while you fry the eggs. Leave the oven door ajar so that the food stays warm but doesn't keep cooking.

6

Heat a frying pan over medium heat and have a cup or mug and a spatula at the ready. Add the remaining oil (there should be about 2 teaspoons left—if not, just add a splash more from the bottle) and let it heat through for 30 seconds. Crack an egg into the cup, then slide it into the oil. Repeat with the second egg.

USE THE FRESHEST EGGS
Always dig to the back of the supermarket shelf and pick the eggs with the longest sell-by or use-by date. If your eggs aren't dated, check their freshness in a glass of water: a fresh egg will sink. If the eggs are older, try scrambling them instead (see page 28).

7

Cook for 3 minutes, using the spatula to carefully drizzle the hot oil over the eggs as they cook, until the whites are set. The eggs should gently sizzle—if they start to spit, turn the heat down a little.

8

Arrange the eggs and all of the other breakfast ingredients on the warmed plates. Season with salt and pepper if desired. Eat immediately.

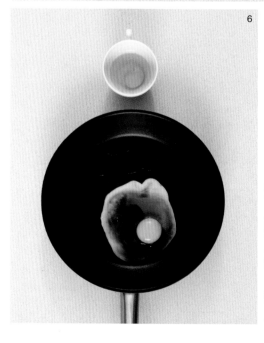

Fruit-Filled Morning Muffins

Preparation time: 15 minutes
Cooking time: 20 minutes
Makes 12

Some morning muffins feel too indulgent, some too worthy. These have the perfect balance: moist, sweet but not too sweet, and full of texture. They'll keep you going until lunch.

¾ cup pecans

½ cup light brown sugar

½ cup mixed seeds (try pumpkin, sesame, and sunflower seeds)

¾ cup rolled oats

12 dried dates

scant ½ cup raisins or golden raisins

2¼ cups self-rising flour

½ tsp ground cinnamon

1 stick (½ cup) unsalted butter

1 cup plain yogurt

2 large eggs

1 large carrot

salt

1
Line a 12-cup muffin pan with paper baking cups and preheat the oven to 400°F. Roughly chop the pecans. Mix 1 tablespoon each of the sugar, seeds, oats, and pecans together in a small bowl and set aside—this will make the topping.

2
Snip the dates into small pieces using kitchen scissors. In a large bowl, mix the dates and raisins with the remaining sugar, seeds, oats and pecans, the flour, cinnamon and a pinch of salt.

LUMPS IN THE SUGAR?
As brown sugar is softer and stickier than other types, it can sometimes clump together. If you need to, rub the dry ingredients through your fingers a few times once the sugar has been added, breaking up any lumps of sugar as you find them.

3
Melt the butter gently in a small saucepan. Remove from the heat, and then, using a fork, beat in the yogurt, followed by the eggs.

4

Coarsely grate the carrot to yield 1½ cups (5 ounces). Add the butter mixture and grated carrot to the flour mixture. Using a spatula or metal spoon, stir everything together quickly, until just combined and still flecked with some dry flour. It's important not to over-work the mix, as this can make the muffins chewy.

5

Scoop generous spoonfuls of the mixture into the muffin cups until you've evenly filled each one. The easiest way to do this is to use 2 spoons. Scoop a big spoonful of batter from the bowl, then push it into the cup using the other spoon. Use all of the mixture, and don't worry, the cups will be very full. Sprinkle with the topping.

6

Bake the muffins for 20 minutes, until risen, golden, and smelling delicious. Let cool for about 5 minutes, then lift the muffins out onto a wire cooling rack. Eat warm or cold.

SURE THEY'RE READY?
Insert a skewer or toothpick into the middle of one of the muffins. It should come out dry. If the skewer comes out coated in sticky mix, return the muffins to the oven for 5 more minutes.

STORING THE MUFFINS
They'll keep in an airtight container for 3–4 days.

Huevos Rancheros (Mexican Spiced Beans with Eggs)

Preparation time: 30 minutes
Cooking time: 10 minutes
Serves 2 (easily doubled)

Start the day with some spice with this brilliantly healthy and filling vegetarian breakfast dish. If you like your eggs with cheese, sprinkle a handful of grated Monterey Jack over the top before broiling at the end of step 5, to melt while the eggs finish cooking.

1 onion

1 red bell pepper

½ green chile

1 clove garlic

1 tbsp vegetable or sunflower oil

1 small bunch fresh cilantro

1 tsp ground cumin

1 (14½-oz) can chopped tomatoes

1 tsp chipotle paste

1 (14½-oz) can pinto beans, drained

2 large eggs

salt and pepper

soft flour tortillas, to serve (optional)

1

Halve and slice the onion. Seed and chop the red pepper into chunky pieces. Slice the chile (leave the seeds in if you like it hot), and crush the garlic. Heat a medium ovenproof frying pan over low heat, then add the oil. After 30 seconds, add the vegetables and stir well.

2

Cook the vegetables gently for 10 minutes, or until softened.

3

While the vegetables soften, finely chop the cilantro stalks. Stir the stalks and the cumin into the pan, then cook for another 3 minutes, until it smells fragrant. Stir the tomatoes, chipotle paste, and pinto beans into the pan, then simmer for 5 minutes, or until the tomato juices have thickened a little. Season with salt and pepper. Preheat the broiler.

CHIPOTLE PASTE
Chipotle paste gives the beans a sweet, smoky, rounded flavor. If you can't find it, add 1 teaspoon tomato paste, 1 teaspoon sugar, and ½ teaspoon paprika or smoked paprika instead.

4

Crack an egg into a small cup. Use a spoon to make 2 hollows in the beans, then slide the egg into one of them. Repeat with the second egg.

5

Cover the pan with a lid, then cook gently for 5 minutes, until the eggs are cooked underneath, but still a little wobbly on the top. To finish cooking the tops of the eggs, put the pan under the broiler for 1–2 minutes, depending on how you like them.

6

To serve the dish, roughly chop the cilantro leaves and sprinkle them over the pan. Serve with warmed flour tortillas.

WARMING TORTILLAS
Soft flour tortillas are available in most grocery stores. To warm them, either give them a quick blast in the microwave, or wrap them in foil and heat in the oven at 350°F for 10 minutes.

Buttermilk Pancakes with Blueberries & Syrup

Preparation time: 10 minutes
Cooking time: 15 minutes
Serves 4 (makes 16 pancakes)

Who can resist a stack of light and fluffy pancakes? Piled high and drenched with maple syrup, they're very hard to refuse.

2¼ cups self-rising flour

3 tbsp fine sugar

2 tsp baking powder

½ tsp kosher salt

1 tbsp unsalted butter, plus extra
   to serve

scant ½ cup milk

scant 1¼ cups buttermilk

1 tsp vanilla extract

2 large eggs

1 organic lemon

2 tbsp or more vegetable
   or sunflower oil, for frying

maple syrup, to serve

1⅓ cups blueberries, to serve

1
Stir together the flour, sugar, baking powder and salt in a large bowl. Make a well in the middle of the mixture using a whisk.

2
Melt the butter in a small pan, then remove from the heat. Whisk in the milk, buttermilk, vanilla and finally the eggs. Finely grate the lemon zest and stir it in.

CAN'T FIND BUTTERMILK?
Buttermilk is slightly acidic, which helps the batter become extra fluffy and light. If you can't find buttermilk, you can use yogurt instead, or simply put 1 cup milk into a bowl or pitcher and add the juice from half a lemon. Let it stand for a few minutes until the milk looks thick and lumpy, then use as above.

3

Pour the wet ingredients into the well in the dry ingredients.

4

Whisk to make a thick, smooth batter. If you plan to cook all the pancakes before serving, preheat the oven to 275°F.

5

Heat a large nonstick frying pan over medium heat. Add 1 teaspoon of the oil, let it heat for a few seconds, then add 3 large spoonfuls of batter, helping each spoonful to spread out with the tip of the spoon. The batter should sizzle gently as the first spoonful hits the oil. Cook the pancakes for 1 minute, or until small holes start to pop on the surface and there's a tinge of gold around the edges.

6

Slide a spatula under a pancake and flip it over. Repeat with the remaining pancakes and cook for a minute on the second side, until they are fluffy and feel springy in the middle. Transfer to a plate. Eat immediately or keep warm in the preheated oven while you cook the rest of the pancakes. Add 1 teaspoon oil to the pan for each batch.

7

Serve the pancakes hot, with a pat of butter, a drizzle of maple syrup, and a handful of blueberries.

TOO MUCH EFFORT FOR THE MORNING?
Although they're always best made fresh, you can make the pancakes the night before and reheat them in the morning. Preheat the oven to 350°F and put the pancakes onto a heatproof dish. Cover with foil and reheat for 10 minutes, then serve with the butter, syrup and berries.

Corn Cakes with Avocado Salsa & Bacon

Preparation time: 20 minutes
Cooking time: about 15 minutes
Serves 4 (makes 12 cakes)

Sizzling corn cakes with crisp bacon and a zingy salsa make a refreshing change from a traditional breakfast or brunch. For the puffiest, lightest corn cakes, cook the batter as soon as it's made.

2 ripe avocados

1 bunch scallions

1 mild red chile

2 limes

1¾ cups self-rising flour

½ tsp baking powder

¼ tsp kosher salt

scant 1 cup milk

2 large eggs

1 (14-oz) can corn, drained

3 tbsp sunflower or vegetable oil

8 strips bacon, dry-cured if you can
   find it (see page 37)

salt and pepper

chili sauce, to serve (optional)

1

Make the salsa first. Cut each avocado in half. To do this, carefully push the blade of a knife into the avocado, until it stops against the pit. Slide the knife all the way around the avocado, keeping the blade against the pit. Pull out the knife, then twist the two halves apart. Scoop out the pit with a spoon. Peel the skin away from the flesh, then cut the flesh into rough cubes, or use a teaspoon to scoop the flesh into a bowl, if that's easier.

CHOOSING AVOCADOS
A ripe avocado should yield slightly to your thumb when pressed at the stalk end. Leave any that feel soft, as these will be overripe.

2

Thinly slice the scallions and seed and chop the chile. Mix half of the scallions and chile with the avocado and season with salt and pepper. Halve the limes and squeeze their juice over the avocado. Stir, then set the bowl aside.

TO SEED A CHILE
Cut the chile along its length, then use the tip of a teaspoon to scrape out the fiery seeds and white pith.

3

Make the corn cake batter. Mix the flour, baking powder, and ¼ teaspoon salt in a large bowl, then add the milk and eggs. Whisk to a smooth, thick batter. Stir the corn and remaining chile and scallions into the batter.

4

Preheat the broiler, ready to cook the bacon later. To cook the corn cakes, heat a large nonstick frying pan over medium-high heat. Add 2 teaspoons of the oil, leave it for 30 seconds to heat up, then spoon in 3 large spoonfuls of the batter, well spaced apart. Leave for 1 minute, or until the edges are golden and the batter starts to bubble on top.

5

Using a frosting spatula or regular spatula, turn the corn cakes over. Cook for another minute, or until the cakes look puffy and feel springy to the touch in the middle. Transfer to a plate and keep warm, either at the bottom of the broiler or in a low oven. Repeat with more oil and batter.

6

Put the bacon onto the rack of a broiler pan, then broil for 3 minutes on each side, or until they are crisp and golden.

7

Serve the corn cakes on warmed plates, with the salsa and bacon. A dash of chili sauce makes a very good addition.

Toasted Ham & Cheese Sandwich

Preparation time: 10 minutes
Cooking time: about 3 minutes
Serves 1 (easily doubled)

Otherwise known as a *croque monsieur*, a simple toasted ham and cheese sandwich is one of life's simple pleasures; unapologetically indulgent but worth every bite. Try it with a few cornichons on the side.

2 oz Gruyère or any good melting cheese, such as Swiss, provolone or Cheddar
2 slices good crusty white bread
1 tbsp soft butter
1–2 slices cooked ham
1 tsp wholegrain mustard
cornichons, to serve (optional)

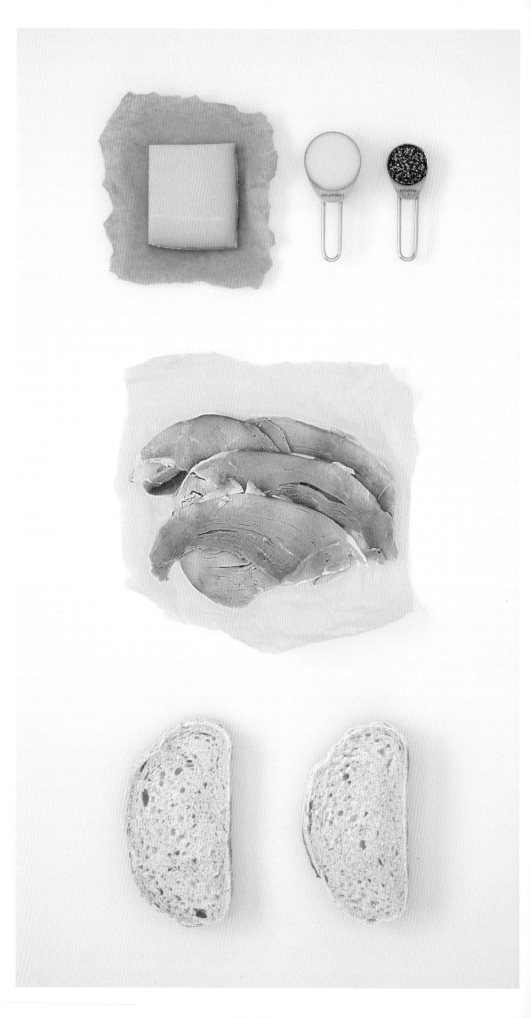

1
Preheat the broiler. Grate the cheese and spread both sides of both pieces of bread with butter. Cover one piece of bread with two-thirds of the cheese and then the ham.

2
Spread the mustard over the other piece of bread, then sandwich it on top of the ham.

3
Put the sandwich on a nonstick baking pan or a pan lined with baking parchment, then broil for 1½ minutes, or until the bread on the top is golden and sizzling. Using a spatula, turn the sandwich over and broil it on the other side.

4
Remove from the broiler, then sprinkle the remaining cheese over the top of the sandwich. Make sure you cover the crusts with the cheese, to prevent them from burning.

5
Broil the sandwich for another 1–1½ minutes, until the cheese is golden and bubbling and melting down the sides. Serve immediately, with the cornichons on the side, if using.

Couscous & Harissa Salad

Preparation time: 25 minutes
Cooking time: 10 minutes
Serves 4

Add a little Moroccan flavor to your lunch and try this aromatic, light salad. It makes a great barbecue or buffet side dish too. Why not add some chickpeas, crumbled feta, or even some flaked smoked mackerel and really make it your own?

---

2 bell peppers (1 yellow, 1 red)

1 pinch saffron threads (optional)

1¼ cups hot vegetable or chicken broth

generous 1 cup couscous

¼ cup dried apricots or ⅓ cup golden raisins

1 tsp ground cinnamon

1 tsp cumin seeds or ground cumin

1 large garlic clove

1 organic lemon

2 tbsp extra-virgin olive oil

scant ½ cup toasted sliced almonds

1 bunch scallions, or ½ red onion

1 cup thick creamy yogurt

1 tsp harissa paste, or more to taste

1 handful fresh mint

salt and pepper

1

Preheat the broiler and lightly oil the broiler pan or a baking pan. Cut the peppers in half through the stalk, then put onto the pan cut side down. Broil for about 10 minutes, or until the skins have turned black.

2

Immediately put the peppers into a plastic food-storage bag and seal, or put into a bowl and cover with plastic wrap. Leave for a few minutes, until cool enough to handle. Peel the skin off the peppers, discard the stalk and seeds, then slice the flesh.

BROILING PEPPERS
Broiling or grilling your own peppers is more economical (and often more flavorful) than buying them ready-prepared in a jar, but if speed is of the essence, by all means use a jar. Choose chargrilled peppers packed in oil, if you can find them.

3

While you wait, mix the saffron (if using) into the hot broth. Put the couscous into a large mixing bowl, add the broth, then cover with plastic wrap. Set aside for 10 minutes.

4

Make the dressing. Put a small pan over low heat and add the cinnamon and cumin. Heat for 1–2 minutes, until the spices smell fragrant, then remove from the heat. Crush the garlic, grate the lemon zest and squeeze the juice. Add the lemon zest and juice, the garlic, and the oil to the pan, and season with salt and pepper.

5

When the couscous has absorbed all of the broth, looks swollen and dry on the surface, fluff it up with a fork to break up any clumps. Stir in the spicy dressing until the couscous is well coated, then add the peppers and toasted almonds. Slice the scallions, add to the bowl, then stir everything together.

TOASTING ALMONDS
If you can't find toasted almonds, spread some almonds on a baking sheet and toast in the oven at 350°F for 5 minutes, or until golden. Alternatively, toast them in a pan over gentle heat for 5 minutes, stirring frequently.

6

Swirl the yogurt and a little of the harissa together. To serve the couscous, tear the mint leaves into the couscous and serve with a dollop of the spicy yogurt sauce.

HARISSA PASTE
A spicy and aromatic ingredient from North Africa, harissa paste is made with chilies, cilantro, garlic, and olive oil. Chili sauce would be a good substitute if you can't find it.

Warm Goat Cheese & Beet Salad

Preparation time: 15 minutes
Cooking time: 15 minutes
Serves 2 (easily doubled)

A bistro-style salad that's hard to improve on—although you can't go wrong by adding a bit of crusty bread and a glass of chilled white wine, too. It also makes a good starter for 4 people.

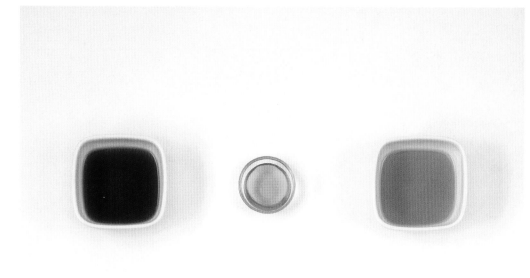

¼ cup pine nuts

½ red onion

2 tbsp red-wine vinegar

2 tbsp extra-virgin olive oil

2 tsp honey

2 (3½-oz) goat cheese disks

2 sprigs fresh thyme

4 medium-size cooked beets
   (not pickled)

3 oz mixed salad greens

salt and pepper

1

Heat a small pan over low heat, then add the pine nuts. Cook very gently for 5 minutes, stirring often, until the nuts are toasted and golden. Transfer them to a plate once they're ready.

2

For the dressing, finely chop the onion and put into a small bowl. Add the vinegar, oil, honey, and some salt and pepper, then set aside.

3

Preheat the broiler. Cut the cheeses in half, then place, cut sides up, onto a nonstick baking pan or a pan lined with parchment paper. Pick the leaves from the thyme and sprinkle over the cheese. Season with salt and pepper.

4

Put the cheeses under the broiler for 5 minutes, or until they start to melt and turn brown around the edges.

5

While the cheese cooks, cut the beets into wedges. Put onto 2 plates with the salad greens. Sprinkle with the pine nuts.

6

Using a spatula, lift the cheeses from the baking pan and onto each plate. Drizzle the dressing, including the chopped onion, over and around each plate. Serve immediately.

Chicken Caesar Salad

Preparation time: 15 minutes
Cooking time: 15 minutes
Serves 4 (easily halved)

Although adding broiled chicken to a classic Caesar salad is not strictly authentic, it certainly makes for a crowd-pleasing lunch. For the tastiest salad, make sure that the lettuce leaves are well coated with the dressing. Use your hands to mix it with the lettuce if you need to.

4 very thick slices good-quality
   white bread, about 9 oz total
2 tbsp olive oil
4 skinless, boneless chicken breasts
1 clove garlic
2 anchovy fillets in oil, drained
½ tsp Dijon mustard
4 tbsp mayonnaise
1 tsp red- or white-wine vinegar
2 oz Parmesan cheese
1 head Romaine lettuce
salt and pepper

1

Preheat the oven to 400°F. Cut the crusts off the bread, then cut into 1-inch cubes. Spread out the bread on a large baking sheet, then drizzle half of the oil over the cubes. Toss thoroughly so that the bread is well coated, then season with salt and pepper.

2

Put the baking sheet in the oven and bake for 15 minutes, until the bread is crisp and golden.

3

Meanwhile, cook the chicken. Place a ridged grill pan over medium heat for a few minutes, until hot but not smoking. Add the oil to the pan. Season the chicken with salt and pepper, then add it to the pan and cook for 5 minutes on each side, until golden and cooked through. Avoid moving the chicken before the 4–5 minutes are up, as the meat needs time to form a crust and brown properly before it will come away cleanly from the base of the pan. Remove from the heat and set aside.

IS IT COOKED?
As the chicken is going to be sliced later on, there's no harm in cutting into the thickest part of one of the pieces to have a look. There should be no sign of pinkness, and the juices should run clear. If necessary, cook it for a few minutes longer.

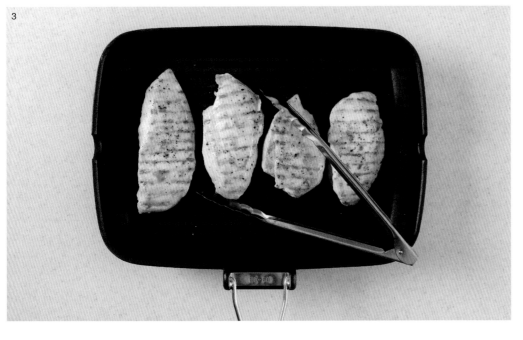

4

Make the dressing while the chicken cooks. Crush the garlic clove, then put it into a bowl. Finely chop the anchovies and add to the garlic, then spoon in the mustard, mayonnaise, vinegar, and 2 tablespoons cold water. Finely grate the cheese and stir half of it in. Season to taste, but be sparing with the salt. The dressing should be spoonable rather than runny, but if it still seems too thick (this can depend on the brand of mayonnaise), stir in a bit more water.

USING ANCHOVIES
Don't be put off from adding anchovies to this recipe—far from tasting fishy, they'll add a deep, savory flavor, giving real backbone to the dressing.

5

Trim the lettuce, removing any tough or wilted outer leaves, then wash and dry the leaves thoroughly. Tear the larger leaves into pieces and leave smaller ones whole. Put them in a large serving bowl.

PREPARING LETTUCE
To wash and dry lettuce, fill a bowl with cold water and add the leaves. Swish them around a little, then drain. Either spin the leaves dry in a salad spinner or dab gently with a clean tea towel or paper towels.

6

Add half the croutons and half the dressing to the bowl, then toss everything together well, coating the leaves in the dressing.

7

Slice the chicken into strips and scatter them over the salad. Sprinkle with the remaining Parmesan and croutons, then drizzle with the rest of the dressing. Serve immediately.

Chicken Noodle Soup

Preparation time: 15 minutes
Cooking time: 25 minutes
Serves 4

Reviving and low in fat, this chicken soup is much better than anything you can buy in a package, and it doesn't take much longer to prepare. Poaching the chicken in the soup means that all its flavor is trapped in the liquid, and the meat won't dry out either.

2 stalks celery

2 medium carrots

2 tbsp butter

½ tsp kosher salt

1 sprig fresh thyme

1 bay leaf

2 skinless, boneless chicken breasts

4¼ cups chicken broth

2½ oz thin egg noodles

1 small handful fresh flat-leaf parsley

½ lemon

salt and pepper

crusty bread, to serve (optional)

1

2

1
Chop the celery and carrots. Heat a medium pan over low heat, then add the butter. Once it's foaming, add the celery and carrots, salt, a few grinds of pepper, the thyme leaves, and bay leaf. Cover with a lid and cook gently for 10 minutes, or until the vegetables are starting to soften, stirring occasionally.

2
Place the chicken breasts on top of the vegetables, then pour in the broth.

3

Bring to a boil, then reduce the heat to a simmer. Cover, then cook for 10 minutes, until the chicken is cooked through and the vegetables are tender. Transfer the chicken to a cutting board. Shred the meat into small pieces using 2 forks, or just chop it into small pieces with a knife, then return it to the pan.

IS THE CHICKEN COOKED?
After 10 minutes, the chicken will have turned from pink to white. If in doubt, lift a piece out, then slice it through its thickest part. The meat should be white all the way through. If not, return it to the pan for a couple of minutes more.

4

Remove the bay leaf from the pan. Add the noodles, separating them with your hands if necessary, then simmer for 4 minutes, until the noodles are tender. Roughly chop the parsley and stir it into the soup. Squeeze in a little lemon juice, taste the soup, then season with salt and pepper. Remove the bay leaf.

5

Enjoy the soup on its own, or with crusty bread and butter.

GETTING AHEAD
If you're making this soup in advance, prepare it to the end of step 3, then stop. Once cool, chill it in the refrigerator. When ready to serve, bring the soup back to a simmer, then add the noodles and continue as above.

Tomato & Thyme Soup

Preparation time: 5 minutes
Cooking time: 20 minutes
Serves 4

It's best to choose canned tomatoes over fresh for a soup like this, as they're packed with the intense flavor it needs.

1 carrot

1 onion

2 tbsp butter

1 sprig fresh thyme

1 large garlic clove

2 tbsp sun-dried tomato paste

3 (14½-oz) cans chopped tomatoes

2½ cups hot chicken or
    vegetable broth

3 tbsp light or heavy cream,
    plus a little more to serve

salt and pepper

crusty bread, to serve (optional)

1
Coarsely grate the carrot and chop the onion. Melt the butter in a medium pan, then add the onion, carrot and almost all of the thyme leaves. Season with salt and pepper, then cover the pan.

2
Keeping the heat low, cook the vegetables for 15 minutes, until soft and sweet, but not browned. Stir them twice during cooking. Thinly slice or crush the garlic and add to the pan during this time.

3
Stir in the sun-dried tomato paste, tomatoes and broth, then simmer gently for 5 minutes, or until the vegetables are tender.

SUN-DRIED TOMATO PASTE
Sun-dried tomato paste is a little sweeter than ordinary tomato paste, and contains oil, which improves the texture of the soup. If you can't find it, use regular tomato paste and add a pinch of sugar.

4
Add the cream, then use an immersion blender to blend the soup until smooth. Alternatively, use a regular blender. Season to taste with salt and pepper.

5
Ladle the soup into bowls, swirl in a little more cream, sprinkle with the remaining thyme, then serve, with crusty bread, if you like.

VARIATION
To serve this soup as a starter, it's good to give it a slightly silkier, smoother texture. After blending, pass the soup through a fine-mesh sieve into another pan. Be careful not to boil the soup when reheating it, as this will affect the texture.

Greek Salad

Preparation time: 20 minutes
Serves 4

Save this classic salad for summer, when tomatoes are at their best. For a light meal, all that's needed is some crusty bread on the side. For a more filling option, drain and rinse a can of lima beans and stir through at the end of step 3. It's also good as a side dish for barbecued lamb or chicken.

8 medium or 4 large vine-ripened
   tomatoes
1 small red onion
1 tbsp red-wine vinegar
⅓ cup extra-virgin olive oil
2 tsp dried oregano
1 cucumber
½ red bell pepper
1 handful fresh flat-leaf parsley
¾ cup pitted kalamata or
   black olives
7 oz feta cheese
salt and pepper
crusty bread, to serve (optional)

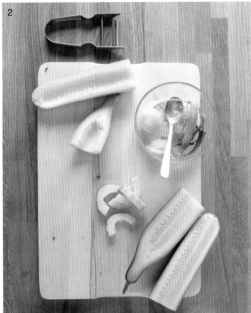

1

Cut each tomato into 6 wedges and finely slice the red onion. Put into a large mixing bowl. Splash on the vinegar and 3 tablespoons of the oil, then add 1 teaspoon of the oregano and season with salt and pepper. Set aside for 10 minutes. This will soften the onion a little and draw some of the juices out of the tomatoes, which will help make a tasty dressing.

CHOOSING TOMATOES
A perfectly ripe tomato will be deep ruby red, yield a little to the touch and smell aromatic. Unless they're a special variety, avoid tomatoes that are still green around the top, or a pale orange-red, as their flavor will be disappointing.

2

Meanwhile, cut the cucumber in half, then halve each piece lengthwise. Peel the skin using a peeler. Scoop out the seeds using a teaspoon, then discard them. This will stop the cucumber from becoming soggy. Slice the cucumber into half-moon slices.

3

Remove the seeds from the pepper, then finely slice it. Roughly chop the parsley, then add it to the bowl along with the pepper, cucumber and olives. Stir. Crumble the cheese into rough cubes.

Spoon the salad onto plates or shallow bowls, then top each bowl with cheese. Sprinkle the remaining oregano over the cheese, then drizzle the remaining oil over and around the salad. Serve with crusty bread.

Shrimp & Mushroom Laksa

Preparation time: 10 minutes
Cooking time: 10 minutes
Serves 4 (easily halved)

Laksa is a spicy noodle soup, and it's a staple quick dish across southeast Asia. If laksa paste is hard to find, use a good quality red or green Thai curry paste instead. Authentic Thai brands will have the best flavor. If you like your food hotter, add a little chopped chile during step 2.

3½ oz rice noodles, either thick
   or thin
5 oz shiitake or oyster mushrooms
1 bunch scallions
2 tsp vegetable or sunflower oil
2 tbsp laksa paste or Thai curry
   paste (red or green)
1 (14-oz) can coconut milk
   (use reduced fat, if desired)
1⅔ cups fish or chicken broth
7 oz large, uncooked shrimp, shelled
   and deveined
2½ cups bean sprouts
1–2 tbsp nam pla (fish sauce),
   to taste
1 lime
½ tsp sugar
1 handful fresh cilantro, to serve

1
Put the noodles into a large bowl, then pour enough boiling water over them to cover. Let soak while you prepare the rest of the recipe. Stir the noodles a few times to separate any that have stuck together.

2
Meanwhile, slice the mushrooms thickly, and thinly slice the scallions. Heat 1 teaspoon of the oil in a pan over high heat. Add the mushrooms and scallions and fry for 2 minutes, until just softened. Transfer to a plate.

3

Lower the heat, then add the remaining oil to the pan. Add the laksa or Thai curry paste to the oil and cook for 3 minutes, stirring frequently, until fragrant.

4

Stir in the coconut milk and broth, then simmer for 2 minutes. Add the shrimp to the pan, then simmer for 3 minutes, or until the shrimp have turned from gray to pink all over.

CHOOSING SHRIMP
Frozen shrimp are just as good, if not better, than chilled shrimp, as they are frozen at sea when very fresh. To quickly defrost frozen uncooked shrimp, put them into a bowl and cover with cold water. Change the water a couple of times over a 10-minute period, after which time the shrimp will be defrosted. Drain well.

5

Squeeze the juice from the lime. Stir in the bean sprouts and return the scallions and mushrooms to the pan. Season the soup with the fish sauce, lime juice, and sugar, then take it off the heat. The bean sprouts should still have lots of texture.

6

Drain the noodles, then divide among 4 serving bowls. Ladle the soup over the noodles, then garnish each bowl with a few torn cilantro sprigs.

Simple Herb Omelet

Preparation time: 5 minutes
Cooking time: 1–2 minutes
Serves 1

Food doesn't get much faster than an omelet. Always use free-range eggs—organic if possible—for the best flavor. Once you've mastered the basic omelet, try the alternative fillings on page 86.

3 large eggs
1 handful fresh chives
1 tbsp butter
salt and pepper

1
Preheat the oven to 275°F and put a plate in the oven to warm up. Crack the eggs into a bowl or measuring cup. Beat with a fork until the whites and yolks are just mixed; stop before they become one uniform yellow. Season generously with salt and pepper.

2
Finely chop the chives, or snip them with scissors if that's easier. Stir them into the eggs.

3

Place a small nonstick frying pan over high heat. Add the butter. Once the butter foams, swirl the pan to make sure it's covered with an even layer.

4

Pour in the eggs and set a timer for 1 minute. As soon as the eggs hit the butter, they will start to set and sizzle. Using the fork, gently and slowly move the eggs around. Thick ribbons of cooked egg will start forming underneath the top runny layer.

5

Keep gently moving the egg around until almost all of it is set, with just a little runny egg on the top. Take the pan off the heat. For the best result, it's important not to overcook the omelet at this stage.

6

Hold the pan over the warmed plate. Shake the omelet out of the pan until half of it is lying on the plate. Use a spatula to help if you like. Now flip the other half over it.

7

Serve immediately.

MUSHROOM OMELET
Thinly slice a handful of mushrooms. Add a little butter to a hot pan, then fry the mushrooms for 5 minutes until softened. Season to taste, then set aside. Cook the omelet as above, then spoon the mushrooms over the omelet before you fold it.

HAM AND CHEESE OMELET
Finely slice a piece of ham and grate 1 ounce Gruyère or Cheddar cheese. Sprinkle over the omelet before folding.

Chicken & Corn Quesadillas

Preparation time: 10 minutes
Cooking time: about 25 minutes
Serves 4

Once you've mastered the basic quesadilla there's no turning back—as long as it goes with cheese, any filling will work.

2½ cups pre-cooked or
   leftover chicken
1 × 14-oz can corn, drained
4 scallions
3 tbsp sliced jalapeño chiles
   from a jar
1 small bunch fresh cilantro
3½ oz sharp Cheddar cheese
3 ripe tomatoes
6 flour tortillas
salt and pepper

1

Remove any skin from the chicken and pull it into small pieces with your hands or finely slice it with a knife. Put the chicken into a bowl and add the corn. Thinly slice the scallions, roughly chop the jalapeños and most of the cilantro leaves, then stir into the mix. Season with salt and pepper.

2

Grate the cheese and slice the tomatoes. Put a tortilla on your work surface, cover one half of it with a little cheese, then some of the chicken mixture and a few slices of tomato. Sprinkle with more cheese, then fold the other side of the tortilla over to make a semi-circle shape. Set aside, then repeat with the remaining tortillas and filling.

3

Preheat the oven to 275°F, ready to keep the quesadillas warm. Heat a large frying pan over medium heat. Add a quesadilla to the pan and cook for 2 minutes, or until the underside is golden and toasted. Turn it over using a spatula, then cook for another 2 minutes, or until the cheese is melting and the quesadilla is crisp all over. Transfer to a baking sheet and keep warm in the oven while you cook the rest.

4

Cut each quesadilla into 3 triangles, pile onto a platter, then serve immediately, garnished with the rest of the cilantro.

Tuna Salad Niçoise

Preparation time: 10 minutes
Cooking time: 20 minutes
Serves 2 as a main course
(easily doubled)

Far more than just a salad, a proper
salade Niçoise is a filling, colorful
meal packed with the classic punchy
flavors of southern France. Quality
of ingredients is important in this
kind of cooking. If you start with
good basics you'll be rewarded with
a dish you'll want to make again
and again.

1 tsp kosher salt
11 oz new potatoes, about the size
   of small eggs
2 large eggs, at room
   temperature
3½ oz thin green beans
1 small clove garlic
5½ oz canned tuna in olive oil
1 tbsp red-wine vinegar
½ small red onion
3½ oz cherry tomatoes
4 canned anchovy fillets
   in oil, drained
½ cup pitted Niçoise or other
   black olives
salt and pepper

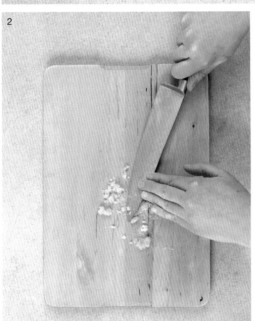

1

Fill a medium pan with water, add 1 teaspoon salt and bring to a boil. Add the potatoes, and set a timer to boil for 20 minutes. With 7 minutes to go, add the eggs to the pan. Trim the stalk end of the beans, then with 5 minutes left, add them to the pan.

NEW POTATOES

New potatoes (sometimes called salad potatoes) have a creamy, firm texture when cooked. A new potato is cooked when a knife slips easily through the flesh.

2

Make the dressing while you wait. First slice the garlic and chop it finely. Sprinkle with some sea salt, then, holding the knife at an angle, scrape and mash the garlic and salt together against the board until the garlic turns into a paste. Work on a little of the garlic at a time until all of the garlic is crushed.

GOT A GARLIC CRUSHER?

There's nothing wrong with using a garlic crusher if you find it easier than crushing with a knife. However, crushing the garlic to a paste with a knife helps to release more of the aromatic oils from within the clove.

3

Drain 3 tablespoons of the oil from the can of tuna into a small bowl. Whisk the vinegar and the garlic into the oil, plus some salt and pepper.

4

Drain the eggs, potatoes, and beans into a colander. Run under the cold tap for 1 minute to cool everything quickly, then set aside.

5

Finely slice the onion into half moons. Cut the tomatoes and potatoes in half. Put into a large bowl and add the beans and olives.

6

Peel the eggs. Crack the shells all over by knocking them gently on the work surface. Peel the shells away from the whites. If they're resistant, peeling the eggs under cold water will help. Cut each egg in half lengthways. Season the cut side of each egg with salt and pepper.

7

Slice the anchovies in half lengthwise. Toss most of the dressing with the vegetables.

8

Spoon the salad onto plates. Top each pile of salad with 2 halves of egg, some tuna and some pieces of anchovy. Drizzle the rest of the dressing around the salad, then serve.

SHOPPING TIP
Traditionally, this recipe would use the small, sourish black Niçoise olives of its region of origin. Greek Kalamata olives make a good alternative if you can't find them.

BLT Sandwich

Preparation time: 5 minutes
Cooking time: 15 minutes
Serves 2 (easily halved or doubled)

A good BLT is hard to beat: the combination of cool lettuce, hot bacon, and crisp toasted bread is enough to make anyone hungry. The mayonnaise in this recipe has added zing with a little mustard and honey, which will bring out the full flavor of the bacon.

---

4 slices good-quality, crusty
   white bread
6 strips bacon
2 tbsp mayonnaise
1 tsp wholegrain mustard
½ tsp honey
2 ripe tomatoes
butter, for spreading
½ head butter lettuce, such as Bibb
   or Boston, washed and dried (see
   page 70)
salt and pepper

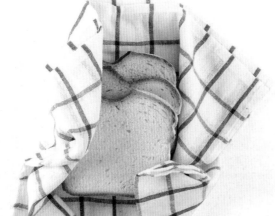

1
Preheat the broiler, then lightly toast the bread on each side. This will take about 5 minutes in total. Keep warm (wrapping it in a clean tea towel works well).

2
Broil the bacon on a rack in a broiler pan for 10 minutes, turning once, until the fat is crisp and golden.

3
Meanwhile, mix the mayonnaise, mustard, and honey together. Thinly slice the tomatoes.

2

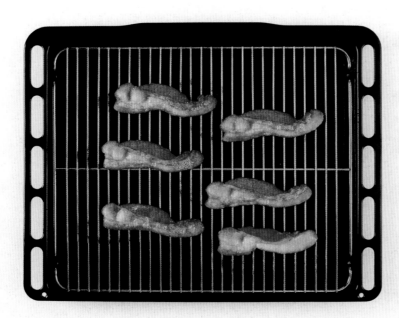

3

4

Lightly butter the toasted bread, then spread each slice with the mustard and honey mayonnaise. Place a few lettuce leaves on top of two of the pieces.

5

Spread out the tomato slices evenly over the lettuce, season with salt and pepper, then top with the bacon.

6

Top with more lettuce leaves and the remaining bread.

7

Cut in half using a sharp knife and serve immediately.

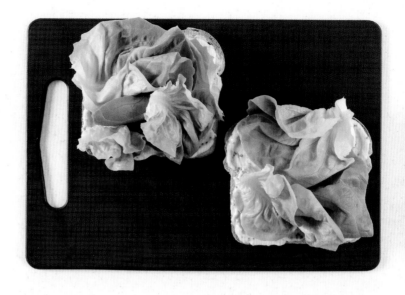

4

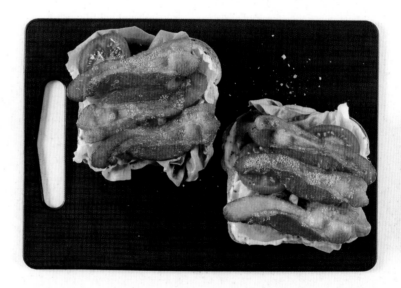

5

6

Spicy Vegetable Soup

Preparation time: 20 minutes
Cooking time: 20 minutes
Serves 4 (with leftovers)

Economical, warming, and delicious, this lightly spiced soup will brighten up even the coldest of evenings. It thickens as it stands, so stir in a little extra water or broth if you need to re-heat it.

2 tsp cumin seeds

¼ tsp dried chili flakes

2 onions

3 cloves garlic

1 thumb-size piece fresh ginger

2 tbsp olive oil

2¼ lb sweet potatoes

1 (14-oz) can chickpeas, drained

3²/₃ cups chicken or vegetable broth

3½ oz baby spinach

salt and pepper

4 tbsp thick plain yogurt, or more, to serve

1 tbsp extra-virgin olive oil, to serve

1
Heat a large saucepan over medium heat. Add the cumin seeds and chili flakes and cook for 1 minute, or until they start to jump around the pan and smell toasty. Scoop half of the spices out of the pan and set aside. Take the pan off the heat while you prepare the vegetables.

2
Chop the onions very roughly, crush the garlic, and finely grate the ginger. Gently heat the 2 tablespoons olive oil in the pan, then add the onions, garlic and ginger and cook gently for 5 minutes until the onions are starting to soften.

PEELING GINGER
There's no need to peel ginger if it's going to be finely grated. Discard any skin and fibrous bits that you're left with on the outside of the grater when you're finished.

3
While you wait, peel and roughly chop the sweet potatoes.

4

Stir the sweet potatoes, chickpeas, and broth into the pan, cover with a lid, and simmer for 15 minutes, until the potatoes are soft.

5

Use a potato masher to mash most of the potato to a pulp to make a thick soup. Season with salt and pepper, then roughly chop the spinach and stir it in. After a few seconds the spinach will wilt.

6

Serve in bowls topped with a spoonful of the yogurt, a sprinkle of the reserved spice mixture, and a drizzle of extra-virgin olive oil.

MAKE IT WITH SQUASH
Butternut squash or pumpkin work wonderfully in this soup, but can take a little while to prepare. Either buy pre-cut cubes or allow 10 more minutes to peel and seed the flesh.

Butternut Curry with Spinach & Cashews

Preparation time: 25 minutes
Cooking time: 35 minutes
Serves 4 (easily halved)

Colorful, fragrant and full of texture, this dish shows you don't need meat to make a good curry. Chickpeas, lentils and nuts add protein to the melting pot of vegetables and spices, for a healthy, balanced meal. It would also make a great side dish to go with the Lamb & Potato Curry (page 238).

2¼ lb butternut squash

1 onion

¼ cup vegetable or sunflower oil

1 tbsp butter

2 cloves garlic

1 thumb-size piece fresh ginger

1 small hot green chile (see note)

1 tsp ground turmeric

1 tsp cumin seeds

1 tsp ground coriander

2 cinnamon sticks

1 tbsp freeze-dried curry
    leaves (optional)

3½ oz red lentils

3 or 4 ripe tomatoes

1 (14-oz) can chickpeas, drained

3½ oz cashew nuts

2 large handfuls baby spinach

salt and pepper

chapattis, naan breads or rice (see
    page 145), to serve (optional)

chutney, to serve (optional)

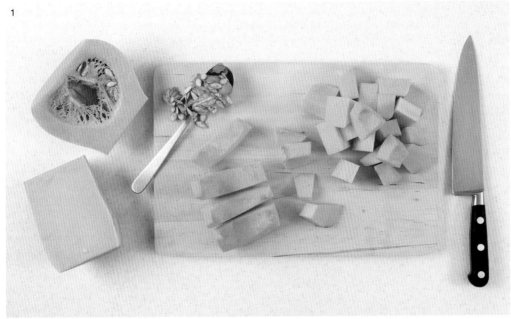

1

Peel the squash using a very good peeler, or a small sharp knife. Be careful, as the skin is tough. Cut the squash into 4 pieces. Scoop out the seeds using a teaspoon. Cut the flesh into large cubes about 1¼ inches across.

2

Halve and slice the onion. Place a large frying pan or wok over a medium-high heat. Add the oil and butter, then after 30 seconds add the squash and onions and season with salt and pepper. Cook for 5 minutes, stirring often, until the vegetables are starting to soften.

3

While the vegetables cook, thinly slice the garlic and finely grate the ginger. Slit the chile, without cutting through the stalk end. If using a larger, milder chile, seed and finely chop it, then add the flesh to the pan.

HOW HOT IS THE CHILE?
Fat chilies tend to be be milder. Smaller chilies, whether thin, finger-length, or small and squat, are usually much hotter. In this recipe, a hot chile is simply split, but not chopped. This is a good way to add a bit of heat and the flavor from a hot chile without having to chop it or remove the seeds. Remember, all chilies vary. So, before you start chopping, slice a little from the end of the chile, touch the cut end with your finger, then touch the tip of your tongue. If it's hotter than you'd like, go easy—if it's milder, use more, or add the seeds too.

4

Stir the garlic, ginger, chile, spices and curry leaves, if using, into the pan and cook for 2 minutes, until the mixture is fragrant and the vegetables are coated in spice. Meanwhile, bring 1¾ cups of water to a boil in a small pan.

5

Stir in the lentils, then pour in the hot water. Stir, then cover and let simmer for 10 minutes, stirring a few times.

6

Preheat the oven to 350°F. Roughly chop the tomatoes, then stir them in with the chickpeas, re-cover the pan, then simmer for 10 minutes more, stirring once or twice. The lentils should be plump and tender. Mash one against the side of the pan to be sure. Season the curry with salt and pepper.

7

Next, toast the cashews. Spread out the nuts on a baking sheet and roast them in the oven for 5 minutes, or until golden.

8

To finish the dish, stir in the spinach leaves and sprinkle the nuts over the top. The spinach will wilt with the heat of the curry. Serve with chapattis, naan breads or rice and your favorite chutney.

Cheeseburgers

Preparation time: 20 minutes
Cooking time: 11–15 minutes
Makes 4 burgers (easily halved)

Start with good-quality beef and you're guaranteed a good burger. The toppings listed here are suggestions rather than instructions—you could add blue cheese, cooked bacon, ketchup, mayonnaise, salsa, or whatever you like. They're great with Chunky Oven Fries (page 312). I've suggested including sliced gherkin in the burger, but feel free to leave them out if your prefer.

1 onion

5 small gherkins or 1 large

1 lb good-quality ground beef

1 tsp Dijon mustard

1 egg

½ tsp kosher salt

¼ tsp black pepper

2 large tomatoes

1 red onion

½ head butterhead lettuce, such as
   Bibb or Boston

4 large hamburger buns

4 slices cheese for melting
   (try Gouda, Havarti or Gruyère)

1

2

3

1

Preheat the broiler. Finely chop the onion and the gherkins, then put them into a large mixing bowl. Add the ground beef, mustard, egg, salt and pepper.

CHOOSING GROUND BEEF
For the juiciest burgers, buy ground beef that is labeled as 80/20, or 80 per cent lean. Broiling the burgers rather than frying or cooking on a griddle will allow much of this fat to drain away, but it will keep the burgers moist. Leaner meat will give you a healthier option, but the burgers may seem a little dry. Buy the best quality meat you can— cheaper meat tends to contain more water and shrinks a lot more when it's cooked.

2

Mix everything together well until thoroughly combined. Using your hands is the easiest way, even if it does seem messy.

3

While it's still in the bowl, roughly divide the meat mixture into 4 sections. Dampen your hands (this makes the mixture easier to shape and handle), then shape the mixture into 4 large burgers, about ¾ inch thick and 4 inches across. Transfer to a plate or chopping board.

4

Put the burgers onto the rack of a broiler pan, then cook for 10 minutes, turning halfway through cooking, until they are dark golden brown. The burgers will be a little pink and juicy in the middle. For well-done burgers, cook for an extra 2 minutes per side.

5

While the burgers cook, slice the tomatoes and red onion, and wash, dry and separate the lettuce leaves (see page 70). Split the buns in half crosswise.

6

When the burgers are cooked, move them to one side of the broiler pan. Put the buns, cut sides up, alongside the burgers. Top each burger with a slice of the cheese. Return to the broiler for 30 seconds to 1 minute, or until the cheese has started to melt and the buns are lightly toasted.

7

Put a little lettuce and tomato onto the bottom half of each bun, top with a burger, then finish with a few onion rings. Serve immediately.

GETTING AHEAD
The burgers can be prepared up to step 3 the day before, left raw, then wrapped in plastic wrap and chilled. Alternatively, sandwich each uncooked burger between pieces of parchment paper and freeze for up to a month.

Chicken Stir-Fry

Preparation time: 15 minutes
Cooking time: 10 minutes
Serves 4 (easily halved)

There's a bit of an art to stir-frying, but this basic recipe is a good place to start. Crisp vegetables and tender chicken are less than thirty minutes away—quicker than ordering in! Serve it with plain boiled rice (see page 145).

2 tsp cornstarch

¼ cup soy sauce

4 boneless, skinless chicken breasts

1 red bell pepper

1 yellow bell pepper

1 bunch scallions

1 thumb-size piece fresh ginger

2 garlic cloves

2 limes

¼ cup honey

2 tbsp vegetable or sunflower oil

3 cups sugar snap or snow peas

½ tsp crushed chili flakes

1 tbsp dry sherry or rice wine

1
Stir together 1 teaspoon cornstarch and 1 teaspoon soy sauce in a medium bowl. Cut the chicken into finger-width strips, then stir into the cornstarch mixture. Set aside for 10 minutes while you prepare the vegetables. Marinating the chicken with cornstarch gives a deliciously tender end result.

2
Halve and seed the peppers, and cut them into slices about ½ inch thick. Finely chop the scallions. Finely grate the ginger and finely chop or slice the garlic.

3
Make the sauce. Squeeze the juice from the limes into a bowl. Stir in the remaining cornstarch and soy sauce, then add the honey.

4

Place a large frying pan or wok over high heat, then add 1 tablespoon of the oil. Add the chicken, let it cook for 1 minute, then stir. Cook for about 3 more minutes, stirring from time to time, until the chicken is turning golden at the edges. Transfer it to a plate and carefully wipe out the pan with a paper towel.

5

Add the remaining tablespoon of oil to the pan, then add the peppers. Cook for 1 minute, then add the peas and cook for another minute, stirring constantly. The vegetables will be just tender. Next, add the garlic, ginger, chili flakes, and half of the scallions. Stir-fry for a minute longer.

6

Now add the sherry or rice wine (it will sizzle and evaporate quickly), then return the chicken to the pan and pour in the soy sauce, lime and honey mixture. Bring the liquid to a boil and cook everything together for 1 minute, or until the chicken is heated through and the sauce has thickened. Scatter the rest of the scallions over the top.

7

Serve in bowls with rice.

STIR-FRYING TIPS
Despite the name, it is important to let the food cook undisturbed when making a stir-fry, as too much stirring slows the cooking down. Cut the vegetables to the same size, so that everything cooks evenly, and add the firmer vegetables to the pan first. Use the largest pan you have and keep the heat high. Don't overcrowd the pan. It's a good idea to cook the meat first, take it out, and then return it to the pan at the end—this prevents it from overcooking and drying out.

Mushroom Risotto

Preparation time: 25 minutes
Cooking time: 20 minutes
Serves 4

A bowl of risotto is one of those wonderful meals that takes no real effort to make, but feels like a bit of a treat. Conveniently, all the ingredients are probably already in your pantry, apart from the fresh mushrooms of course. Choose a mixture of wild mushrooms if you're lucky enough to see them at the grocer.

1¼ oz dried porcini mushrooms
1 onion
2 cloves garlic
1 tbsp mild olive oil
¾ stick (6 tbsp) butter
5 cups chicken broth
2 cups risotto rice (see page 118)
scant ½ cup dry white wine
2 oz Parmesan cheese (about
   ⅔ cup grated)
9 oz cremini mushrooms, or a mix
   of cremini and wild or cultivated
   mushrooms such as oyster and
   enoki (about 3½ cups chopped)
salt and pepper

1

Pour ⅔ cup boiling water into a measuring cup. Stir in the dried porcini mushrooms and push them under the water level. Let stand for 15 minutes. The mushrooms will start to swell.

WHAT ARE PORCINI?
Porcini (also known as cèpes), are highly flavored mushrooms often used in Italian cooking. Fresh porcini are seasonal and expensive; dried porcini are more economical, and have the same great flavor. They must be soaked, after which they can be used to add flavor to sauces, pasta, and meat dishes. Mixed wild dried mushrooms make a good substitute.

2

Meanwhile, finely chop the onion and crush the garlic. Heat a frying pan or shallow saucepan over low heat, then add the olive oil and 4 tablespoons of the butter. Add the onion and garlic and cook gently for 10 minutes, stirring occasionally, until the onions are soft and translucent.

3

Scoop the mushrooms out from their soaking liquid, and put them onto a cutting board. Strain the mushroom liquid through a fine-mesh sieve into another pan. Add the broth to the pan, set it over medium heat and keep it at a simmer.

4

Roughly chop the soaked mushrooms, then add them to the pan with the onions. Stir in the rice. Cook for 2 minutes, stirring, until the rice is well coated in the butter and starting to turn a little translucent. Pour in the wine, then let it bubble until most of it has evaporated. This will happen quite quickly.

5

Add one ladle of the broth to the pan, then stir until the rice has absorbed it. Don't have the heat too high under the rice, or the liquid will bubble and evaporate instead of being absorbed into the rice.

6

Continue adding the broth little by little, stirring all the time, until the rice becomes plump and just tender and surrounded by a creamy sauce. Taste the rice—it should be just soft, without any chalkiness in the middle. Try not to rush it; the whole process should take no less than 20 minutes.

7

Once all the broth has been added, take the pan off the heat. Grate the Parmesan, then stir half of it into the rice. Dot half the remaining butter over the rice.

8

Cover the pan and set aside for 5 minutes. While the risotto rests, thickly slice the large fresh mushrooms, leaving the small ones whole. Melt the remaining butter in another pan over high heat. Add the mushrooms, season with salt and pepper and sauté them for 2–3 minutes, stirring frequently, until golden.

9

Serve the risotto in shallow bowls, topped with a spoonful of hot, buttery mushrooms and a little of the remaining Parmesan.

RISOTTO RICE
There are three main types of risotto rice, all of which have a small, round grain: Arborio, Carnaroli and Vialone Nano. For the beginner cook, Carnaroli is a good choice. Arborio is the most commonly found but it's easy to overcook. Vialone Nano takes longer to cook and is harder to track down.

Chicken & Chorizo Casserole

Preparation time: 15 minutes
Cooking time: 35 minutes
Serves 4 (easily halved)

This hearty one-pot dish makes a perfect winter meal to curl up with. You can use canned beans instead of the chickpeas, if that's what's in the cupboard.

1 lb 2 oz skinless, boneless
   chicken thighs
5 oz chorizo (see note)
1 tbsp olive oil
1 onion
2 cloves garlic
1 red bell pepper
1 tsp ground cinnamon
2 tsp sweet smoked paprika
1 tsp dried thyme
3 tbsp dry sherry or white wine
1 (14½-oz) can chopped tomatoes
scant 1 cup chicken broth
1 (14½-oz) can chickpeas, drained
1 handful fresh flat-leaf parsley
1 tbsp extra-virgin olive oil,
   to serve (optional)
salt and pepper
crusty bread, to serve (optional)

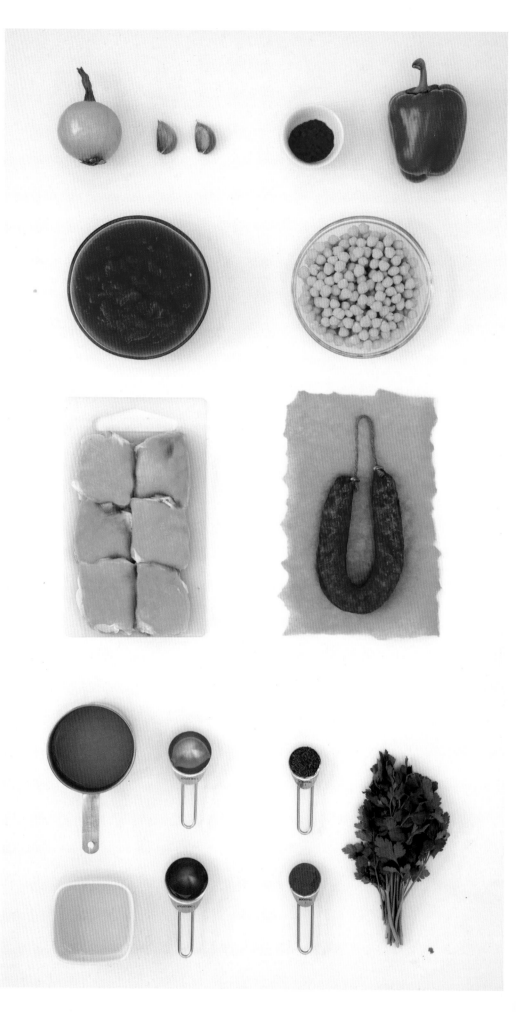

1

Cut the chicken into bite-size chunks and the chorizo into thin slices. Place a large heavy frying pan or shallow flameproof casserole dish over medium-high heat, then add 1 tablespoon olive oil. After 30 seconds, add the chorizo. Fry for 3 minutes, stirring occasionally, until the chorizo is starting to crisp and has released some of its red oil.

CHORIZO

Chorizo is a spicy Spanish sausage flavored with paprika and garlic. There are two types: cooking chorizo, which is soft, like a regular sausage, and cured chorizo, which is firm and dry, and is eaten raw, like salami. Either type will work in this recipe, but choose cooking chorizo if there's a choice.

2

Transfer the chorizo to a plate and set it aside. Add the chicken to the pan, season with salt and pepper, then fry for 5 minutes, stirring often, until golden.

3

While the chicken cooks, start preparing the vegetables. Thinly slice the onion and garlic, then seed the pepper and cut it into chunky strips. Add them to the pan, then reduce the heat. Cook gently for 10 minutes until the onions, peppers and garlic have softened, stirring every few minutes.

4

Stir in the cinnamon, paprika, and thyme and fry for 1 minute, until fragrant.

5

Reduce the heat to medium. Now pour in the sherry or wine—it will sizzle and reduce down to almost nothing—then add the tomatoes and broth. Stir, then simmer, uncovered, for 15 minutes, until the sauce has thickened a little and the chicken is tender.

6

Add the chickpeas and chorizo to the pan, stir well, then simmer for 2 more minutes, until heated through.

7

Roughly chop the parsley leaves, add to the casserole, then stir to combine. Season to taste with salt and pepper. Drizzle with the extra-virgin olive oil, if using. Serve with crusty bread.

Breaded Fish
& Tartar Sauce

Preparation time: 20 minutes
Cooking time: 12–15 minutes
Serves 4 (easily halved)

Home-breaded fish is so much fresher tasting than frozen fish sticks or fillets, and it doesn't have to be fried either. To make the sauce for a special occasion, replace half of the mayonnaise with crème fraîche or sour cream—or for kids, simply serve with ketchup.

4 thick slices white bread (day-old bread is best), about 7 oz
1 handful fresh flat-leaf parsley
2 tablespoons light olive oil
2 oz Parmesan cheese
1 organic lemon
1¾ lb sustainably sourced thick white fish fillet, such as cod, haddock, pollack, or whiting
3 tbsp all-purpose flour
1 large egg
2 tsp capers
5 small gherkins or 1 large
½ cup good-quality mayonnaise
salt and pepper
salad greens or peas, to serve

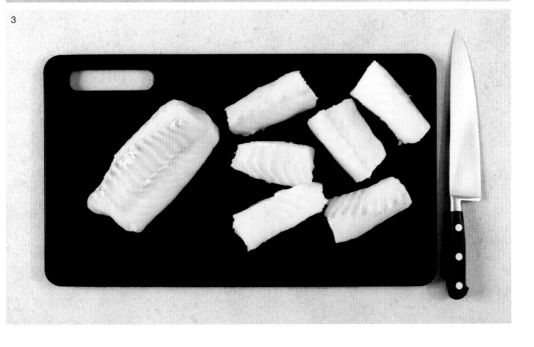

1
Preheat the oven to 425°F. Cut the crusts off the bread and discard. Put the bread into a food processor with half of the parsley—stalks and all—and all of the oil.

2
Pulse everything together to make oily, herby bread crumbs. Finely grate the Parmesan and the lemon zest, then mix into the crumbs with salt and pepper. Transfer to a bowl.

MAKE BREAD CRUMBS
FOR NEXT TIME
If you have more bread going stale, why not make double the bread crumb mixture and freeze half of it? Defrost overnight then use as above.

3
Cut the fish into chunky "fingers" about 1¼ × 1¼ × 4 inches.

4

Put the flour onto a plate and season it generously with salt and pepper. Break the egg into a bowl, add salt and pepper to this too, then beat it with a fork. Dust a piece of fish with the flour, then dip it into the egg. Let the excess egg drip off into the bowl below, then roll and pat the fish in the bread crumb mixture until covered in an even layer.

5

Place it onto a nonstick baking sheet and repeat with the rest of the fish. Rinse and dry your hands every now and again, as they can get a bit sticky.

6

Bake the fish for 12–15 minutes, until crisp and golden. Meanwhile, make the tartar sauce. Cut the lemon in half, squeeze one half and cut the other into wedges. Finely chop the remaining parsley leaves, the capers, and gherkins and put into a bowl. Add the mayonnaise and 1 tablespoon lemon juice. Season with salt and pepper.

7

Serve the fish with the tartar sauce, the lemon wedges, some salad greens or some just-cooked peas.

SHOPPING FOR FISH
It can be hard to tell if fillets of fish are fresh, especially if they're packaged. For that reason, it's best to buy from the fish counter. Fresh fish should look shiny and bright, not dull or dry. It should be firm when pressed (don't be afraid to ask), and smell like the sea. Anything that smells overly fishy is best avoided.

Macaroni & Cheese

Preparation time: 25 minutes
Cooking time: 30 minutes
Serves 4 (easily halved)

So comforting, simple, and economical, a hunger-busting pot of mac and cheese is always a winner with families. The tomatoes baked on top of this macaroni give a pleasant little tang here and there.

1 onion

1 bay leaf

3 cups milk

1 tsp kosher salt

12 oz macaroni, or other tube-
   shaped pasta

½ stick (¼ cup) butter

scant ½ cup all-purpose flour

7 oz sharp Cheddar cheese

2 oz Parmesan cheese

2 tsp Dijon mustard

nutmeg, for grating (optional)

4 ripe tomatoes

salt and pepper

1

Bring a large pan of water to a boil for the pasta. While it's heating, start the sauce. Cut the onion into a few rough chunks, then put into a pan with the bay leaf and the milk. Bring the milk to a boil over medium heat. As soon as small bubbles start to pop at the sides of the pan, take it off the heat. Let infuse for 10 minutes (or longer, if there's more time). This will give the cheese sauce a good depth of flavor.

2

Add the salt to the pasta water, then add the macaroni. Return to a boil, stir once, then cook for 8 minutes. Reserve a cupful of the cooking water, then drain the macaroni in a colander. It will be a little undercooked.

3

Once the milk has infused, remove the onion and bay leaf with a slotted spoon. Add the butter and sift in the flour.

4

Cook on medium-high heat, stirring with a whisk for about 5 minutes, until the sauce comes to a boil and is thickened and smooth. Meanwhile, preheat the oven to 350°F. Grate the Cheddar and Parmesan cheese.

5

Stir the mustard, ¼ teaspoon finely grated nutmeg (if using), and two-thirds of the Cheddar and Parmesan into the sauce. Season to taste with salt and pepper. If the pasta has stuck together a little, pour the reserved cup of pasta water into the colander, then stir to loosen. Pour the pasta into a baking dish. Pour the sauce over the pasta, and stir well.

6

Sprinkle the remaining cheese on top of the macaroni, then slice the tomatoes and place them on top. Season with salt and pepper.

7

Bake for 30 minutes, or until golden and bubbling. Serve immediately.

GETTING AHEAD
Make the cheese sauce up to 2 days ahead. Cover the surface with plastic wrap, then cool. Reheat gently, pour it over just-cooked pasta, then follow the recipe from step 6. If you make the whole dish in advance, the pasta tends to absorb a little too much of the sauce and makes the dish dry.

Lamb Chops with Tomato & Mint Salad

Preparation time: 20 minutes,
plus optional marinating time
Cooking time: 8–10 minutes
Serves 2 (easily doubled)

This mouthwatering lamb dish makes a fabulous summer meal, and it's smart enough for entertaining too. Bring out a hunk of crusty bread to mop up the juices.

1 organic lemon

2 tbsp extra-virgin olive oil

1 tsp sugar

1 tbsp capers

1 clove garlic

2 tsp light olive, sunflower, or
  vegetable oil

4 lamb chops, cutlets, or leg steaks,
  at room temperature

1 (14-oz) can lima beans, drained

½ red onion

1 bunch cherry tomatoes

1 handful fresh mint

salt and pepper

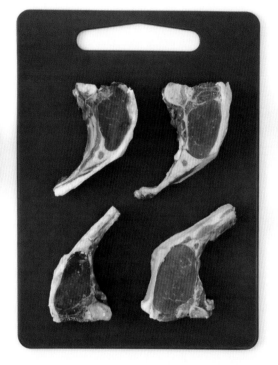

132

1

Squeeze the juice from half of the lemon into a small bowl, then add the extra-virgin olive oil and stir in the sugar and capers. Set aside.

2

Crush the garlic and put it into a small bowl. Finely grate the zest of the lemon, add to the garlic, then mix together with 1 teaspoon of the light oil. Season with salt and pepper. Rub this mixture all over the lamb. The lamb can be left to marinate for anything from 5 minutes to several hours at this point, if you have time. Keep the meat chilled in the refrigerator if you do want to do this well ahead. Remember to let the meat come up to room temperature before cooking.

3

Place a frying pan over medium heat. Add the second teaspoon of the light oil, wait 30 seconds, then add the chops. The first piece should sizzle immediately. If it doesn't, take it out and let the pan heat up a for little longer. Cook the lamb for 6 minutes, turning it halfway for meat that's medium-rare (pink and juicy in the middle). Cook for 2 minutes longer if you prefer lamb well done.

4

Transfer the meat to a warm plate, cover loosely with foil, and leave for a few minutes while you make the salad. Set the pan aside for later. To make the salad, put the beans into a large bowl. Thinly slice the red onion and halve the cherry tomatoes. Pick the leaves from the mint, tear them roughly, then stir the onion, tomatoes and mint through the beans. Season with salt and pepper.

5

Return the pan to medium heat, then add the lemon and caper mixture prepared in step 1. Scrape up any tasty bits from the bottom of the pan, then add the juices that have pooled under the lamb.

6

Spoon the salad onto plates, then nestle the lamb on top. Spoon the warm caper dressing over the lamb and the salad and serve immediately.

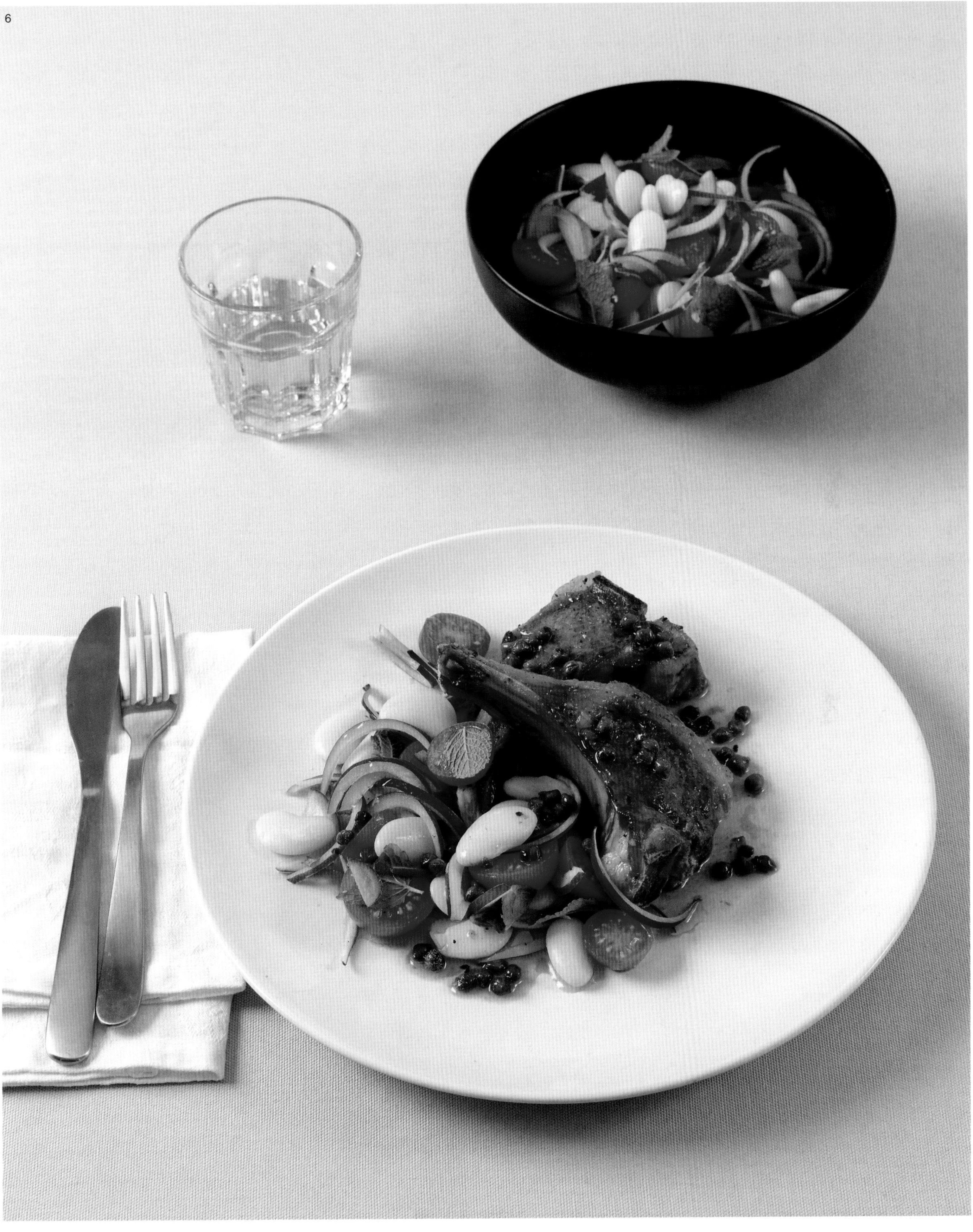

Sausages & Mashed Potatoes with Onion Gravy

Preparation time: 15 minutes
Cooking time: 30 minutes
Serves 4 (easily halved)

This is an old-fashioned recipe with one modern touch: a dash of balsamic vinegar that enriches and lifts the gravy at the end of cooking. Serve with a spoonful of Dijon mustard. For a traditional British variation known as Toad in the Hole, see page 138.

1 tbsp olive oil

8 good-quality pork sausages

2 onions

2 tbsp butter

1 generous sprig fresh thyme

1 kg (2¼ lb) medium-size baking
   potatoes, such as russets

1 tsp kosher salt

½ tsp sugar

1 tbsp all-purpose flour

2 tsp balsamic vinegar (optional)

generous 2 cups beef broth

½ cup milk

salt and pepper

1
Preheat the oven to 350°F. Heat a large frying pan over low heat, then add the oil. Fry the sausages in the oil for 5 minutes, turning them every minute or so, until well browned. Remove the pan from the heat. Transfer the sausages to a baking sheet and cook them in the oven for 25 minutes.

2
Meanwhile, start the gravy. Halve and thinly slice the onions. Return the pan to low heat, and add half the butter to the sausage juices. When it foams, add the onions and the leaves from the thyme. Cook for about 15 minutes, stirring occasionally with a wooden spoon, until softened and starting to turn golden.

3
While the onions cook, peel and quarter the potatoes. Put them into a large pan, cover with cold water, add the salt, then bring to a boil. Once the water is boiling, turn the heat down and simmer the potatoes for 15 minutes, until tender. The potatoes are ready when a table knife slices easily through the flesh. Always start baking potatoes in cold water and bring them to a boil, rather than adding them to boiling water.

4
When the onions have softened, turn up the heat, add the sugar, then cook for 2–3 minutes, stirring, until the onions are sticky, dark brown, and smell sweet.

5
Add the flour to the pan, then stir it around until it disappears into the onions. Cook for 2 more minutes, until the flour smells sweet and feels sandy between the spoon and pan as you stir.

6

Stir in the balsamic vinegar, if using, and one-third of the broth. The mixture will be a bit lumpy at first, but keep stirring until a smooth, thick paste comes together.

7

Gradually stir in the rest of the broth to make a thin, smooth gravy. Once the gravy comes to a boil, it will thicken. Remove from heat and set aside.

8

Check the sausages: They should be dark golden brown and sizzling. Turn the oven off. Drain the potatoes in a colander. Put the remaining butter and the milk into the potato pan, then heat it until the milk starts to boil and the butter melts. Add the potatoes, then remove from heat.

9

Mash the potatoes using a potato masher or a potato ricer. It's important to mash the potatoes while they're still piping hot. If left to cool, they'll turn gluey. Heating the milk and butter will also help you to achieve the best texture.

10

Spoon the mashed potatoes onto plates, then place 2 sausages on top. Spoon the onion gravy over, then eat immediately.

TO MAKE TOAD IN THE HOLE
Preheat the oven to 425°F. Brown the sausages in the frying pan, then transfer to a medium roasting pan. Add 2 tablespoons more oil, then put the dish into the oven to heat while you make the Yorkshire pudding batter (see page 274). Pour the batter around the sausages and cook for 30 minutes, until the batter is puffed and golden. Meanwhile, prepare the gravy as above. Cut into squares and serve with the gravy.

Penne with Tomato & Olive Sauce

Preparation time: 10 minutes
Cooking time: 12 minutes
Serves 2 (easily doubled)

A simple tomato sauce is one of the most useful (not to mention economical) recipes to know by heart. There are endless ways to vary this easy sauce: see page 142 for some ideas.

---

1 tsp kosher salt

8 oz penne pasta

2 cloves garlic

1 small bunch fresh basil

2 tbsp olive oil

1 (14½-oz) can chopped tomatoes

½ tsp sugar

25 g (1 oz) Parmesan cheese

½ cup pitted black olives (buy 3½ oz
    if you want to pit your own)

salt and pepper

1
Place a large pan of water on high heat and bring it to a boil. Add the salt and the pasta. Stir once, turn the heat down just a little, then boil for 10–12 minutes (check the instructions on the package), or until the pasta is just tender.

IS THE PASTA COOKED?
The best way to check if pasta is cooked, no matter what its shape, is to lift a piece out of the pan with a fork and bite it. It should be firm but not chewy.

2
While the pasta cooks, make the sauce. Thinly slice or crush the garlic and finely chop the basil stems. Heat the oil in a frying pan, keeping the heat low. Add the garlic and stems to the pan, then sauté very gently for 3 minutes, until softened.

MAKING THE MOST OF HERBS
Throughout this book you'll find recipes using the stems from a bunch of soft herbs (such as basil, parsley, and sage), as well as the leaves. By adding the chopped stems early on in the cooking, you'll be layering flavor into the dish from the beginning, ready to finish with a flourish of just-chopped leaves at the end.

3
Turn the heat to medium, then pour the tomatoes into the pan. Season with the sugar and simmer for 5 minutes, until slightly thickened.

4

Finely grate the Parmesan. Set a few basil leaves aside, then roughly tear the rest and stir them into the sauce. Roughly chop the olives, then stir these and half the cheese into the sauce. Season with salt and pepper.

PITTING OLIVES
To remove the pits from whole olives, squash each olive under the flat of your knife. Pluck out the pit, then chop the olive flesh.

5

Drain the pasta in a colander as soon as it's cooked, reserving a cup of the cooking water.

6

Stir the pasta and 2 tablespoons of its cooking water into the sauce. Add more water to thin it, if you need to.

7

Spoon the pasta onto plates or bowls, scatter the rest of the cheese and basil leaves over it, then eat immediately.

VARIATIONS
For a spicy pasta, add a pinch of dried chili flakes to the garlic as it softens. For a puttanesca-style sauce, swap the basil for flat-leaf parsley and sauté 2 chopped anchovy fillets with the garlic. Alternatively, make it creamy by adding a few spoonfuls of mascarpone, cream cheese, or crème fraîche. To serve it with fish or chicken, add chunky fillets of white fish or chicken breasts directly to the sauce. Fish will cook in about 10 minutes, and chicken breasts in 15–20 minutes.

Salmon with Garlic, Ginger, Greens & Rice

Preparation time: 15 minutes
Cooking time: 20 minutes
Serves 2

A quick, energizing supper for weary souls. Using a plate set in a frying pan is a clever way to steam without needing a special steamer basket. If you do have one, simply sit the plate in the basket over a large pan of water instead.

¾ cup basmati rice

1 large red chile

1 large clove garlic

1 thumb-size piece fresh ginger, about 1¼ inches

2 heads bok choy

2 fillets skinless salmon

2 tbsp soy sauce, plus more to serve, if desired

1 tsp toasted sesame oil

salt

1

First, prepare the rice. Put the rice into a medium pan, then cover with cold water. Swish the rice around in the water a few times; the water will become cloudy. Carefully drain the water away from the rice, then repeat this several times until the water runs clear.

WHY RINSE RICE?
Rice is naturally surrounded by starchy molecules, which expand when they're boiled and can make rice sticky. In some cases, such as risotto, it's important to keep the starch. But for fluffy basmati, rinsing is essential.

2

Cover the rice with double its volume of water, about 1¼ cups, or just enough to cover the rice by a fingertip. Season with salt, then put the pan over high heat and bring to a boil. Once boiling, reduce the heat to a simmer, stir the rice, then cover it with a tight-fitting lid. Cook the rice for 10 minutes. Meanwhile, start the vegetables.

NEED TO INCREASE
THE QUANTITY?
It's easy to increase these quantities if you're cooking for more than two. Allow 2¾ oz rice per person and cover it with double the quantity of water, or enough to cover it by a fingertip's depth. The cooking time will be the same, even for a large panful.

3

Halve and seed the chile, then thinly slice it. Thinly slice the garlic and finely grate the ginger. Cut the green leafy parts of the bok choy away from the white stalks, and set them aside. Then cut the stalks in half lengthwise.

4

If you have a steamer, put a plate into its base. Half-fill a saucepan the same size as the steamer with water, then sit the steamer on top. Alternatively, put a dinner plate into a large frying pan, then add enough water to come halfway up the outside of the plate. Bring the water to a boil. Put the salmon and bok choi onto the plate, then scatter the chile, garlic and ginger over them. Spoon the soy sauce over and around the fish and greens.

Cover the steamer or frying pan, then steam for 5 minutes. Nestle the bok choi leaves alongside the fish and replace the lid. Steam for another 5 minutes.

5

Meanwhile, check the rice. When it has finished cooking, take it off the heat and let it sit with the lid on for 10 minutes (or longer, it won't spoil). The rice will be cooked and fluffy.

6

The salmon and greens are cooked when the bok choy leaves are wilted. the stems are tender and the salmon flakes easily in the middle. Drizzle with the sesame oil.

7

Lift the salmon and greens onto warmed plates, then spoon over some of the tasty cooking juices. Splash with more soy sauce to taste. Fluff up the rice with a fork and serve alongside the fish.

Spaghetti with Pesto

Preparation time: 10 minutes
Cooking time: 10 minutes
Serves 4

Fresh homemade pesto has so
much more flavor than store-bought
pesto in jars. Although best eaten
as soon as it's made, any leftover
pesto will keep in the refrigerator,
covered with a layer of olive oil, for
a week or so.

½ tsp kosher salt

14 oz spaghetti (although any
    pasta shape will work)

¼ cup pine nuts

1 clove garlic

1 large bunch fresh basil

⅔ cup extra-virgin olive oil

2 oz Parmesan cheese,
    plus a little extra to serve

salt and pepper

1

Place a large pan of water on high heat and bring it to a boil. Add ½ teaspoon salt and the pasta and bring to a boil. Stir once, turn the heat down a little, then boil for 10 minutes, or until the pasta is just tender (check the cooking instructions on the package). See page 141 for how to tell if the pasta is cooked. Meanwhile, start the pesto. Heat a medium pan over low heat. Add the pine nuts and cook them for 3 minutes, stirring frequently, until they are golden and smell nutty. Transfer to a plate and let cool for a few minutes.

2

Very roughly chop the garlic and the basil stems and leaves, then put them into a food processor. Add the pine nuts and olive oil to the bowl and season with salt and pepper.

3

Pulse the ingredients together until a bright green, slightly textured sauce comes together. Finely grate the cheese, then pulse it into the sauce a couple of times.

4

Reserve a cup of the pasta cooking water, then drain in a colander. Return the pasta to the pan. Spoon half the pesto, plus a couple tablespoons of the reserved water, into the pasta. Toss well, using a pair of tongs if you have them. If the pasta seems at all dry, add a little more of the reserved cooking water. Adding a little of the pasta's cooking water to the pan helps the sauce and pasta to marry together.

5

Serve the pasta topped with a little more Parmesan, shaved thinly with a vegetable peeler, if you like.

Cajun Chicken with Pineapple Salsa

Preparation time: 30 minutes,
plus optional marinating time
Cooking time: 12 minutes
Serves 4

Brighten up your weeknight with
this lively and healthy meal. The
spice rub is aromatic rather than hot
(although there's nothing wrong with
adding a sprinkle of chili powder),
and it works beautifully with pork
chops, steak, or even chunky fillets
of fish too.

For the chicken

4 skinless, boneless chicken breasts

2 cloves garlic

2 tsp dried thyme

2 tsp paprika

1 tsp black pepper

2 tsp ground allspice

1 tbsp sunflower or vegetable oil

salt and pepper

boiled rice (see page 145), to serve
    (optional)

For the salsa

1 medium, ripe pineapple

1 small red onion

1 green chile

½ red bell pepper

1 handful fresh cilantro

1 lime, plus more to serve in
    wedges, if you like

1
First, prepare the chicken. Preheat the broiler. Slash each breast 3 times using a sharp knife, cutting about a third of the way through the flesh.

2
Crush the garlic, then put it into a small bowl with the dried thyme, paprika, black pepper, allspice, and oil. Season with salt and mix well.

3
Rub the spice mixture all over the chicken and down into the slashes. The chicken can be left for up to 24 hours in the refrigerator in this marinade, if you like. When ready to cook, put the chicken onto the rack of a broiler pan. Broil the chicken for 12 minutes, turning it once or twice during cooking.

4
While the chicken cooks, start the salsa. Cut the ends off the pineapple. Cut the pineapple into quarters lengthwise, then slice off the strip of hard, pale core that runs along the middle of each quarter.

HOW TO CHOOSE
A RIPE PINEAPPLE
A juicy, sweet pineapple will smell fragrant and fruity. Pull one of the leaves from the center of the crown of leaves. If it comes out with a gentle tug, the pineapple is ripe.

5

Cut criss-cross lines about ½ inch apart across each pineapple quarter, cutting all the way down to the skin. Then, starting with the knife about ½ inch away from the skin, run the knife between the flesh and the skin to release the small cubes into a large bowl.

6

Finely chop the onion. Seed, then finely chop the chile and the pepper. Add to the pineapple and mix. Roughly chop the cilantro leaves, add to the salsa, then squeeze in the juice from the lime and stir. Season with salt and pepper.

7

After 12 minutes' cooking, the chicken should be dark golden brown—almost black in places—and cooked through. If you haven't yet finished chopping the salsa ingredients, don't worry—the chicken will benefit from resting for a while, covered with foil to keep it warm.

IS THE CHICKEN COOKED?
Slashing the meat will have helped the heat to travel into the chicken. If you're not sure if the chicken is cooked, insert a sharp knife into the thickest part of the chicken breast. When you remove it, the juices that come out of the meat should be clear, without a trace of pink. The tip of the knife should feel hot too—if not, return to the broiler for a few minutes more, then test again.

8

Serve the chicken with spoonfuls of salsa, wedges of lime, and some plain rice, if you like.

Stuffed Chicken with Tomatoes & Arugula

Preparation time: 20 minutes
Cooking time: 25 minutes
Serves 4 (easily halved)

Bring this delicious one-pot meal straight to the table—not only because everyone will be impressed, but also because the cooking juices are well worth soaking up with good bread once the chicken is all gone.

---

2 sprigs fresh rosemary

4 medium skinless, boneless
   chicken breasts

3½ oz soft goat cheese
   (or any full-fat soft cheese)

8 strips dry-cured smoked bacon

1 tbsp sunflower or vegetable oil

4 large or 6 smaller ripe tomatoes

1 clove garlic

2 tbsp extra-virgin olive oil

3½ oz arugula or other
   leafy salad greens

½ lemon

salt and pepper

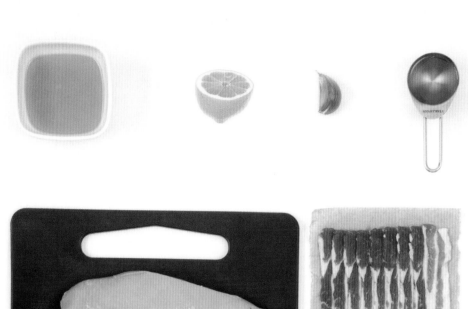

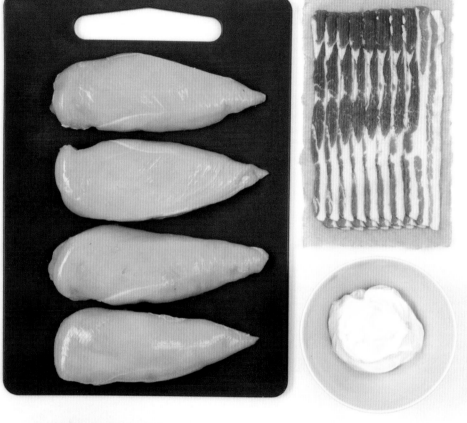

1
Preheat the oven to 400°F. Finely chop the needle-shape leaves from the rosemary. Put the chicken onto a cutting board. Using a small sharp knife, cut a slit into the thickest part of each chicken breast, then poke down inside the chicken to make a pocket. Spoon the cheese into each pocket, using your fingers to help, then seal the pocket up as well as you can.

2
Season the chicken with salt and pepper, then sprinkle with half of the rosemary. Wrap 2 strips of the bacon tightly around each piece of chicken, tucking in any loose ends.

3
Place a shallow, flameproof casserole over high heat, then add the sunflower or vegetable oil. After 30 seconds, add the chicken. Cook for at least 2 minutes on each side, until the bacon is starting to turn golden. Kitchen tongs are useful here.

4

Meanwhile, very thickly slice the tomatoes and thinly slice the garlic. Add the tomatoes to the casserole, then sprinkle them with the remaining rosemary and the garlic. Season with salt and pepper and drizzle with about ½ tablespoon of the olive oil. Put the pan into the oven for 25 minutes.

Remove the pan from the oven and set aside for a couple of minutes to let the chicken rest. The chicken will be surrounded with delicious tomato-flavored juices.

5

Put the arugula into a large bowl. Squeeze the juice from the lemon over it and drizzle with the remaining olive oil. Season with salt and pepper.

6

Serve the chicken with the salad, drizzling some of the warm pan juices around around each plate.

Steak with Garlic Butter

Preparation time: 15 minutes,
plus 10 minutes for chilling
Cooking time: 5–7 minutes
Serves 2

Cooking steaks well is surprisingly
easy. Buy good meat and follow a few
basic rules, and you'll be rewarded
with something very special. The garlic
butter recipe will make more than
you need, but you can keep the rest
wrapped in the refrigerator for a week,
or in the freezer for a month. Serve
with Chunky Oven Fries (page 312).

---

1 clove garlic

1 handful fresh flat-leaf parsley

4 tbsp unsalted butter, softened

¼ tsp kosher salt

2 sirloin steaks, about ¾ inch thick,
   at room temperature

1 tsp vegetable or sunflower oil

salt and pepper

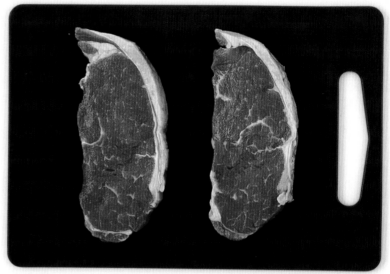

1

Make the garlic butter first. Crush the garlic and roughly chop the parsley. Put these into a small bowl. Add the butter, the ¼ teaspoon salt and season with pepper, then mix well with a fork.

2

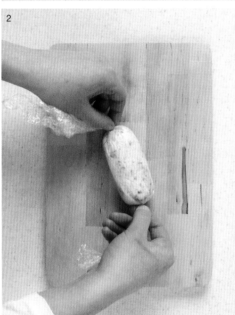

Unroll a sheet of plastic wrap onto the work surface. Spoon the butter onto the plastic in a rough rectangle shape. Roll the plastic wrap around the butter, then twist the ends to make a tight sausage. Chill in the freezer for 10 minutes until firm (or for longer in the refrigerator, depending on how much time you have).

3

Meanwhle, trim any excess fat off the steak (too much will just cause the kitchen to get smoky), leaving a layer about ¼ inch thick. Snip into this fat edge with a pair of kitchen scissors to prevent the steaks from curling up too much as they cook.

4

When you're ready to cook the steaks, rub them with the oil, then season generously with salt and pepper. Heat a ridged grill pan or frying pan over medium heat until hot but not smoking. Put the steaks into the pan, then cook, without moving them around, for 2 minutes. The steak should give a loud sizzle as the first edge hits the pan; if not, the pan isn't hot enough. Give it another minute to heat up, then try again. Press down a few times on the surface of the steaks with a spatula or tongs as they cook, to encourage a deep, golden crust underneath.

5

Turn the steaks over and cook for another 2 minutes for medium rare—that is, pink and juicy in the middle. Press down on the meat as before to encourage good color and a crusty exterior. After 2 minutes on each side, press the steak. Rather than feeling very soft or very bouncy, a medium-rare steak will just yield to your finger. For medium steak, allow 3 minutes per side. To cook the fat along the edge of the steak, use tongs to hold the steak, fat-edge down against the pan. Hold the steak for about 30 seconds, until the fat turns golden.

6

Transfer the steaks to a warm plate and take the pan off the heat. Cover the steaks very loosely with foil then let stand for a couple of minutes. While you wait, preheat the broiler.

7

Return the steaks and their resting juices to the pan. Unwrap the butter and slice off 2 thick disks. Put them on top of the steaks.

8

Place the steaks under the broiler for 30 seconds, or until the butter starts to melt over the steaks and into the juices below.

9

Serve the steaks with the buttery juices, and enjoy immediately.

GOLDEN RULES

Always take the steak out of the refrigerator an hour before cooking. The thickness of steak is more important than its weight: A thinner steak will cook more quickly than a thicker steak. Always err on the side of caution with cooking times. You can't undo an overcooked steak, but you can put an undercooked steak back under the broiler.

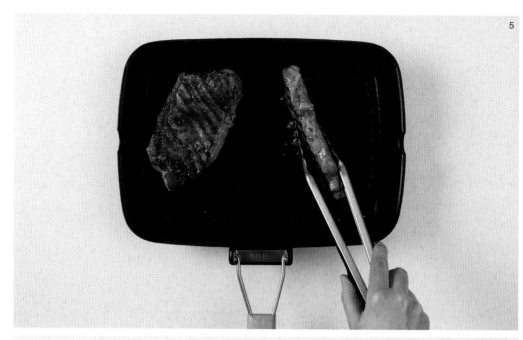

Spaghetti Carbonara

Preparation time: 10 minutes
Cooking time: 10–12 minutes
Serves 2 (easily doubled)

Just six ingredients come together to create this quick and indulgent dish. For an extra touch of luxury add a dash of cream—just two tablespoons or so—to the Parmesan and eggs before mixing with the pasta.

1 tsp kosher salt

7 oz spaghetti

1 clove garlic

4 strips smoked dry-cured bacon,
    or 3½ oz smoked bacon lardons,
    or pancetta cubes

1 tbsp light olive oil

1½ oz Parmesan cheese (about
    ½ cup grated)

3 large eggs

salt and pepper

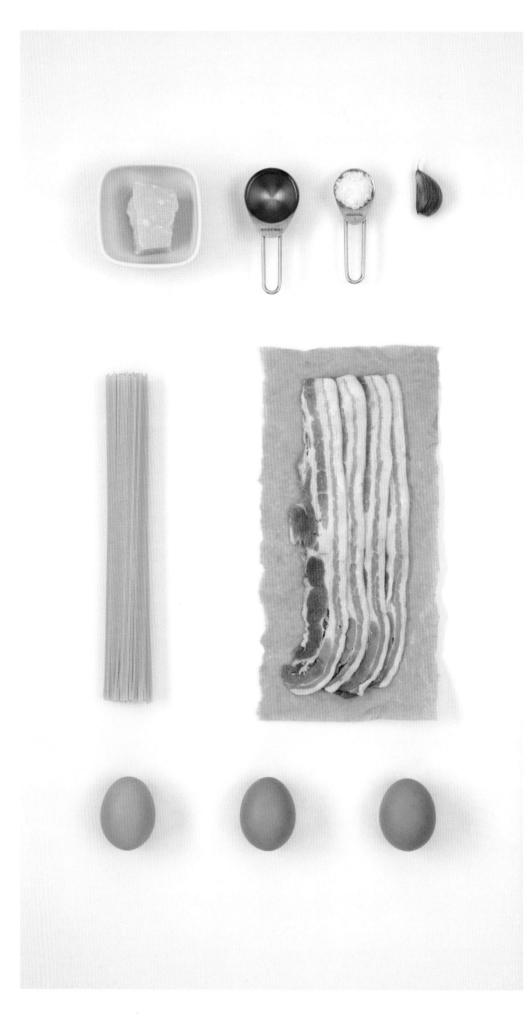

1

Put a large pan of water over high heat and bring it to a boil. Add the salt, then add the spaghetti and bring back to a boil. Stir once, turn the heat down a little, and boil for 10 minutes, or until the pasta is just tender (see page 141).

2

While the pasta cooks, start the sauce. Smash the whole garlic clove without peeling it. You can do this by simply bashing it with the bottom of a pan keeping it in one piece. Chop the bacon into small pieces. Heat a large frying pan over medium heat, then add the oil. After 30 seconds, add the chopped bacon and the garlic. Fry for 8–10 minutes, or until the bacon is golden and crisp and the fat has run out. Discard the garlic and take the pan off the heat.

3

While the bacon cooks, finely grate the Parmesan cheese and beat the eggs in a measuring cup with a fork. Mix half of the Parmesan into the eggs. Season with salt and pepper.

4

When the pasta is just tender, reserve a cup of its cooking water, then drain it in a colander. Add the pasta to the bacon pan, add 2 tablespoons of the reserved cooking water, then pour the egg and cheese mixture over it. Toss everything together quickly (tongs are useful here), so that the egg mixture, bacon and its juices coat the pasta. The residual heat in the pan and the pasta will be enough to just cook the eggs to a creamy sauce within about 1 minute.

5

Scoop the pasta into warmed bowls, then sprinkle with the rest of the cheese and a little black pepper, and serve immediately.

Shrimp Pad Thai

Preparation time: 15 minutes
Cooking time: 10 minutes
Serves 4

Give tofu a try in this quick Thai café classic. Leftover cold roast chicken could be added to the noodles too.

14 oz wide rice noodles

12 oz firm tofu, drained

3 fat cloves garlic

1 bunch scallions

1 small bunch fresh cilantro

1 tbsp vegetable or sunflower oil

3 tbsp tamarind paste (optional)

3 tbsp sweet chili sauce

3 tbsp nam pla (Thai fish sauce)

1½ tbsp sugar

1 handful roasted peanuts (optional)

4 large eggs

7 oz uncooked shrimp, shelled and
    deveined

½ tsp dried chili flakes
    (or more if you like)

2 limes

3½ oz bean sprouts

1
Put the noodles into a large bowl, then pour enough boiling water over them to cover. Stir gently and let soak until you get to step 8.

WHAT TO DO IF YOUR NOODLES STICK TOGETHER
Sometimes rice noodles just want to stick together as they soak. If this happens, rinse the noodles in a colander under cold water and separate the strands with your fingers.

2
While you wait, cut the tofu into cubes about ¾ inch across. Crush the garlic and thinly slice the scallions. Pick the leaves from the cilantro.

3
Put a large nonstick frying pan or wok over medium-high heat. Add the oil, then the tofu. Fry for 6 minutes, stirring frequently, until the tofu is golden all over. Transfer the tofu to a plate covered with paper towels using a slotted spoon. This will absorb any excess oil.

4
Meanwhile, put the tamarind paste (if using), chili sauce, fish sauce, and sugar into a small measuring cup and stir together. Roughly chop the peanuts, if using. Crack the eggs into a bowl and loosely beat them with a fork.

TAMARIND PASTE
This is a fairly runny brown paste made from the tamarind pod. Tamarind has a uniquely sourish taste and adds piquancy to many Asian recipes. It's stocked in many grocery stores, but if you can't find it, simply be more generous with the lime juice.

5

Put the pan back over high heat. It shouldn't need more oil. Carefully add the shrimp and fry for 2 minutes, until they turn completely pink. Now add the garlic, chili flakes and half the scallions. Cook for 1 minute, stirring, until the garlic and scallions smell fragrant.

6

Transfer the shrimp to a plate, then add the beaten eggs to the pan. Cook for 30 seconds to 1 minute, moving the eggs around the pan a little with a wooden spoon until just set, like an omelet.

7

Lift the omelet out of the pan and transfer it to a cutting board. Roll it up like a pancake, then cut across the roll to make long thin strips. Take the pan off the heat if you feel like you need to concentrate on this bit.

8

Return the pan to the heat, drain the noodles and add them to the pan. Add the sauce, most of the cilantro leaves, the shredded egg, tofu, shrimp, the remaining scallions and a squeeze of lime juice, then toss well.

GETTING A GRIP
A pair of tongs is a great tool here, as they will help you to turn and toss the noodles in the sauce. If you don't have tongs, try using 2 wooden spoons—holding them as you would salad servers—instead.

9

For an authentic look, serve the peanuts and beansprouts in little piles alongside the noodles, then scatter the remaining cilantro over the dish. Cut the remaining lime into wedges and put a wedge on each plate.

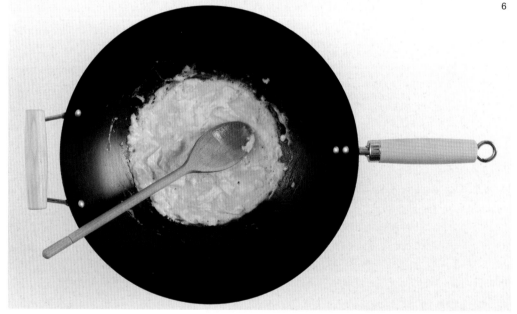

Thai Curry with Beef

Preparation time: 15 minutes
Cooking time: 16 minutes
Serves 2 (easily doubled)

Revive the senses with a bowl of
fragrant Thai curry—so easy
to make instead of ordering take-
out. If you want to make this with
chicken or shrimp, see page 170
for instructions. For the perfect
fluffy basmati rice to go with your
curry, turn to page 145.

2 fat cloves garlic

1 thumb-size piece fresh ginger

11 oz sirloin or rump steak

1 cup green beans

5 baby eggplants (or
    1 ordinary eggplant)

2 tbsp sunflower or vegetable oil

1½ tbsp Thai red or green
    curry paste

1 tsp light brown sugar

1 (14-oz) can coconut milk (use
    reduced fat if desired)

4 freeze-dried kaffir lime
    leaves (optional)

1 large red chile

1 small handful fresh cilantro

2 tbsp nam pla (Thai fish sauce)

1 lime

boiled rice, to serve (optional)

1

Crush the garlic and finely grate the ginger. Slice the steak into thin strips. For the most tender result, cut across the grain of the meat. Trim the ends of the beans, then cut them in half. Cut the eggplant into thick slices.

2

Place a large frying pan over high heat, then add the oil. After 30 seconds, add the garlic, ginger and steak. Fry for 2 minutes, or until the steak has changed color, then remove the meat from the pan, leaving most of the ginger and garlic behind.

3

Stir the curry paste into the pan, then cook for 2 minutes until sizzling and fragrant.

4

Add the sugar, coconut milk, a scant ½ cup of water, the beans, eggplant and lime leaves, if using, then simmer for 10 minutes, until the vegetables are just tender.

KAFFIR LIME LEAVES
These unassuming leaves will plump up and add an intense lime scent and flavor to your curry. If you can't find them, finely grate the zest of the lime and add that instead.

5

Meanwhile, finely slice the red chile and tear the cilantro leaves from their stalks. When the vegetables are tender, stir the fish sauce into the curry and squeeze in the juice from the lime. Taste the sauce— it should have a balance of sweet, salty, hot and sour, without one flavor particularly dominating the others. Return the beef to the pan, and warm through for 1 minute.

6

Sprinkle with the sliced chile and cilantro leaves.

7

Ladle into bowls and serve with boiled rice.

VARIATIONS
For a chicken curry, slice 2 chicken breasts thinly, then fry as for the beef, until all the pink meat has turned white. Proceed as above, then return to the pan halfway through step 4. For a shrimp curry, follow the recipe through the end of step 5. Then add 11 ounces uncooked shrimp, and simmer for a few minutes, until the shrimp have turned completely pink and are cooked through.

FOOD

FOR

Sticky Barbecue Ribs

Preparation time: 10 minutes,
plus 1 hour for marinating
Cooking time: 2½ hours
Serves 6

Making a tasty barbecue marinade
from scratch is as simple as opening
a jar. Let the ribs and marinade cook
slowly in the oven, and the sauce
takes care of itself. Look for ribs
surrounded with plenty of meat and
fat around the bone.

1 clove garlic

3 tbsp tomato purée

6 tbsp soy sauce

3 tbsp honey

2 tbsp red-wine vinegar

2 tbsp dark brown sugar

½ tsp kosher salt

½ tsp pepper

½ tsp paprika

½ tsp Tabasco sauce

2 tbsp Worcestershire sauce

18 meaty pork spare ribs,
    about 4½ lb

1

Crush the garlic, then put it into a large bowl. Add all of the other ingredients except for the ribs, then stir together. Now add the ribs, and toss them well in the marinade. Let stand for at least 1 hour at room temperature, or up to 24 hours in the refrigerator.

2

Preheat the oven to 350°F. Transfer the ribs and all of their marinade into a large roasting pan, spreading them out evenly. Cover the pan tightly with foil, then bake the ribs for 1½ hours. Remove the foil, then return the ribs to the oven for 1 hour more, turning them in the sauce every 20 minutes or so with a pair of tongs.

3

When they're cooked, the ribs will be meltingly tender and coated with a dark, sticky sauce. Serve them on their own, with finger bowls if desired, and napkins.

Chicken Wings & Blue Cheese Dip

Preparation time: 15 minutes
Cooking time: 40 minutes
Serves 6 (easily doubled)

Chicken wings are cheap to buy and have lots of flavor. In this version of the famous Buffalo Wings, the crisp wings are tossed with chili sauce, then served with a creamy blue cheese dip and crisp celery— a time-honored and very moreish combination.

2¼ lb chicken wings

¼ tsp kosher salt

¼ tsp pepper

¼ tsp cayenne pepper

2¾ oz strong blue cheese, such as
    Stilton or Gorgonzola

5 tbsp plain yogurt

¼ cup good-quality mayonnaise

1 bunch celery

scant ½ cup chili sauce

1

Preheat the oven to 400°F. If the tips of the chicken wings haven't already been removed, cut them off with kitchen scissors, then cut each wing into 2 pieces through the joint using a sharp knife.

2

Put the wings into a large baking pan, then add the salt, pepper, and cayenne. Rub the seasonings all over the chicken using your hands.

3

Put the chicken into the oven and roast for 40 minutes, or until crisp and golden, turning once. Meanwhile, make the blue cheese dip. Put the blue cheese in a large bowl, then mash with a fork. Add the yogurt and the mayonnaise and season with salt and pepper. Mix well and chill in the refrigerator until needed.

4

Trim the base off the bunch of celery, then separate out the stalks. Trim off any leaves. Cut the celery into finger-length sticks.

5

When the chicken wings are crisp all over and tender, pour the chili sauce over them and stir well to coat.

6

Serve the chicken with the dip and celery sticks, with plenty of napkins for sticky fingers.

Antipasti with Tapenade & Tomato Bruschetta

Preparation time: 35 minutes
Cooking time: 4 minutes
Serves 6

This dish is a bit of a hybrid, but it's a very good one. Antipasti are a very Italian way to start a meal (it literally means "before the meal") along with bruschetta, which are crisp, tomato-topped toasts. Tapenade is a traditional French olive paste, but it's also very popular in Italy and goes beautifully with the other elements and flavors on the antipasti board.

¾ cup good-quality pitted black or
   green olives
2 tbsp capers in brine, drained
2 canned anchovy fillets, drained
3 sprigs fresh thyme
2 tbsp extra-virgin olive oil,
   plus extra to serve
½ lemon
3 medium ripe tomatoes, about
   9 oz in total
1 handful fresh basil
14 oz crusty sourdough, or other
   good-quality bread, sliced
1 clove garlic
salt and pepper
your choice of cured meats,
   such as prosciutto or salami
   (allow 3–4 slices per person)
cornichons, caperberries and
   marinated artichokes, to serve

1
To make the tapenade, put the olives, capers, anchovies, thyme leaves, and oil into the bowl of a food processor. Squeeze the lemon and add the juice.

2
Pulse until a thick, chunky paste comes together. The sides of the bowl might need scraping down a few times before the mixture reaches the right texture.

3

For the bruschetta, roughly chop the tomatoes and put them into a bowl. Roughly chop the basil leaves and stir them into the tomatoes. Season with salt and pepper and a little extra-virgin olive oil. Set aside.

GETTING THE BEST FROM YOUR TOMATOES
Tomatoes taste so much better at room temperature than chilled. As long as they're kept away from direct sun and heat, they will keep at room temperature for a few days, and as a bonus they will ripen at the same time. If your kitchen is very warm, then chill your tomatoes—but remember to take them out of the refrigerator a few hours before use.

4

Cut each slice of bread in half or into 3 pieces, depending on its size. Preheat the broiler. Put the bread onto a large baking sheet and broil for 2 minutes on each side, until crisp and golden.

5

Cut the garlic clove in half, then rub one of the cut sides sparingly over one side of each piece of toast. Drizzle a little oil over the garlicky sides.

6

Serve the toasts on a large board, with the cured meats, cornichons, caperberries, artichokes, chopped tomatoes, and tapenade, ready for everyone to help themselves. Spoon the tomatoes on top of the toasts to make bruschetta, or spread with a little of the tapenade.

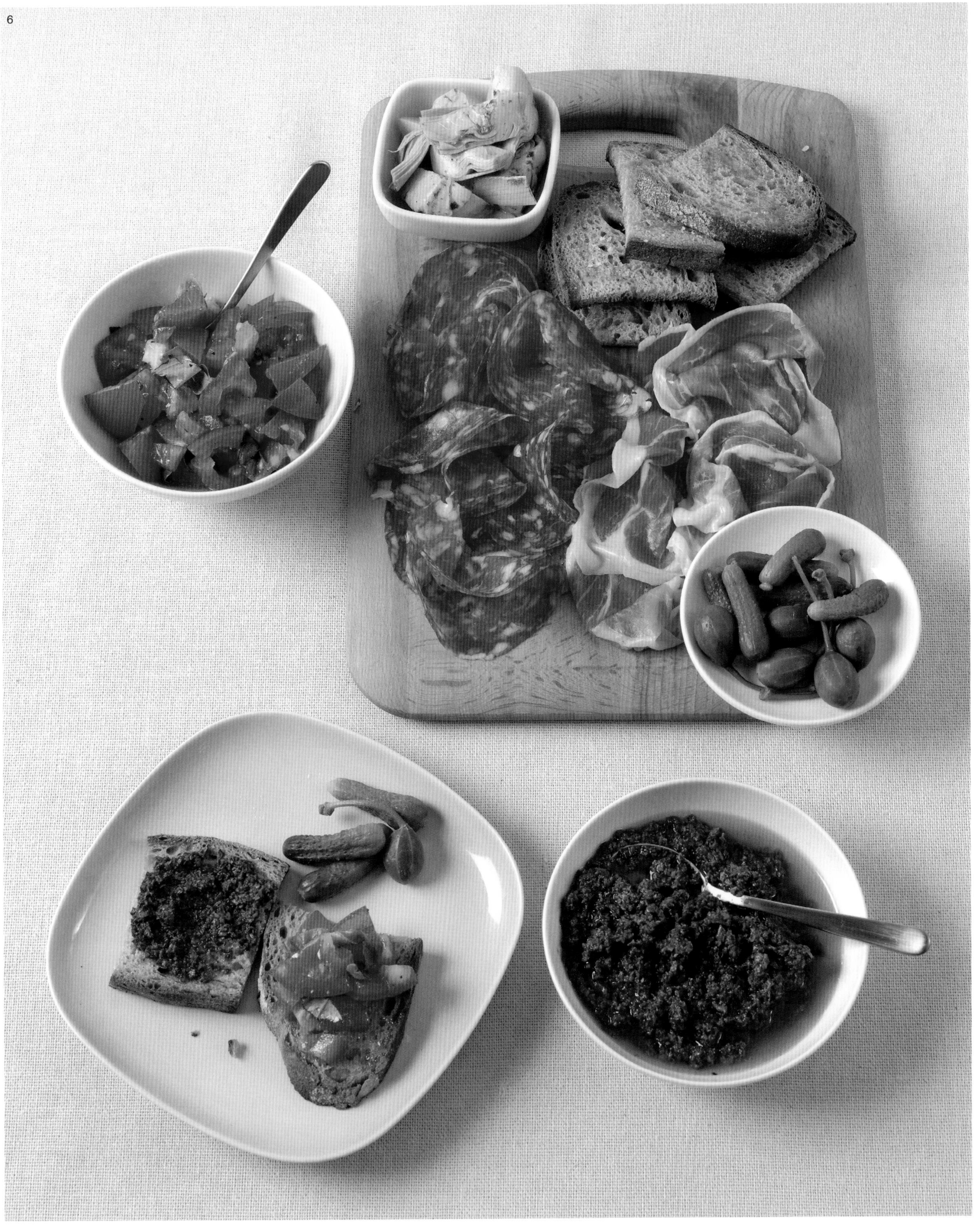

Cheese Nachos with Guacamole

Preparation time: 30 minutes
Cooking time: 7 minutes
Serves 6

Crisp nachos are always popular, and make a great choice for a snack if you're not sure who does or doesn't eat meat. Layering the sauce, tortilla chips and beans means that every chip should have something tasty on it, right down to the bottom of the dish.

1 clove garlic

3 tbsp extra-virgin or light olive oil

1 (14½-oz) can chopped tomatoes

3 ripe avocados (see note)

1 small bunch fresh cilantro

1 red onion

1 ripe tomato

2 limes

8 oz Cheddar cheese, shredded

14 oz tortilla chips, lightly salted
  or original flavor

1 (14-oz) can black beans, drained

1 handful sliced jalapeño chilies
  from a jar, drained

7 fl oz sour cream

salt and pepper

1
Make the tomato salsa for the nachos first. Thinly slice the garlic. Put a pan over low heat and add 2 tablespoons of the oil. After about30 seconds, add the garlic and let it sizzle very gently for 2 minutes. Don't let it color.

2
Turn up the heat, then add the canned tomatoes. Simmer, uncovered, for 15 minutes, until the mix is thickened and reduced by about a third. Season with salt and pepper, then cool. The sauce can be made well ahead, or frozen.

3
For the guacamole, cut each avocado in half. Scoop out the pit with a teaspoon, then spoon the flesh into a large bowl.

CHOOSING AND PREPARING AVOCADOS
To choose a ripe avocado, gently press the stem end. If it yields slightly, the avocado is ripe. If it's squishy, it will be past its best.

To cut an avocado in half, very carefully push the blade of a knife into it, until it stops against the pit. Slide the knife all the way around the avocado, keeping the blade against the pit. Pull out the knife, then twist the two halves apart.

4

Mash the avocado against the side of the bowl using a fork. Finely chop the cilantro stems and roughly chop most of the leaves. Finely chop the onion and roughly chop the fresh tomato. Stir into the avocado with the remaining olive oil. Squeeze the juice from the limes and stir it in. Season with salt and pepper. You can keep the guacamole chilled and covered tightly with plastic wrap for up to 24 hours.

5

Preheat the oven to 400°F. Grate the cheese. Put half the tortilla chips into 2 large ovenproof dishes. Haphazardly spoon half of the tomato salsa over them, then scatter half the beans, a few jalapeños, and a little of the cheese over the top. Repeat to make more layers, ending with cheese.

6

Bake the nachos for about 7 minutes, or until the cheese has melted. Sprinkle with more jalapeños and the remaining cilantro leaves. Spoon some of the guacamole and sour cream on top and serve the rest on the side.

Pizza Margherita

Preparation time: 25 minutes,
plus 1 hour for rising
Cooking time: 30 minutes
Serves 6 (makes 2 pizzas)

Homemade pizza doesn't get much
easier than this recipe, with its
virtually no-knead dough and no-
cook tomato sauce. Children will
love to lend a hand with the making,
just as much as the eating!

2½ cups bread flour, plus extra
   for rolling out
1 tsp kosher salt
1 tsp fast-rising yeast
2 tbsp extra-virgin olive oil, plus
   extra for oiling and drizzling
1 clove garlic
1 handful fresh basil
½ cup tomato purée (crushed and
   strained tomatoes)
1 tsp dried oregano
1 handful cherry tomatoes
4 oz fresh mozzarella cheese,
   drained
1½ oz Parmesan cheese
   (about ½ cup grated)
salt and pepper

1
Make the dough first. Put the flour, salt, and yeast into a large bowl, then mix well. Measure 7 fl oz warm water into a cup, then add the oil.

2
Pour the oil and water over the flour and yeast, then quickly mix together to make a rough, sticky dough. Set aside for 10 minutes.

3
Lightly dust your work surface with a little flour and also flour your hands. Turn the dough out, then roll and knead it on the work surface for about 1 minute, until the dough is smooth and bouncy. Thanks to the standing time earlier, this will only take about 30 seconds or so.

HOW TO KNEAD
Hold the left edge of the dough down, then grab the edge farthest away from you with your other hand, and push the dough away from you. Fold the stretched dough back on top of itself, press it down with your palm, then turn the dough through 90 degrees. After a few turns, the dough will be smooth and elastic. Sprinkle the work surface with a little flour if the dough sticks.

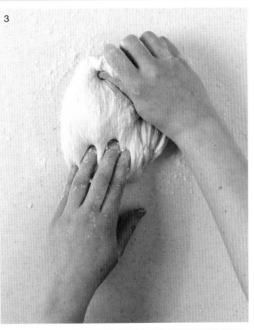

4
Shape the dough into a ball, ready for rising.

5
Rub a little oil around the inside of the bowl, then put the dough into it. Lightly oil a sheet of plastic wrap, then cover the dough and leave in a warm (not hot) place, for 1 hour, until the dough has doubled in size.

6

Meanwhile, make the sauce. Crush the garlic and put it into a bowl. Reserve some of the smaller basil leaves for later, then roughly chop the rest of the leaves and add them to the bowl. Stir in the tomato purée and oregano, and season with salt and pepper.

7

Cut the tomatoes in half, then thinly slice the mozzarella. Finely grate the Parmesan.

8

Once the dough has risen, preheat the oven to 475°F. Flour the work surface again and scrape the dough onto it, using your hand. The dough will be very bubbly underneath. Use a large knife to cut the dough in half.

9

Scatter a little flour over 2 flat baking sheets. Lift a piece of dough onto one of the sheets, then press it out with your hands to a rough round, about 12 inches across. This can take some time—the dough will spring back as you stretch it. Repeat with the second piece.

10

Use the back of a spoon to spread the tomato sauce over the pizzas, leaving a border around the edge for the crust. Arrange the mozzarella and tomatoes on top, sprinkle with Parmesan, then drizzle with a little oil. Season with salt and pepper. The pizzas can be prepared to this stage in advance and stored for about 2 hours in the refrigerator before baking.

11

Bake the pizzas one at a time for 12–15 minutes, or until the crust is crisp and brown and the cheese sizzling. Top with the remaining basil, then cut into wedges to serve.

Hummus with Marinated Olives & Pitas

Preparation time: 20 minutes
Cooking time: 2 minutes
Serves 6

Add a few flavorings to a pot of olives and whip up some hummus, and a mezze platter to share is ready in minutes. The key to good hummus is lots of oil and lots of seasoning—don't be surprised how much you may need to add.

2 cups mixed olives
   (pitted, if you like)
1 large red chile
2 organic lemons
8 oz feta cheese
1 tsp red- or white-wine vinegar
6 tbsp extra-virgin olive oil
1 handful fresh flat-leaf parsley
3 cloves garlic
2 (14-oz) cans chickpeas, drained
1 tsp kosher salt
3 tbsp tahini (see note)
6 pita breads, to serve
1 pinch cayenne pepper or paprika,
   to serve

1

Put the olives into a bowl. Seed and finely chop the chile and finely grate the zest of 1 lemon. Cut the feta into small cubes. Stir the feta into the olives, then add the vinegar and 2 tablespoons of the oil. Roughly chop the parsley leaves and stir in. Set aside to marinate.

2

For the hummus, chop the garlic cloves very roughly. Squeeze the juice from the lemons (there should be about 6 tablespoons in total). Put all but 2 tablespoons of the chickpeas into the bowl of a food processor with the garlic, lemon juice, 3 tablespoons of oil, the salt, and tahini.

WHAT IS TAHINI?
Tahini is a paste made from ground sesame seeds, which is often used in Middle Eastern cooking. It will add a silky texture and a deep nutty flavor to your hummus.

3

Process the ingredients together
to make a smooth, thick hummus.
You may need to scrape the sides
of the bowl down a few times as you
go. If the hummus seems too thick,
add a little water, starting with
2 tablespoons. Taste and season
with salt and pepper if necessary.

4

When ready to eat, warm the pita
breads. Preheat the broiler. Put
the pitas onto a baking sheet, then
broil for 1 minute on each side,
or until the breads puff up a little.
Cut into strips.

5

To serve the hummus, scoop it
into a serving bowl, top with the
rest of the chickpeas, then drizzle
1 tablespoon olive oil over it.
Sprinkle with the pinch of cayenne
pepper or paprika and serve
with the marinated olives and pita
bread strips.

Crispy Duck Pancakes

Preparation time: 20 minutes
Cooking time: 1½ hours
Serves 6 (easily doubled)

There's no secret to making this classic Chinese dish—all that's needed is the patience to wait while the duck slowly cooks to crisp melting perfection.

2 tsp Chinese five-spice powder

2 tsp kosher salt

½ teaspoon pepper

4 duck legs

1 large cucumber

2 bunches scallions

24 Chinese pancakes

½ cup hoisin sauce

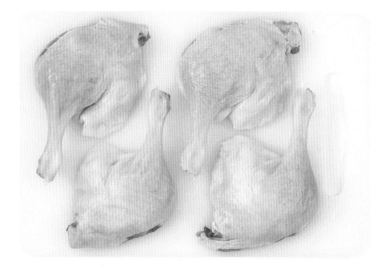

1
Preheat the oven to 325°F. Mix the five-spice powder with the salt and pepper. Put the duck legs into a roasting pan. Rub the duck legs all over with the salty spice.

2
Roast the duck for 1½ hours, or until the skin is very dark golden and crisp and the meat is very tender. The fat will have run out of the skin. A convection oven will give a really crisp result, so if you have the option, use a convection oven, not forgetting to reduce the temperature by 50°F.

3

Meanwhile, cut the cucumber into thin sticks. Cut off the dark green parts of the scallions, reserving them for another use. Finely shred the scallions lengthwise, using the tip of a sharp knife to make thin strips.

4

Cover the pancakes with foil and put into the oven for 10 minutes to warm through (or follow the package instructions). When the duck is cooked, use 2 forks to pull the duck flesh and skin away from the bones. It should come away from the bone very easily. Keep the duck warm on a plate in the oven. Don't cover it with foil, or the skin will lose its crispness.

5

Spoon the hoisin sauce into a serving dish. Serve the sauce, shredded duck, sliced cucumbers, scallions, and pancakes separately and let everyone assemble their own. To assemble, spoon about 1 teaspoon of hoisin sauce onto a pancake, then spread it out with the back of the spoon. Arrange a couple sticks of cucumber, a few shreds of onion and a little duck in a line across the middle of the pancake. To roll, tuck the bottom of the pancake up, then roll the sides over, leaving the top open.

CHINESE PANCAKES
If you can't find the thin Chinese pancakes in the supermarket, try small flour tortillas instead. Chinese pancakes are also made with flour, so the flavor is very similar. If the tortillas are larger, cut them in half and wrap around the filling in a cone shape, rather than a roll.

Chicken Satay
with Peanut Sauce

Preparation time: 20 minutes,
plus at least 30 minutes for
marinating
Cooking time: 7 minutes
Serves 6

It's doubtful many Thai street-food
sellers use peanut butter in
their satay, but it's a great shortcut
ingredient for us, and tastes
pretty authentic. For the juiciest,
most flavorful satay, let the chicken
marinate for a few hours.

4 large, skinless boneless
   chicken breasts
1 thumb-size piece fresh ginger
1 tsp ground turmeric
1 tsp ground coriander
2 tbsp nam pla (Thai fish sauce)
2 tbsp sugar
1½ tsp ground cumin
¼ cup coconut milk
1 large green chile
1 onion
2 cloves garlic
1 stalk lemon grass
2 tbsp vegetable or sunflower oil
4 heaping tbsp crunchy
   peanut butter
1 handful fresh cilantro, to serve
20 wooden or metal skewers

1
Cut each chicken breast into 5 long strips along its length.

2
Finely grate the ginger and put it into a large bowl. Mix in the turmeric, ground coriander, 1 tablespoon of the fish sauce, 1 tablespoon of the sugar, 1 teaspoon of the cumin and 1 tablespoon of the coconut milk. Add the chicken, stir, then cover and marinate for 30 minutes at room temperature, or up to 24 hours in the refrigerator.

3
If you're using wooden skewers, soak them in cold water while you wait for the chicken to marinate. This will stop them from burning too much under the broiler. Next, make the peanut sauce. Seed and very roughly chop the chile. Roughly chop the onion, garlic and lemon grass. Put them all into the bowl of a food processor with the remaining cumin, sugar, 1 tablespoon of the oil and 2 tablespoons water.

2

3

4

Process the ingredients together to make a smooth paste. Heat the remaining oil in a pan, add the paste, then fry over a high heat for 4 minutes, until fragrant. Stir it as it cooks.

5

Add the peanut butter and a scant ½ cup water into the pan and stir. The sauce will boil and thicken quickly. Season with the remaining fish sauce. Set aside while you cook the chicken; add a splash of hot water if it starts to thicken up.

GETTING AHEAD
You can make the sauce ahead of time while the chicken marinates. Keep it covered in the refrigerator, then warm it gently in a pan, adding a little water, as it will have thickened as it cooled.

6

After the marinating time, thread each piece of chicken onto a skewer. Put the skewers onto a large baking sheet, well spaced apart. Preheat the broiler.

7

Broil the chicken for about 7 minutes, turning the skewers half way through cooking, until they start turning golden and are cooked through. Spoon a little of the remaining coconut milk over the chicken as it cooks. Serve drizzled with more of the coconut milk, sprinkled with the cilantro leaves and with the peanut sauce ready for dipping.

Chicken Tikka &
Raita Lettuce Cups

Preparation time: 20 minutes,
plus 30 minutes for marinating
Cooking time: 15 minutes
Serves 6

Lightly spiced and refreshing, this
healthy nibble also makes a great
starter for an Indian feast. For a
barbecue, try using the marinade on
larger pieces of chicken or chunks
of lamb threaded onto kebobs.
Raita is a cucumber and yogurt dip
that's great to serve on the side.

3 cloves garlic

1 thumb-size piece fresh ginger

½ tsp garam masala

¼–½ tsp chili powder (depending
   how hot you like it)

½ tsp ground turmeric

1 tsp kosher salt

1 tbsp tomato paste

1 lime

2½ cups Greek yogurt

6 boneless, skinless chicken thighs

1 red onion

½ cucumber

1 small bunch fresh mint
   or cilantro

2 very small heads butterhead
   lettuce, such as Bibb or Boston

salt and pepper

1
Crush the garlic and finely grate the ginger into a large bowl. Add the spices, salt, and tomato paste. Squeeze the juice of the lime and add the juice along with ¾ cup of the yogurt.

2
Stir well to make a marinade. Cut the chicken into bite-size chunks, then mix into the marinade. Let stand for at least 30 minutes at room temperature, or for up to 4 hours in the refrigerator.

3

Meanwhile, make the raita. Finely chop the onion. Peel and seed the cucumber (see page 79), then coarsely grate it. Roughly chop the mint or cilantro leaves. Stir everything together with the remaining 1¾ cups yogurt. Season with salt and pepper. The raita can be made a few hours ahead of time and kept in the refrigerator until needed.

4

When the chicken has marinated, preheat the broiler, then line a large baking pan with foil, or use a broiler pan. Lift the chicken pieces out of the marinade and place them on the pan, well spaced out.

5

Broil the chicken for 15 minutes, turning once during cooking, until golden and charred in places and cooked through. Spoon any leftover marinade over the chicken halfway through the cooking time, if you like. Set the lettuce leaves out on a serving platter. Put a little of the raita into each leaf, then add a chunk of chicken to each one. Enjoy immediately.

Patatas Bravas (Spicy Potatoes) with Chorizo

Preparation time: 20 minutes
Cooking time: 40 minutes
Serves 6

A classic tapas dish of potatoes with tomato sauce, made that little bit tastier with some crisp fried chorizo. Serve with olives, salted almonds, and good bread for a Spanish-style feast.

3¼ lb potatoes, such as Yukon Gold

3 tbsp light olive oil

9 oz chorizo (see note)

3 garlic cloves

2 sprigs fresh thyme

½ tsp paprika, either smoked
 or regular

2 tbsp dry sherry, optional

1 (14½-oz) can chopped tomatoes

1 handful fresh flat-leaf parsley

1¾ cups olives (preferably Spanish),
 to serve

1½ cups salted almonds, to serve

salt and pepper

crusty bread, to serve (optional)

1
Preheat the oven to 400°F. Peel the potatoes, then cut them into large cubes about 1¼ inches across. Put the potatoes into a large roasting pan, drizzle with 1 tablespoon of the oil, season with salt and pepper, then toss well. Roast for 40 minutes.

2
Meanwhile, make the sauce. Cut the chorizo into chunky slices. Place a large frying pan over medium heat, then add the remaining oil. After 30 seconds, add the chorizo. Fry it for about 5 minutes, stirring often, until it is golden and sizzling and has released lots of red oil. Meanwhile, thinly slice the garlic. Remove the chorizo from the pan and set aside.

CHORIZO
Chorizo is a spicy Spanish sausage flavored with paprika and garlic. There are two types: cooking chorizo, which is soft, like a regular sausage, and cured chorizo, which is firm and dry, and is eaten raw, like salami. Either type will work in this recipe, but choose cooking chorizo if there's a choice.

3
Put the pan back on low-to-medium heat, then add the sliced garlic and the leaves from the thyme sprigs. Cook for 1 minute, until the garlic has softened.

4

Add the paprika to the pan, cook for another minute, then add the sherry, if using, and tomatoes. Simmer the sauce for 10 minutes, or until it has thickened a little. Season with salt and pepper.

5

After 40 minutes, the potatoes should be crisp and golden. Stir the potatoes and chorizo into the hot sauce. Roughly chop the parsley leaves and sprinkle them over.

6

Serve the patatas bravas with the bread, olives, and almonds.

Stuffed Potato Skins
with Sour Cream Dip

Preparation time: 1½ hours
Cooking time: 20 minutes
Serves 6

These won't last long when they
reach the table. Substitute any well-
flavored cheese, such as Cheddar,
for the blue cheese if you prefer.

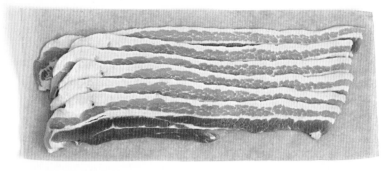

2 tbsp vegetable or sunflower oil

6 large baking potatoes (such as
　　russets), 8–9 oz each

1 tsp kosher salt

6 strips bacon

1 cup sour cream

1 handful fresh chives

1 bunch scallions

5 oz blue cheese (any type)

salt and pepper

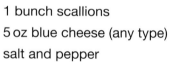

1

Preheat the oven to 400°F. Rub
1 teaspoon of the oil over the
potatoes, then put them in a large
roasting pan. Sprinkle with the
salt. Bake for 1½ hours, until the
potatoes are golden and crisp.
Turn the potatoes over halfway
through cooking.

2

While you wait, chop the bacon
into small pieces. Place a frying pan
over medium heat, then add
2 teaspoons of the oil. After
30 seconds, add the bacon. Fry for
10 minutes, stirring often, until the
bacon has released its fat, and
is crisp and golden. Drain on paper
towels to absorb the excess fat.

3

Make the dip. Put the sour cream
into a bowl, then snip in the chives
using a pair of kitchen scissors, and
stir them in. Season with salt and
pepper, then chill in the refrigerator
until needed.

4

When the potatoes are ready,
remove from the oven and let stand
until cool enough to hold. Cut each
potato in half lengthwise. Use a
spoon to scoop out the soft fluffy
potato from the middles, leaving
a shell of potato skin about ½ inch
thick all the way around.

LEFTOVER POTATO
The cooked potato scooped from
the middle of each skin can be
mashed and kept in the refrigerator
for future use.

5

Cut each potato skin in half lengthwise. Put the skins into the pan, skin side down. Use a pastry brush to brush them with the rest of the oil. Return the skins to the oven and bake them for 15 minutes, or until crisp and golden. Meanwhile, finely slice the scallions and cut or crumble the cheese.

6

When the skins are ready, increase the heat to broil (or turn the oven off and preheat the broiler if you have separate units). Sprinkle the cheese and the scallions over the skins, then top with a little bacon.

7

Broil the skins for 5 minutes, until the cheese is melted and bubbling. Serve with the sour cream and chive dip.

GETTING AHEAD
The potatoes can be baked and the skins scooped and crisped the day before. The dip can be mixed and chilled ahead of time too. Reheat the skins under a hot broiler for a few minutes, then top with the cheese and scallions and finish as above.

Chilli Con Carne with Baked Potatoes

Preparation time: 30 minutes
Cooking time: 1½ hours
Serves 6

As the nights get colder, thoughts turn to comfort food—and to chilli con carne. Spoon it over a crisp baked potato, or if you prefer, a bowl of rice. See page 145 for how to cook the perfect pan of basmati.

2 onions

2 cloves garlic

2 red bell peppers

1 tbsp olive oil, plus 1 tsp

1 lb 2 oz lean ground beef

½ tsp ground cumin

½ tsp ground cinnamon

½ tsp ground coriander

1–2 tsp chili powder, depending
    on your taste

1 tsp mixed dried herbs

scant ½ cup red wine

2 (14½-oz) cans chopped tomatoes

2 tbsp tomato paste

scant 1 cup beef broth

6 large baking potatoes, such
    as russets

1 tsp kosher salt

1 (14-oz) can red kidney beans
    in water, drained

1 (1-inch) square dark chocolate

salt and pepper

1 handful fresh cilantro, to serve

creamy natural yogurt or sour
    cream, to serve

1
Chop or slice the onions and garlic, then seed the peppers and cut them into chunky strips. Heat a large frying pan or flameproof casserole over low heat. Add 1 tablespoon oil, then the vegetables.

2
Cook the vegetables gently for 10 minutes, until softened. Transfer to a plate, then wipe out the pan with a paper towel.

3
Turn the heat to high, then add the ground beef. It should sizzle in the pan, rather than stew. Break up the meat with a wooden spoon as it cooks.

4
After 10 minutes, the meat will have changed color from pink, to gray, to golden brown. If the meat releases water as it cooks at first, keep the heat up and it will boil away, leaving the meat to brown.

5
Return the vegetables to the pan, then stir in the cumin, cinnamon, coriander, chili powder and dried herbs, and cook for 2 minutes until they smell fragrant.

6
Now add the wine, tomatoes, tomato paste, and broth, then stir. Partly cover the pan, then simmer the chilli gently for 1½ hours.

7
Meanwhile, bake the potatoes. Preheat the oven to 400°F. Rub 1 teaspoon of the oil over the potatoes, then put them into a large baking pan. Sprinkle with the kosher salt. Bake for 1½ hours, until the potatoes are golden and crisp. Turn the potatoes over halfway through cooking.

8
When the chilli has 30 minutes' cooking time left, stir in the beans. Then, just before serving, add the chocolate, let it melt, and stir to incorporate. Season with salt and pepper. Roughly chop the cilantro.

CHILLI WITH CHOCOLATE?
Melting a little dark chocolate into the sauce before serving will give your chilli extra richness and give the sauce a well-rounded flavor. Choose chocolate with a high cocoa content, around 70% cocoa. Anything with less cocoa will be a little too sweet for the sauce. Don't get carried away—add just 1 square.

9
Split the baked potatoes in half and serve the chilli spooned over them. Top with spoonfuls of yogurt or sour cream and sprinkle with the cilantro.

Pan-Fried Fish with Salsa Verde

Preparation time: 15 minutes
Cooking time: 30 minutes
Serves 6

Crisp-skinned, tender fish with vibrant salsa verde makes one of the best simple suppers, and it's great for entertaining. The fish won't overcook if you follow these instructions—just make sure everything else is prepared before you start. Choose any sustainably caught, fresh white fish.

1 clove garlic
3 canned anchovy fillets, drained
1 organic lemon
1 small bunch fresh flat-leaf parsley
1 small bunch fresh basil
2 tbsp capers in brine, drained
3 tbsp extra-virgin olive oil
1 tsp kosher salt
2¼ lb new potatoes
6 white fish fillets, skin on and
    scales removed
2 tbsp all-purpose flour
2 tbsp sunflower or vegetable oil
1 tbsp butter, plus a little extra for
    the potatoes, if desired
salt and pepper

1
Preheat the oven to 275°F. Bring a large pan of water with 1 teaspoon salt to a boil, ready for the potatoes. While it heats, make the salsa verde. Very roughly chop the garlic and anchovies. Finely grate the zest from the lemon and squeeze the juice. Put the parsley and basil leaves, capers, anchovies, garlic, lemon zest and juice, and extra-virgin olive oil into the bowl of a food processor.

2
Process the ingredients to make a slightly chunky, bright green sauce. This sauce can be made up to a day ahead and kept covered in the refrigerator.

USING A MORTAR AND PESTLE
Traditionally, this sauce is made using a mortar and pestle, and the anchovies, garlic, capers and herbs would be pounded together to release their aromas. Feel free to make it that way if you have a mortar and pestle, but a food processor makes it quicker.

3
Carefully put the potatoes into the boiling water, then boil for 20 minutes. They're ready when the tip of a knife slips easily through one of the potatoes. If you're not sure, then lift one out, slice it and taste it.

4

While the potatoes are boiling, start the fish. Dry the fillets with a paper towel, then slash the skin on each fillet 3 times using a sharp knife. Pour the flour onto a plate, then season generously with salt and pepper. Dust the fish fillets in a fine layer of flour, then set aside. The flour coating will give the fish a tasty crisp coating and also protect the delicate fish from the heat of the pan.

CHOOSING FISH FILLETS
A good, fresh fish fillet should look and feel firm, and won't smell fishy. Buy fresh fish on the day you intend to cook it, or buy frozen and defrost in the refrigerator when you need it.

5

When the potatoes are ready, start cooking the fish. Have a plate ready, lined with paper towels. Place a nonstick frying pan over medium-high heat, then add half the oil and half the butter. After 30 seconds, slide in 3 fish fillets, skin side down. Without moving the fish, cook for 3 minutes, until the skin is golden and crisp and the flesh has turned white almost all the way to the top.

6

Carefully turn each piece of fish over with a spatula, then cook for another 30 seconds. It shouldn't stick as you turn it. If the fish shows any sign of sticking, give it a little longer; it will come away from the pan when it's ready. Now transfer the fish to the plate and keep warm in the oven. Wipe out the pan with paper towels, then heat the rest of the butter and oil and fry the second batch.

7

Drain the potatoes and toss them with a little more butter, if you like. Serve the fish with spoonfuls of the salsa verde and potatoes on the side.

Eggplant Parmigiana

Preparation time: 45 minutes
Cooking time: 30 minutes
Serves 6

First softened in a pan, then layered
with a rich herby sauce, eggplant
becomes a hero ingredient in this
homey recipe. The cheesy crust and
the saucy layers below make for a
rich and satisfying dish, and it makes
a wonderful vegetarian alternative
to lasagne.

---

4 large eggplants, about 3¼ lb

scant ½ cup light olive oil

2 cloves garlic

a few sprigs fresh oregano,
    or 1 tsp dried

1 tbsp tomato paste

2 (14½-oz) cans chopped tomatoes

¼ tsp sugar

1 small bunch fresh basil

2 slices white bread (about 3½ oz)

3 oz Parmesan cheese

4 oz fresh mozzarella cheese

salt and pepper

1

Cut the eggplants into slices about ¼ inch thick. Use a pastry brush to paint the top of each slice with some of the olive oil.

2

Heat a large frying pan over medium heat. Add several slices of eggplant, oiled side down. Fry for 5 minutes, or until golden and softened underneath. Brush the tops of the slices with oil, then turn them over and cook for another 5 minutes, or until completely tender. Set aside and repeat with the rest of the slices.

3

While the eggplants are cooking, start the sauce. Thinly slice the garlic. Heat a pan over a medium heat, then add 2 tablespoons of the oil. Add the garlic and cook for 1 minute, until softened. Add the tomato paste, chopped tomatoes, sugar, and half the oregano leaves. Tear in the basil leaves, then simmer for 10 minutes. Season with salt and pepper.

4

To make the crumb topping, tear the bread into the bowl of a food processor, discarding the crusts. Finely grate the Parmesan, then add half of it to the bread. Add the remaining oregano leaves.

5

Process until you have bread crumbs flecked with green.

IF YOU DON'T HAVE
A FOOD PROCESSOR
You can make the bread crumbs by grating the bread instead. Finely chop the herbs, then stir them together with the crumbs and Parmesan.

6

Preheat the oven to 350°F. Layer the eggplant slices and tomato sauce in an ovenproof dish, seasoning the eggplants with salt and pepper as you go.

7

Chop the mozzarella into small pieces. Scatter the mozzarella and remaining Parmesan over the top, then finish with the crumbs and a drizzle of oil.

8

Bake for 30 minutes, or until golden and bubbling. Remove from the oven and let stand in the dish for 10 minutes before serving.

GETTING AHEAD
This dish can be prepared up to the end of step 7, then covered and chilled in the refrigerator for up to 2 days. If cooking from chilled, add an extra 10 minutes to the cooking time and cover it with foil if the topping browns before the time is up.

Coq au Vin
(Chicken with Red Wine)

Preparation time: 1 hour 10 minutes
Cooking time: 55 minutes
Serves 6

A very considerate dish, this one, as it builds in 24 hours for you to get ahead if you're entertaining. During this time its flavors will improve and marry wonderfully under the lid. If you'd rather use skinless chicken, that's fine, although you'll need to brown it for slightly less time and the sauce will be a little less rich.

18 small onions or shallots, about 1 lb 2 oz

2 onions

2 stalks celery

3 carrots

6 strips bacon

3 tablespoons light olive oil

2 cloves garlic

½ cup all-purpose flour, plus 1 tbsp

6 chicken thighs and 6 drumsticks

5 tbsp butter

1⅔ cups full-bodied red wine

2 cups chicken broth

11 oz mixed mushrooms, such as button and cremini

salt and pepper

1

Put the small onions or shallots into a bowl, then pour in enough just-boiled water to cover. Leave for 5 minutes, then drain and let cool. Trim the root ends and peel off the skins.

2

Finely chop or slice the large onions and finely slice the celery. Cut the carrots into thick slices and the bacon into bite-size pieces. Heat a large ovenproof pan over medium heat, then add 1 tablespoon of the oil. Add the vegetables and bacon to the pan.

3

Fry the vegetables and bacon for 10 minutes, until softened.

4

Turn up the heat, then cook, stirring frequently, for 10 minutes until everything is golden. Meanwhile, crush the garlic, then add it to the pan and cook for 1 minute. Transfer everything from the pan to a bowl and set aside.

5

Mix the ½ cup flour with some salt and pepper in a plastic bag. Put the chicken pieces into the bag, seal it and shake to coat the meat.

6

Add 1 tablespoon butter and 1 tablespoon of the remaining oil to the pan. Cook one-third of the chicken pieces for 10 minutes, turning halfway, until golden brown. It's important not to crowd the pan, or the chicken will start to sweat rather than fry. After browning the first batch, spoon off any excess fat, then add a splash of water. Scrape up the bits from the bottom of the pan, adding them to the vegetables in the bowl. These juices contain lots of flavor. Brown the remaining chicken pieces in the same way.

7

After browning and removing all the chicken pieces, pour in the wine, then let it bubble for 5 minutes, or until it has reduced in volume by a quarter.

8

Return all the chicken, vegetables, and juices to the pan, then pour in the broth (it's fine if the chicken is not completely covered with liquid). Partially cover the pan with a lid and simmer the chicken for 50 minutes.

9

When the chicken is tender (check this by cutting into one of the pieces—it should be easy to pull the meat away from the bone), scoop the chicken and vegetables out of the pan using a slotted spoon, and put them into a large bowl. Mix the remaining tablespoon of flour and 1 tablespoon butter together until smooth. Whisk into the sauce, then simmer for 5 minutes, until the sauce is glossy and thickened.

10

To finish the dish, fry the mushrooms. Cut any large ones in half. Heat the remaining butter in a frying pan, and once it foams, add the mushrooms. Fry for 2–3 minutes on a high heat, until the mushrooms are golden and just tender. Season with salt and pepper.

11

Gently stir the chicken and vegetables back into the pan, scatter the mushrooms over the top, then serve.

GETTING AHEAD

If you make the Coq au Vin in advance, let it cool, then chill for up to 2 days. Warm the pan gently and add a splash more broth or red wine to loosen the sauce if you need to, stirring gently. Fry the mushrooms and add them just before serving.

Creamy Fish Pie

Preparation time: 1 hour
Cooking time: 40 minutes
Serves 6

Perfect for informal get-togethers, a fish pie makes a luxurious but simple meal. Feel free to vary the fish, or to replace the dill with flat-leaf parsley. Do use smoked haddock if you can find it; its gentle smokiness gives a backbone of flavor to the whole dish. If not, substitute more white fish and add a little smoked salmon at step 9.

3¼ lb potatoes, such as russets

1 tsp kosher salt

scant 3⅔ cups whole milk

1¼ cups heavy cream

1 bay leaf

4 cloves

1 onion

14 oz smoked haddock fillet, skin on
    if possible

1 lb 5 oz chunky white fish fillets,
    skin on

¾ stick (6 tbsp) butter

½ cup all-purpose flour

1 whole nutmeg, for grating

1 small bunch fresh dill

7 oz large uncooked shrimp, shelled
    and deveined

1 oz Parmesan cheese

salt and pepper

1

Peel, then quarter the potatoes. Put into a large pan, just cover with cold water, add the salt, then bring to a boil. Once the water is boiling, turn the heat down and simmer the potatoes for 15 minutes, or until tender.

2

Meanwhile, start the sauce. Pour 2 cups of the milk and all the cream into a pan, then add the bay leaf and cloves. Cut the onion into quarters and add to the pan. Place the pan over low heat and bring to a simmer.

3

Once small bubbles start to appear, slide the fish fillets into the milk, skin side down. Cover, then cook the fish very gently for 5 minutes, until the flesh has changed color and flakes easily. Carefully lift the fish from the pan and onto a plate. Turn off the heat under the pan, then leave the milk and flavorings to infuse for 10 minutes.

SKIN ON?
It's best for the fish to have skin on for this recipe, as it helps protect it from overcooking in the milk, and also keeps it in one piece, ready for flaking into big pieces later.

4

Drain the potatoes in a colander. Put 2 tablespoons of the butter and the remaining milk into the potato pan, then place over medium heat until the milk starts to boil and the butter is melting. Add the potatoes, then remove from the heat.

5

Mash the potatoes using a potato masher, or a potato ricer if you have one. Do this immediately, as they need to be hot for the best, fluffiest result. Season with salt and pepper.

6

Heat another pan over medium heat, then add the flour and remaining butter. Allow the butter to melt, then cook together, stirring, for 2 minutes, or until the flour starts to turn golden. Remove from the heat.

7

Strain the infused milk through a fine-mesh sieve into a measuring cup, then gradually whisk it into the flour and butter mixture. It will be thick at first, but keep whisking and a smooth sauce will come together. Return the pan to the heat and whisk until the sauce thickens.

8

Season generously with salt, pepper, and about ¼ teaspoon finely grated nutmeg. Chop the delicate dill fronds, then stir into the sauce.

9

Preheat the oven to 350°F. Flake the fish into a large ovenproof dish, discarding the skin and keeping the fish in chunky pieces. Discard any bones. Pat the shrimp dry with a paper towel, then scatter them around the dish.

10

Spoon the sauce over the fish. Cover with spoonfuls of mashed potato, then smooth and swirl them together with a fork. Finely grate the Parmesan over the top. The pie can be chilled for up to 2 days at this point.

11

Bake the pie for 40 minutes, or until the top is golden and the sauce bubbling around the edges. Let stand for 10 minutes before serving.

Lamb & Potato Curry with Fragrant Rice

Preparation time: 1 hour
Cooking time: 2½ hours
Serves 6

Like almost all stews, this rich lamb curry improves in flavor if made the day before and then reheated. Chill it overnight, then bring it slowly to a simmer the next day, ready to serve with a bowl of scented spiced rice. For a real Indian feast, try starting your meal with the Chicken Tikka & Raita Lettuce Cups on page 204.

3 onions
4 cloves garlic
2 tbsp vegetable oil
4 tbsp butter
1 tsp kosher salt
1 large green chile
1 small bunch fresh cilantro
1 large chunk fresh ginger,
    or 3 thumb-size pieces
2 tsp ground turmeric
2 tsp ground cumin
2 tsp ground coriander
½ tsp ground black pepper
2¼ lb boneless lamb shoulder,
    trimmed of excess fat and cut into
    matchbox-size pieces (a butcher
    will be happy to do this)
2 tbsp tomato paste
1 (14½-oz) can chopped tomatoes
2 medium potatoes, about 9 oz

For the rice
2½ cups white basmati rice
6–7 cardamom pods
2 cinnamon sticks

1

Preheat the oven to 325°F. Thinly slice the onions and garlic. Place a wide, deep, ovenproof pan over low heat. After 30 seconds, add the oil and half of the butter. Once the butter foams, add two-thirds of the onions, all of the garlic and ½ teaspoon salt. Sauté gently for 10 minutes, stirring occasionally, until softened and turning golden.

2

Meanwhile, seed and finely chop the chile, and finely chop the cilantro stems. Finely grate the ginger. Add these to the pan with the turmeric, cumin, ground coriander, and black pepper, then turn up the heat a little and cook for 3 minutes, stirring, until golden and fragrant. Be careful not to let the spices burn.

3

Add the lamb and stir to coat with the spices. Cook for 5 minutes, stirring occasionally, until the lamb has changed color all over. It doesn't need to be browned.

4

Stir in the tomato paste, tomatoes and ½ cup water.

5

Put the lid on the pan, leaving a little gap for steam to escape. Transfer the pan to the preheated oven and cook for 1¼ hours. Covering the pan this way lets the sauce cook down and reduce a little without becoming dry. While the curry cooks, peel the potatoes, then cut them into large chunks. Stir the potatoes into the curry and return to the oven for another 1¼ hours.

6

With about 45 minutes' cooking time left, start the rice. Heat a large pan over medium heat, then add the remaining butter. When it foams, add the remaining onions. Sauté for 15 minutes, until the onions are golden and soft, stirring often.

7

While the onions cook, put the rice into a fine-mesh sieve, then rinse it under cold water, until the water runs clear. Let drain.

8

Stir the cardamom pods and cinnamon sticks into the onions, then add the drained rice. Stir until everything is well coated with butter. Pour in 2½ cups cold water (or just enough to cover the rice by a fingertip's depth), then add the remaining ½ teaspoon salt.

9

Bring to a boil, stir once, then cover and cook over medium heat for 10 minutes. Remove the pan from the heat without removing the lid, and let it stand for 15 minutes. The rice should be cooked through with no water remaining. If it seems slightly undercooked, add a splash of water, cover and return to a low heat for 5 minutes, then remove and let stand for 5 minutes.

10

Fluff the rice with a fork to separate the grains, then re-cover the pan until ready to serve.

11

To finish the curry, spoon off any excess fat that has risen to the top and season with salt and pepper. Roughly chop the cilantro leaves, and stir some of them through the curry. Sprinkle more cilantro leaves over the top and serve with the rice.

Cheese & Onion Tart

Preparation time: 1 hour 10 minutes,
plus 50 minutes for chilling
Cooking time: 30 minutes
Serves 8–10 (makes 10 slices)

A delicate, slightly wobbly homemade
tart is a simple pleasure to cook
and eat, and a great option for
lunches, buffets and picnics, as it can
be transported in its pan. If you
don't want to make your own crust,
use store-bought pie crust instead.
To make this into a Quiche Lorraine,
see the instructions on page 244.

---

4 large eggs

scant 1½ cups all-purpose flour,
   plus extra for rolling

¼ tsp kosher salt

1 stick (½ cup) cold unsalted butter

3 large onions

1 tbsp light olive oil

5 oz Gruyère or Cheddar cheese

1¼ cups heavy cream

scant ½ cup milk

salt and pepper

1

Make the crust first. Separate 1 egg yolk and white by gently cracking the shell against the side of a small bowl. Slowly pull the shell apart as cleanly as possible along the crack, pouring the yolk into half of the shell. Let the white drain away into a bowl below. Drop the yolk into another small bowl.

2

Add 2 tablespoons ice-cold water to the yolk, then beat together with a fork. Put the flour into a large bowl, and add the salt. Cut 7 tablespoons of the butter into cubes, then scatter them over the flour.

3

Rub the ingredients together. To do this, use both hands to lift the butter and flour from the bowl, then gently pass them between your fingers and thumbs as they drop back into the bowl. As you repeat the action, the butter will gradually work its way into the flour. Lift the mixture up as you go, to keep it cool and aerated. The mixture will end up looking like fine bread crumbs.

MAKING THE CRUST WITH A FOOD PROCESSOR

If you'd rather use a food processor, process the butter and flour together for about 10 seconds, until the mixture resembles fine bread crumbs and no flecks of butter remain. Add the yolk mixture and pulse a few more times, until balls of dough come together in the bowl.

4
Add the yolk mixture to the bowl, then, using a knife, quickly stir it into the crumbs to make a rough dough.

5
Press the clumps of dough firmly together with your hands, then turn it out onto the work surface and shape it into a flat disk, paying particular attention to the edge, pinching any cracks together to keep it in a smooth round. Wrap the dough in plastic wrap, then chill in the refrigerator for at least 30 minutes, until firm but not rock hard.

6
While the dough chills, make the filling. Thinly slice the onions. Place a frying pan over low heat, then add the remaining butter and the oil. When the butter starts to foam, add the onions.

7
Cook the onions for 10 minutes, until soft, then turn up the heat a little and cook for 10 more minutes, until they take on a tinge of gold. Stir the onions often to prevent them catching on the bottom of the pan. Meanwhile, break the remaining 3 eggs into a large measuring cup, then beat with a fork. Grate the cheese. Add the cream, milk, and 4 ounces of the cheese to the eggs, then season with salt and pepper.

TO MAKE A QUICHE LORRAINE
Turn your tart into a quiche lorraine by frying 6 chopped strips of bacon until golden and adding them to the filling with the cheese. Alternatively, just tear in 4 large slices of cooked ham.

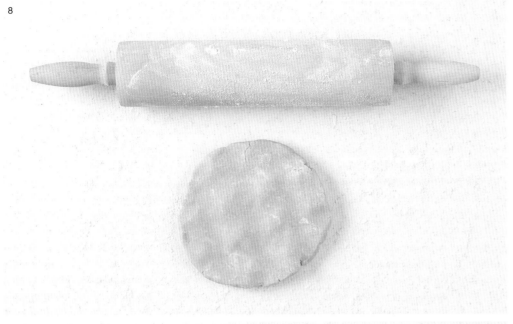

8
Dust the work surface and a rolling pin with flour. Have ready a 9-inch round, loose-bottom tart pan. Using a rolling pin, press shallow ridges evenly across the dough, then rotate it by a quarter turn. Repeat this until the dough is about ½ inch thick. This will help it to stretch without becoming tough.

9
Now roll out the dough. Push the rolling pin in one direction only, turning the dough by a quarter turn every few rolls, until it's less than ¼ inch thick. Using a rolling pin to help, lift the dough over the pan.

10
Ease the dough gently into the pan, then press it gently into the fluted edge, using your knuckles and fingertips.

ANY HOLES?
If your dough has ripped or small holes have appeared, don't panic. Dampen a little of the leftover dough and stick it down well to seal the gap.

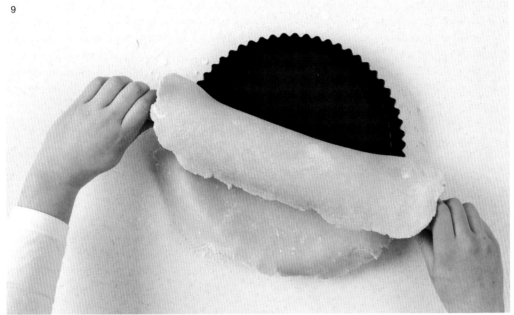

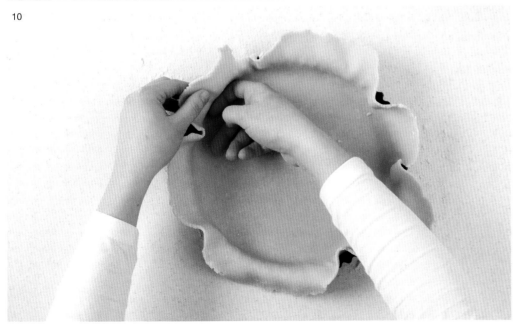

11

Trim the top of the crust with a pair of scissors so that it just overhangs the pan. Place onto a baking sheet, then chill in the refrigerator for 20 minutes, until firm. Put an oven rack in the middle of the oven and preheat it to 400°F.

12

Tear a sheet of parchment paper large enough to completely cover the pan and overhanging dough. Crumple the paper, then unfold it to cover the crust. Cover the paper with a layer of pie weights, mounding them up a little at the edges. Bake the pie crust, still on the baking sheet, for 15 minutes.

PIE WEIGHTS
Pie weights are actually small ceramic balls, used to weigh down the crust as it cooks, which helps it to keep its shape. Ceramic weights are the most effective, but dried chickpeas or rice can be used instead. Cool and re-use them for baking only.

13

Remove the paper and the pie weights. The crust should be pale but feel dry and be turning gold at the edges. Return to the oven and cook for another 10 minutes, or until the base is starting to brown. Remove from the oven. Turn the oven down to 325°F.

14

Scatter the onions over the base of the tart, then pour over the creamy filling. Make sure that the cheese is evenly distributed. Sprinkle the rest of the cheese over the top.

15

Bake for 30 minutes, or until the filling is set, with just a slight wobble in the middle. Once cooled, remove the tart from the pan, then cut into wedges to serve.

Lasagne

Preparation time: 30 minutes
Cooking time: 40 minutes
Serves 6

Lasagne is one of the ultimate
comfort foods. This recipe produces
the ultimate, classic version with just
the right amount of creamy richness.

2½ cups milk

4 tbsp butter

scant ½ cup all-purpose flour

3½ oz Parmesan cheese

1 whole nutmeg for grating (optional)

4 oz fresh mozzarella cheese

1 quantity Bolognese sauce
  (see page 262)

about 9 oz lasagna noodles or
  lasagna verde (about 9 sheets—
  the quantity will depend on
  the shape of the dish and the
  lasagna noodles)

salt and pepper

1

To make the cheese sauce, put the milk and butter into a medium pan. Sift in the flour, then place the pan over medium heat. Stir with a whisk for about 5 minutes, until the sauce comes to a boil and is thick and smooth. This all-in-one method is a quick and easy way to make a white sauce. However, if you end up with lumps in your sauce, pass it through a fine-mesh sieve into another pan and whisk until thickened.

2

Grate the Parmesan cheese and finely grate ¼ teaspoon of the nutmeg, if using. Stir two-thirds of the Parmesan into the sauce. Season the sauce with salt and pepper and the nutmeg. Tear the mozzarella into pieces, ready for using later.

COOKING WITH MOZZARELLA
Choose a mid-priced mozzarella for cooking. Very cheap brands tend to be rubbery, but the finest buffalo mozzarella is best enjoyed in salads or on its own.

3

Preheat the oven to 350°F. Assemble the lasagne in a large ceramic dish. Start with a layer of Bolognese sauce, then spoon a little of the cheese sauce over it.

4

Add a layer of lasagna noodles, snapping the sheets to fit the dish if needed. Now build up the layers, first Bolognese sauce, then cheese sauce, then pasta, and so on. The final layer should be cheese sauce. Make sure you have enough left over to completely cover the top of the dish.

CHOOSE THE RIGHT LASAGNA
For this recipe, buy dried lasagna noodles that don't need pre-cooking in water before use. Check the back of the pack if you're not sure.

5

Cover with the remaining Parmesan and mozzarella.

6

Bake for 40 minutes, until golden and bubbling. Check that the pasta is cooked through in the middle by inserting a skewer or small sharp knife. If it goes through without resistance, it's ready. If not, and the topping is already golden, cover with foil and return to the oven for 10 minutes. Let the lasagne rest for 10 minutes before serving.

GETTING AHEAD
Lasagne is a great get-ahead meal, as it can be frozen whole before baking (if the Bolognese sauce has not previously been frozen), or chilled for up to 3 days. If frozen, defrost it in the refrigerator for a day. Add an extra 10 minutes to the cooking time, covering the top with foil as soon as the topping is golden.

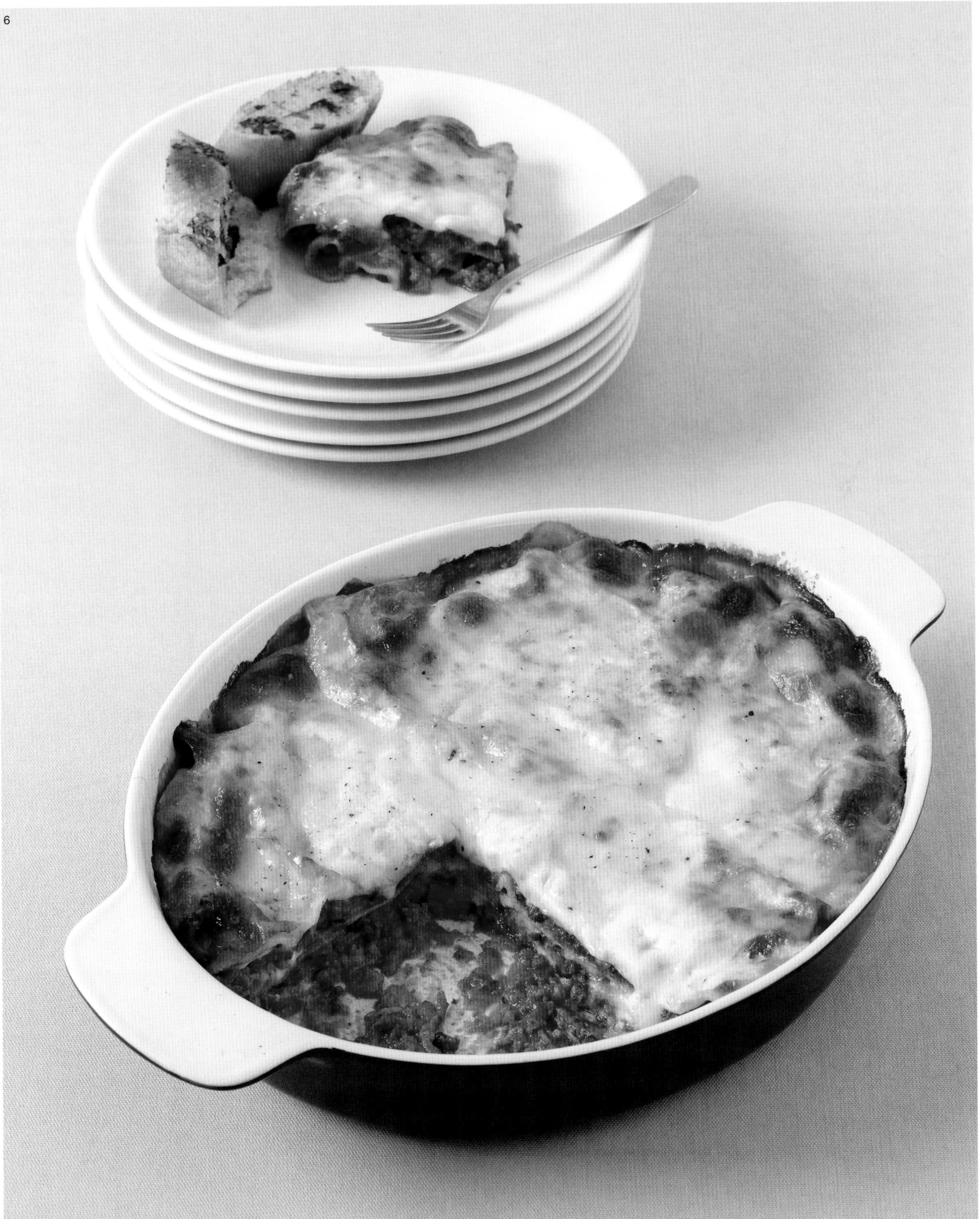

Roast Chicken with Lemon & Leek Stuffing

Preparation time: 1 hour
Cooking time: 1 hour 50 minutes
Serves 4–6

A good roast chicken is hard to beat, especially when served with crisp stuffing balls and rich gravy. For a traditional Sunday dinner with all the fixings, serve with Roast Potatoes (page 306) and a bowl of Glazed Carrots (page 314). This recipe can easily be adapted for turkey—see the note on page 256.

1 large free-range chicken,
    about 4 lb
2 organic lemons
1 head garlic
several sprigs fresh thyme
1 tbsp butter
2 onions
3 tbsp extra-virgin olive oil,
    plus extra for oiling
2 slim leeks
5 oz crustless white bread,
    about 5 slices
1 handful fresh flat-leaf or
    curly parsley
1 handful fresh sage
1 medium egg
6 strips smoked bacon
1 tbsp all-purpose flour
scant ½ cup dry white wine
1¼ cups chicken broth
salt and pepper

1

Preheat the oven to 400°F. If the chicken has an elastic string around it, snip it off and throw it away. Remove the bag of giblets from the cavity. Set the bird in a heavy-based roasting pan so that it fits fairly snugly. Finely grate the zest from the lemons, then set the zest aside. Halve one of the lemons and put one half inside the chicken cavity (the big hole between the legs). Cut the garlic head in half through the middle. Put one half of the garlic, plus a couple of the thyme sprigs, inside the chicken.

2

Tie the chicken's legs together: draw a long piece of string under the breast meat then around to the legs, then tie with a bow. Spread the butter over the breast and legs, sprinkle with salt and pepper and a few thyme leaves. Finally, cut 1 onion into chunky slices and scatter around the bird. Drizzle everything with 1 tablespoon of the oil. Put the chicken into the oven and roast for 1½ hours. Drizzle the second half of the garlic with a little oil and add it to the pan halfway through cooking.

3

While the chicken cooks, make the stuffing. Trim and discard any tough green leaves from the leeks and rinse them well. Slice the white and pale green part thinly into rounds, then thinly slice the second onion. Place a frying pan over low heat, add the remaining oil, then the onion and leeks. Cover and cook for 10 minutes, stirring occasionally, until softened.

4

Tear the bread into big chunks and put into the bowl of a food processor with the parsley and sage. Strip the leaves from the stems of the remaining thyme, then add to the bowl.

5

Pulse to make fine, herby crumbs.

6

Squeeze the juice from the remaining lemon half into a small bowl and lightly beat the egg into another. Stir the bread crumb mixture, lemon zest and juice, and the egg into the cooked leeks and onions, and season with salt and pepper. Allow to cool for a few minutes.

7

Stretch each bacon strip a little by holding one end of a strip, then running the edge of a knife along its length. It will increase in size by about 50 percent. Repeat with each strip, then cut them in half to make 12 pieces.

8

Lightly oil a baking pan. Shape the stuffing into golfball-sized balls, then wrap each one in a piece of bacon. Put the balls into the pan with the loose bacon ends down so that they don't unravel as the stuffing cooks.

9

When the chicken is ready, the onions and garlic will have caramelized into the fat and juices in the pan, creating the basis of a tasty gravy. Lift the bird out of the pan and onto a serving board or platter using two wooden spoons. Put 1 spoon into the cavity of the chicken to lift it from the pan, and use the other to support its weight. Catch any juices that come out of the chicken in the pan below as you tilt it. Let the chicken stand for 20–30 minutes. Don't cover the chicken, or the skin will get soggy. Don't worry, it will stay hot. Increase the oven temperature to 425°F. Put the stuffing balls in the oven to cook for 20 minutes.

IS IT COOKED?
To check whether the chicken is cooked, wiggle the legs a little — if they feel loose, this means that the meat around the joints has cooked. Next, insert a skewer into the thickest part of the thigh. Pull it out and look at the juices; if they're clear, the chicken is ready. If they're pink, return to the oven for 15 minutes, then test again.

10

Meanwhile, start the gravy. Degrease the gravy by spooning any excess fat from the roasting pan, then set it over low heat. Sprinkle in the flour and cook for 2 minutes, stirring constantly, to make a thick paste, then add the wine, stirring constantly. Let it come to a boil as you stir, until you have a thickish, smooth mixture and the raw wine smell has faded.

11

Add the broth gradually, stirring constantly, until you have a thin, lump-free gravy. Keep stirring and simmering until the gravy thickens.

12

If you like, strain the gravy through a fine-mesh sieve into a warmed measuring cup and cover the top to keep in the heat. Press the onion against the mesh of the sieve to extract as much of its flavor as you can. Add any resting juices that have collected under the chicken, too.

13

Serve the chicken with the stuffing balls and gravy, along with the soft roasted garlic, ready to squeeze onto your plate and mash into the juices.

TO ROAST A TURKEY

To use this recipe for a 10–12-pound turkey (enough to serve 8 with leftovers), coat the turkey with 4 tablespoons butter and roast, covered with foil, at 375°F for 20 minutes per pound. Uncover the turkey for the last 90 minutes of cooking. Double the stuffing recipe and cook it while the turkey rests for at least 30 minutes. Double the gravy quantities, and be sure to add all of the resting juices to the gravy. Serve with cranberry sauce and your favorite vegetables.

10

11

12

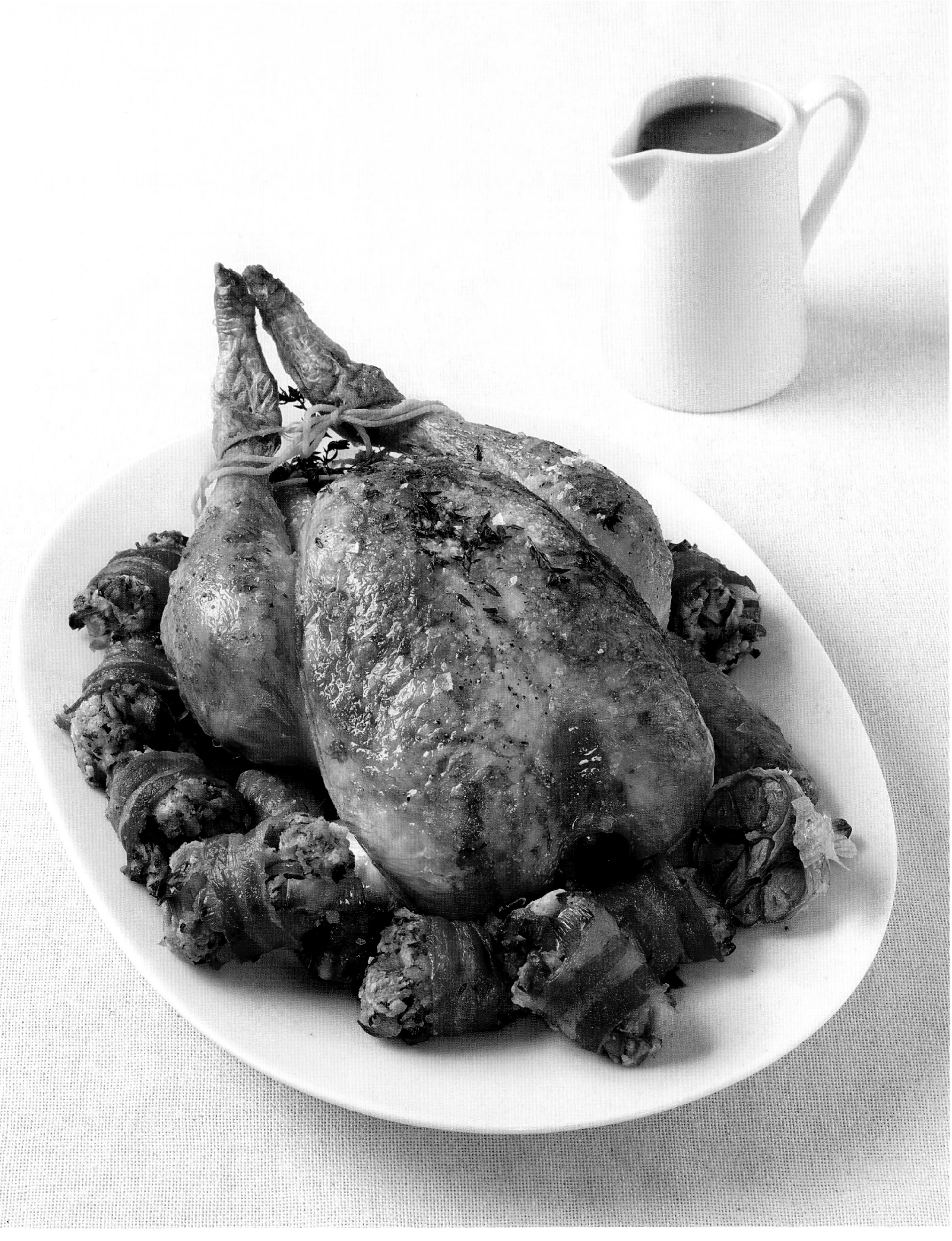

Shepherd's Pie

Preparation time: 45 minutes, plus
1½ hours for simmering
Cooking time: 25 minutes
Serves 6

A shepherd's pie is made with ground
lamb, and a cottage pie is made
with beef—but both are comfort-
cooking classics. If you'd like to try
cottage pie, just make a direct swap
of beef for lamb: the two meats are
interchangeable. You'll need to
add some oil when frying the ground
beef, though, as it's leaner than
ground lamb.

1 lb 2 oz ground lamb

2 onions

2 stalks celery

3 carrots

1 tbsp light olive oil

4 tbsp butter

2 tbsp tomato paste

2 tbsp Worcestershire sauce

few sprigs fresh thyme

2 tsp Dijon mustard

2¼ cups lamb or beef broth

2¼ lb baking potatoes

1 tsp kosher salt

scant 1 cup milk

1 tbsp all-purpose flour

salt and pepper

1

2

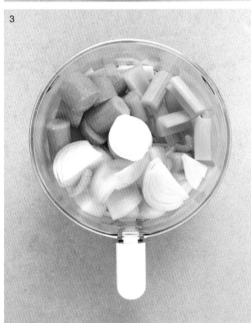

3

4

5

6

1
Heat a large frying pan or shallow flameproof casserole over high heat, then add the ground meat. Break it up with a wooden spoon as it browns.

2
After 10 minutes, the meat will change from pink to gray to golden brown and dry. It's possible that the meat will release water as it cooks at first, but keep the heat up and it will boil away, leaving the meat to fry. Transfer the meat to a bowl lined with paper towels, to absorb any excess fat.

3
While the meat browns, very roughly chop the onions, celery, and carrots and put them into a food processor.

4
Pulse the food processor until the vegetables are finely chopped. If you don't have a food processor, you can finely chop the vegetables by hand, but you might need to cook them for a little bit longer.

5
Place the pan over low heat, then add the oil and half the butter. When the butter foams, add the chopped vegetables. Cook gently for 10 minutes, until softened.

6
Stir the meat back into the pan, then add the tomato paste, Worcestershire sauce, thyme leaves, and 1 teaspoon of the mustard. Cook for 1 minute, then add the beef broth. Stir until the mixture comes to a boil. Partially cover the pan, then simmer for 1½ hours, until the meat is tender and surrounded with a rich sauce.

7

While the meat sauce simmers, make the mashed potato topping. Peel and quarter the potatoes. Put them into a large pan, just cover with cold water, add the salt, then bring to a boil. Once it comes to a boil, turn the heat down a little and cook for 15 minutes, or until tender.

8

Drain the potatoes in a colander. Put the remaining butter and the milk into the potato pan, then place over medium heat and cook until the milk starts to boil and the butter is melting. Add the cooked potatoes, then take the pan off the heat.

9

Mash the potatoes using a potato masher, or, if you have one, a potato ricer. It's important to mash the potatoes while they're still piping hot. Stir in the remaining mustard, then season with salt and pepper.

10

Mix the flour with 2 tablespoons cold water to make a smooth paste, then stir into the meat sauce. Bring the sauce back to a boil, stirring until the sauce thickens. Preheat the oven to 350°F.

11

Spoon the meat sauce into a large baking dish. Dot spoonfuls of mashed potato over the meat sauce (if you put it all in one place it will sink into the sauce).

12

Spread out and swirl the mashed potato with a fork. Bake the pie for 25 minutes, until the potato is golden and the sauce bubbles at the sides of the dish. Serve hot. It's good with Buttered Green Vegetables (page 330).

Tagliatelle with Bolognese Sauce

Preparation time: 40 minutes
Cooking time: 1½ hours
Serves 6 generously

A rich and meaty Bolognese sauce, or *ragù*, is a fabulous thing, but it can't be rushed. Ground meat is usually made from the tougher parts of the animal, so it needs long, slow cooking to become really tender. Browning the meat properly at the start is crucial to build up an intense flavor, so take your time.

---

1 tbsp light olive oil

1 lb 2 oz lean ground beef

2 onions

2 stalks celery

1 carrot

2 cloves garlic

8 strips bacon, or pancetta

1 handful fresh basil or 1 tsp dried
    mixed herbs

2 tbsp tomato paste

1 bay leaf

⅔ cup white wine

⅔ cup milk

2 (14½-oz) cans chopped tomatoes

1 lb 2 oz tagliatelle

salt and pepper

chunk of Parmesan cheese, to serve

1
Heat a large frying pan or flameproof casserole over high heat, then add the oil. After 30 seconds, add the meat. Make sure the heat is high enough that the meat sizzles in the pan, rather than stews. Break up the meat with a wooden spoon as it browns.

2
After 10 minutes, the meat will have changed color from pink, to gray, to golden brown. It's possible that the meat will release water as it cooks at first, but keep the heat up and it will boil away, leaving the meat to brown. Transfer the meat to a bowl.

3
While the meat browns, very roughly chop the onions, celery, carrot, and garlic cloves. Put them into the bowl of a food processor.

4
Pulse the blades of the food processor in short bursts until the vegetables are quite finely chopped. A food processor will save lots of time here, but if you don't have one, chop the vegetables by hand. You may have to cook them for a little bit longer.

5
Chop the bacon or pancetta, add it to the pan, then fry gently for 8–10 minutes, until the fat has run out of the meat, and it's crisp and golden. Pancetta will take slightly less time to crisp than bacon.

6

Add the vegetables to the bacon, then turn the heat down. Cook gently for another 10 minutes, until the vegetables have softened.

7

Return the meat to the pan and tear in the basil leaves, if using, or add the dried herbs. Stir in the tomato paste, bay leaf, and wine, then let the mixture simmer for 2 minutes. Stir in the milk and tomatoes, plus a scant ½ cup of water, then season with salt and pepper.

8

Partially cover the pan, then simmer for 1½ hours, until the meat is tender and surrounded with a rich, thick sauce. Taste to check the seasoning, and add salt and pepper if necessary.

9

Just before serving, boil the pasta for 10 minutes (see page 141 for a full description if you need one). Reserve a cup of the cooking water, then drain. Finely grate some Parmesan cheese.

WHY TAGLIATELLE?
In Bologna, Italy, this sauce is served with tagliatelle, rather than spaghetti. You can use spaghetti if you like.

10

Remove the bay leaf from the sauce. Add the pasta to the sauce, along with a couple of tablespoons of the reserved pasta cooking water, then toss well and serve, topped with grated or shaved Parmesan.

GETTING AHEAD
This meat sauce is a great recipe to double and keep in the refrigerator or freezer, ready to serve with pasta or make into Lasagne (page 248). If you double the quantity you will need to brown the meat in batches.

Roast Lamb & Rosemary Potatoes

Preparation time: 30 minutes
Cooking time: 2 hours 10 minutes
Serves 6

Although some cuts of lamb, such as a rack, are best served very pink, the leg is a slightly tougher cut that benefits from a little more cooking. These timings give juicy and slightly pink meat. Choose a part-boned leg (also called a short leg or three-quarter leg) if possible, as this makes carving so much simpler.

10 cloves garlic

1 handful fresh rosemary sprigs

1 (4½-lb) short leg of lamb

1 stalk celery

1 carrot

1 onion

3 tbsp light olive oil

4½ lb potatoes, such as Yukon Gold

scant ½ cup good red wine

2 cups good-quality lamb
   or beef broth

1 tbsp red currant or cranberry jelly

salt and pepper

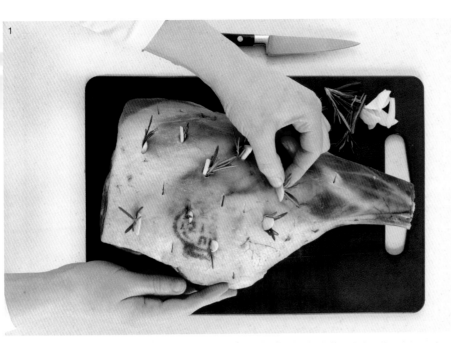

1

Preheat the oven to 425°F. Slice 5 of the garlic cloves into thin slivers. Pick small tufts of rosemary from the stalks. Using a small, very sharp knife, carefully poke about 25 holes into the lamb, cutting down about ¾ inch or so into the meat each time. Poke a sliver of garlic and a tuft of rosemary into each slit. Season well with salt and pepper.

2

Chop the celery, carrot, and onion into big chunks. Put them into a heavy roasting pan. Set the lamb among the vegetables, drizzle 1 tablespoon of the oil over the lamb and vegetables, then put the pan into the middle of the oven and roast the lamb for 20 minutes. Turn the oven down to 375°F, pour scant ½ cup water over the lamb, then set the timer for 1 hour. If at any point the garlic, rosemary or lamb look as though they are coloring up too much, cover the pan with foil.

3

While the lamb roasts, peel the potatoes and cut them into small chunks. Put these into a large roasting pan, then add the remaining garlic cloves, still in their skins. Chop 1 tablespoon of rosemary, and sprinkle it over the potatoes, along with plenty of salt and pepper. Drizzle the rest of the oil over the pan, then rub the oil around the potatoes with your hands.

4

After the lamb has cooked for 1 hour, put the potatoes into the oven on the upper rack. Cook the lamb for 30 minutes more. The vegetables around the lamb will have softened and caramelized.

5

As soon as the lamb is cooked, take it out of the oven and turn up the heat in the oven to 425°F and cook the potatoes for 20 minutes more. Transfer the lamb from the pan to a cutting board or platter and let it rest, uncovered.

6

Spoon the excess fat from the roasting pan, leaving a tablespoon or so behind, then place the pan over medium heat. Add the red wine and broth, scraping up any bits from the bottom of the pan. Simmer until reduced by half, or until the sauce looks a little syrupy, then stir in the red currant or cranberry jelly to make a glossy sauce. Season to taste, and add any resting juices.

7

Strain the sauce into a pitcher or gravy boat. Serve the lamb with the potatoes, sauce, and your favorite vegetables, such as Glazed Carrots (page 314).

PERFECT TIMING

If you want to cook a different-size piece of lamb, follow these timing guidelines. Always start with 20 minutes at 425°F. For lamb that's golden brown on the outside and just pink nearer the bone, calculate an additional 20 minutes cooking per pound of meat (the weight includes the bone). For rare lamb, calculate 15 minutes, and for well done, 25 minutes. As with all meat, cook the lamb from room temperature, or at least not straight from the refrigerator.

Mediterranean Fish Stew

Preparation time: 30 minutes
Cooking time: 40 minutes
Serves 6

The seafood and sunshine of Provence, France, come together in this rich and tasty fish stew, flavored with a twist of orange and a slight hint of anise. Finish the stew with this easy version of *rouille*, a traditional garlicky mayonnaise that melts into the sauce, ready for mopping up with good crusty bread.

---

2 onions

3 large cloves garlic

3 stalks celery

2 red bell peppers

2 tbsp light olive oil

1 orange

1 star anise

2 bay leaves

½ tsp crushed dried chilies

2 tbsp tomato paste

⅔ cup dry white wine

1 (14½-oz) can chopped tomatoes

generous 2 cups fish broth

2¼ lb sustainably caught skinless
   chunky white fish fillet

14 oz clams or mussels

1 fat red chile

1 cup good-quality mayonnaise

7 oz large uncooked shrimp, shelled
   and deveined

1 handful fresh flat-leaf parsley

salt and pepper

crusty bread, to serve (optional)

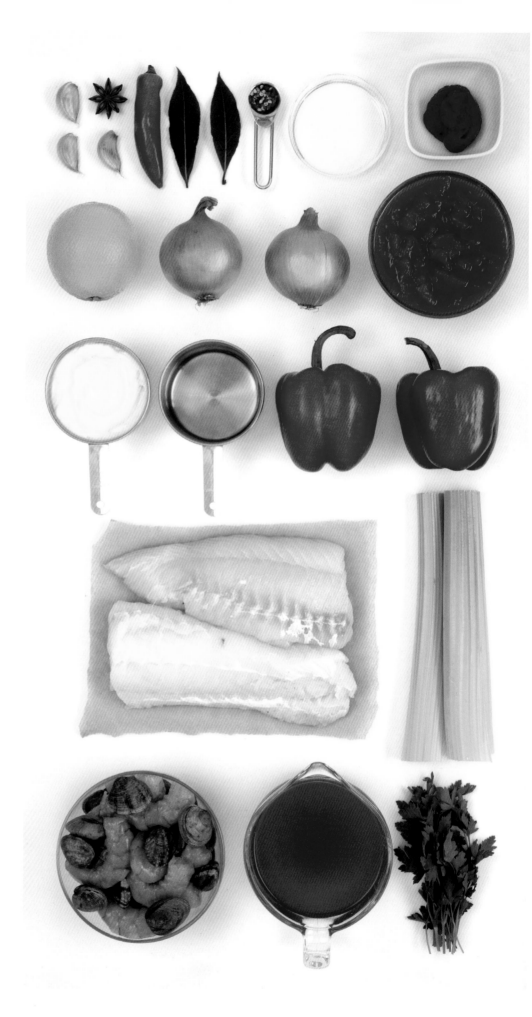

1

2

3

1

Thinly slice the onions, 2 garlic cloves, and the celery, then seed and slice the bell peppers into chunky strips. Heat a large pan over low heat, then add the oil. Add the vegetables, then cook gently for 10 minutes, until softened but not colored.

2

Pare a strip of zest from the orange (trying not to include any of the white pith) using a vegetable peeler. Stir this, the star anise, the bay leaves, and dried crushed chilies into the pan, then cook, uncovered, for another 10 minutes, or until the vegetables are very soft and slightly colored.

3

Turn up the heat to medium, stir in the tomato paste, cook for about 2 minutes, then pour in the wine. Let the wine bubble down to almost nothing in the bottom of the pan. Add the tomatoes and broth, then simmer for 10 minutes, until slightly thickened. Season with salt and pepper.

4

While the sauce cooks, cut the fish into very chunky pieces. Scrub the clams or mussels and pull any stringy threads away from the mussels (these are known as beards), if using. Sharply tap any that are open. Any that don't close within a few seconds should be discarded, along with any that feel strangely heavy, as they may be full of grit.

5

To make the rouille, seed, then very roughly chop the chile, as well as the remaining garlic. Put the mayonnaise, chile and garlic into the bowl of a small food processor.

6

Pulse the ingredients together until the mayonnaise is flecked with chile. Alternatively, finely chop the chile and crush the garlic, then stir into the mayonnaise. Spoon into a serving bowl.

7

Add the chunks of fish and the shrimp to the stew. Bring back to a boil, then cover and simmer for 2 minutes. Add the mussels or clams, then cover and cook for about 2–4 minutes longer, or until the shells have opened, the fish has turned opaque, and the shrimp are pink all the way through. Discard any shellfish that remain closed. Season the sauce with salt and pepper.

8

When ready to serve, roughly chop the parsley leaves and sprinkle over the stew. Serve with crusty bread, with the rouille on the side.

Roast Beef &
Yorkshire Puddings

Preparation time: 20 minutes
Cooking time: 2 hours 20 minutes
Serves 6

There's nothing like bringing out
roast beef for a special occasion!
Ideally the beef should be aged for
at least 21 days—quality really
does make all the difference when
meat is cooked simply. Rib roast,
also called prime rib or standing rib,
is an expensive cut, so if you prefer,
choose a bone-in sirloin instead.

2- or 3-rib beef rib roast, about
  5½ lb
1 cup all-purpose flour, plus 2 tbsp
2 tsp English mustard powder
1½ tsp kosher salt
1 tsp pepper
1 handful fresh thyme sprigs
3 large eggs
1¼ cups milk
¼ cup sunflower or vegetable oil
2¼ cups good beef broth
salt and pepper

1
Preheat the oven to 425°F. Wipe the meat dry with some paper towels. Mix 1 tablespoon of the flour, the mustard powder, 1 teaspoon of the salt, and the pepper in a small bowl, then rub the mixture all over the beef.

ON THE BONE
It's best to use a bone-in rib roast, which will give the meat and gravy more flavor. Ask the butcher to remove the chine bone, but leave the ribs attached.

2
Scatter the thyme sprigs across the middle of a roasting pan, then set the beef on top, fat side uppermost.

3
Roast the beef for 20 minutes. After 30 minutes, turn the heat down to 325°F and roast for 1 hour 40 minutes for meat that's medium rare (in other words, juicy and still pink in the middle). If you like your meat cooked differently, see page 278 for more information on timings.

While the beef is cooking, start the Yorkshire pudding batter. Pour the 1 cup flour and ½ teaspoon salt into a mixing bowl and stir together. Make a well in the middle of the flour, then crack in the eggs and add 1 tablespoon of the milk.

4

Use a whisk to beat the mixture to a thick, smooth paste. If it looks lumpy, keep beating.

5

Once all lumps have been beaten out, gradually whisk in the rest of the milk to create a smooth, thin batter. Set aside until needed.

6

Remove the beef from the oven, and set aside to rest, covered loosely with foil, while you bake the Yorkshire puddings. The internal temperature of the beef will continue to rise a little as it rests, so don't be tempted to add on more cooking time, as you could risk overcooking it.

7

Turn the oven up to 425°F. Pour 1 teaspoon of the oil into each of the 12 cups of a nonstick muffin pan. Put the pan into the oven and let the oil heat up for 10 minutes. When the oil is hot, carefully remove the pan from the oven. Pour the batter carefully and evenly into the oil, working as quickly as you can. Bake the Yorkshire puddings for 15–20 minutes. Avoid opening the oven door before 15 minutes have passed.

8

Make the gravy while you wait. Transfer the beef to a platter or cutting board, then spoon off any excess fat from the juices, leaving about 1 tablespoon. Tilt the pan to help. Place the pan over medium heat, then add the remaining tablespoon flour. Stir for 2 minutes. It will thicken up. This method gives a traditional, thicker-style gravy. If you prefer yours thinner, leave out the flour, and move on to step 9.

9

Gradually stir the broth into the pan, adding a little at first to make a smooth base, then stirring in the rest to make a smooth, thin gravy. Once the gravy comes to a boil, it will thicken. If you haven't used flour, boil the gravy for a few minutes until it's syrupy. Stir in any resting juices from the beef, season to taste, then strain into a gravy boat.

10

When the puddings have had 15 minutes in the oven they will be puffed, dark golden and crisp.

11

If you like, cut away the ribs before you carve the meat by carefully running a knife between the meat and the bones. This makes it easier to carve.

12

Serve the beef with the Yorkshire puddings, gravy, and vegetables, such as Roast Potatoes (page 306) and Buttered Green Vegetables (page 330).

PERFECT TIMING

To cook a different-size piece of beef, weigh it and follow these timings. Start the cooking with 20 minutes at 425°F. After this, turn the oven down to 325°F. For rare beef (soft and red in the middle) add 15 minutes per pound. For beef that's medium-rare (firmer, but still pink and juicy), add 18 minutes per pound. For medium (a hint of pink in the middle), add 20 minutes per pound. For well-done (not recommended, as this results in dry meat), add 25 minutes per pound. The beef should be cooked from room temperature, or at least not straight from the refrigerator.

Since joints of beef vary a lot in size and shape, these timings are only a guide. To be absolutely sure, use an instant-read meat thermometer, inserted into the thickest part of the meat, away from the bone. When ready, rare beef will be around 122°F, medium-rare 131°F, medium 140°F, and well-done will be 158°F. As the meat rests, its internal temperature will rise a few degrees and complete the cooking. These temperatures also apply to roast lamb.

Paella

Preparation time: 30 minutes
Cooking time: 50 minutes
Serves 6

This classic Spanish rice dish is a great dish to cook for friends. The mix of seafood is up to you, but shrimp, mussels, and squid (don't fear—it's simple to cook) give great color and texture. Make sure you use the largest pan you can, as the rice swells up a lot as it cooks.

3½ oz chorizo (see note)

2 tsp light olive oil

6 skinless, boneless chicken thighs

2 onions

3 cloves garlic

2 red bell peppers

2 cups paella or risotto rice
    (see page 282)

1 tsp smoked or regular paprika

generous pinch saffron threads,
    about ½ tsp

scant ½ cup white wine

4¼ cups chicken or fish broth

6 small cleaned squid (optional)

11 oz mussels

12 large shell-on uncooked shrimp,
    with heads on or off

1 handful frozen baby peas
    (petits pois)

1 handful fresh flat-leaf parsley

1 lemon

salt and pepper

1

Thinly slice the chorizo. Put a large frying pan or flameproof casserole (or a paella pan if you have one) over medium heat, then add the oil. After 30 seconds, add the chorizo. Fry for 5 minutes, until golden all over and the chorizo has released its red oil. Remove from the pan and set aside. While the chorizo cooks, cut the chicken into bite-size chunks.

CHORIZO
Chorizo is a spicy Spanish sausage flavored with paprika and garlic. There are two types: cooking chorizo, which is softer, and needs cooking like a regular sausage, and cured chorizo, which is firm and dry, and is eaten raw, like salami. Either type will work in this recipe, but choose cooking chorizo if there's a choice.

2

Add the chicken to the pan, season with salt and pepper, and fry for 5 minutes, turning occasionally, until golden.

3

While the chicken cooks, finely slice or chop the onion and garlic. Seed the peppers and cut them into chunky slices. Add the onions, garlic and peppers to the chicken, stir, then cook gently for 10 minutes, until the onions and peppers are softened.

4

Add the rice and turn up the heat. Stir well to coat with the oil, then add the paprika, saffron, wine, and broth and season with salt and pepper. Simmer the rice for 20 minutes, or until it is nearly soft. Stir several times as it cooks.

PAELLA RICE
Spanish cooks use a short, round-grained rice for paella, which looks similar to risotto rice. It's either labeled as "paella rice" or as one of the two most common varieties, Calasparra or Bomba. If you can't find it, use risotto rice.

5

Meanwhile, slice the squid tubes into thick rings, if using. Leave the tentacles whole. Scrub the mussels and pull any stringy threads away from them (these are known as beards). Tap any open mussels sharply on the work surface. Any that don't close after a few seconds must be discarded.

6

Add the shrimp to the pan, tucking them into what sauce is left around the rice. Cover with a lid and cook for 5 minutes, then scatter the squid, mussels, peas, and chorizo over the top. Cover and cook for another 2 minutes, or until the mussels have opened and the squid has turned from translucent to white. The rice will have absorbed the broth.

7

Discard any mussels that haven't opened. Roughly chop the parsley leaves, then sprinkle over the paella, which is best served in the pan right on the table. Serve with lemon wedges to squeeze over the paella.

Chicken, Bacon & Vegetable Pot Pies

Preparation time: 1¼ hours,
plus 30 minutes for cooling
Cooking time: 20 minutes
(or 30 for a large pie)
Makes 6 individual pies
or 1 large pie

Individual pot pies are easy to
put together, without any pastry
crimping. Serve with simple
cooked vegetables such as Glazed
Carrots (page 314), or mashed
potatoes (page 136), for an ideal
family supper.

---

12 skinless, boneless chicken thighs

8 strips bacon

1 tbsp mild olive oil

2 onions

2 stalks celery

3 medium leeks

several fresh thyme sprigs

1 tbsp butter

7 oz white mushrooms

2 tbsp all-purpose flour, plus extra
    for rolling

1⅔ cups chicken broth

7 fl oz crème fraîche

1 tsp Dijon mustard

1 (17-oz) package frozen puff
    pastry, defrosted

1 medium egg

salt and pepper

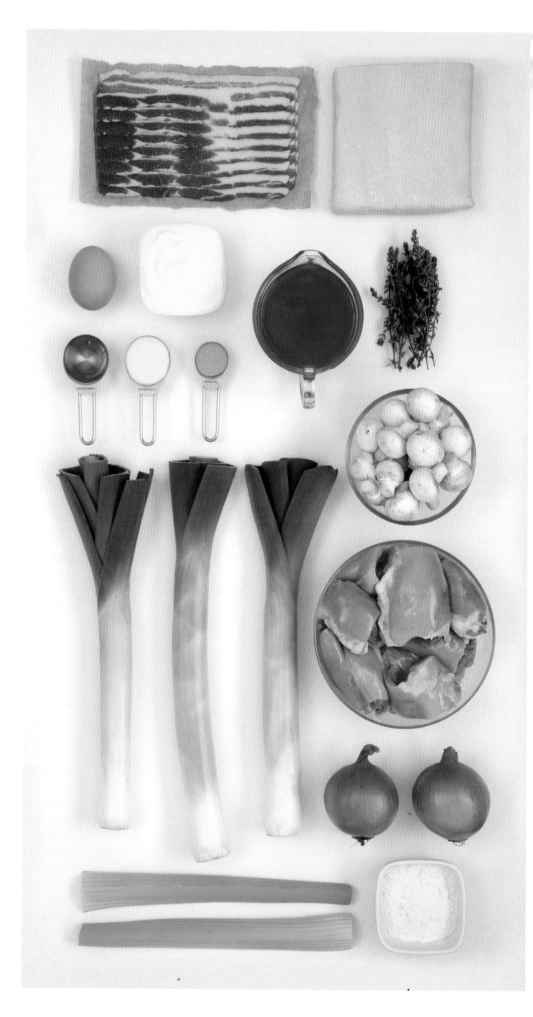

1
Cut the chicken thighs and bacon into bite-size pieces.

2
Heat a large frying pan or shallow heatproof casserole over medium heat and add the oil. After 30 seconds, add half of the chicken and bacon to the pan and season with salt and pepper. Fry for about 8–10 minutes, stirring often, until golden all over. Transfer to a plate using a slotted spoon, then repeat with the second batch.

CAN'T FIND CHICKEN THIGHS? Most grocery stores now sell boned chicken thighs. They're better than breasts for a recipe like this because the meat stays moist, they have more flavor, and they are also better value. If you can't find chicken thighs, use breasts cut into chunks. Brown them, then return them to the pan during step 5, simmering for 5 minutes only, until the chicken is cooked through.

3
While the chicken cooks, finely slice the onions, celery, and leeks (white parts only). Once both batches of chicken are cooked and set aside, add the vegetables to the pan, then cover and cook gently for about 10 minutes, until soft.

4
Pick the thyme leaves from their stems. Turn the heat back up a little, then add the butter, mushrooms and thyme. Fry, stirring, for about 3 minutes, until the mushrooms and vegetables take on a golden tinge. Return the chicken to the pan.

5
Take the pan off the heat, then stir in the flour. Add the broth gradually to make a smooth sauce. Simmer for 20 minutes, until the chicken is tender.

6

Stir the crème fraîche and mustard into the pie filling.

7

Taste the sauce for seasoning before adding any salt (the bacon will have added plenty). Season with pepper. Spoon the chicken pie filling into 6 individual pie dishes, leaving at least 1 inch at the top so that the filling can bubble without escaping. Let cool.

8

Lightly flour the work surface, then roll out the puff pastry sheets slightly. Cut each into 3 rectangles, each a little wider than the tops of the pie dishes. Use a fork to beat the egg with 1 tablespoon water to make a glaze. Dampen the rim of each dish with a little of the glaze. Press the pastry over the top.

9

Lightly brush the glaze over the pastry. Make a few small slashes in the top of each pie with a small sharp knife. The pies can be chilled for up to 2 days at this point.

GETTING AHEAD
Use fresh pastry rather than frozen, then freeze the pies, unbaked, for up to 1 month. Defrost overnight in the refrigerator before baking.

10

Preheat the oven to 400°F. Put the pies onto a baking sheet and bake for 20 minutes, or until the pastry is golden and the filling is bubbling up in the middle. Pies cooked straight from the refrigerator will take a few minutes longer to cook.

TO MAKE A LARGE PIE
Put the filling into a large pie dish, and cover with the pastry. Slash the top, then bake for 30 minutes, until risen and golden.

Beef Stew with Herb Dumplings

Preparation time: 45 minutes
Cooking time: 2½–3 hours
Serves 6

Recipes like this were made for winter. If you can, make the stew a day ahead to let the flavors intensify, then reheat it very gently (don't boil it), pop in the dumplings, and cook until crisp on top and fluffy inside. The dumplings aren't essential, but they're wonderfully comforting.

1¼ cups all-purpose flour,
    plus 3 tbsp
½ tsp kosher salt
2¼ lb stew beef, trimmed of excess
    fat and cut into large cubes (a
    butcher will be happy to do this)
3 tbsp light olive oil
2 onions
2 stalks celery
4–5 large carrots, or about 1 lb 5 oz
5 tbsp cold unsalted butter
several sprigs fresh thyme
1 bay leaf
1 tbsp tomato paste
1¼ cups full-bodied red wine
1⅔ cups good beef broth
2 oz sharp Cheddar cheese
½ tsp baking powder
5 tbsp milk
salt and pepper

1

Mix 3 tablespoons flour, the salt and some pepper in a resealable plastic bag, then add the beef. Shake the bag to coat the beef in the flour.

STEW BEEF

Packaged stew meat tends to be cut too small (and can be too lean) for proper long, slow cooking, so it's better to choose a large piece and cut it yourself, or ask the butcher to do it for you. I have used flat-iron steak here, but anything labeled chuck, shank, skirt, blade, or just plain old stew beef will do.

2

Place a large ovenproof casserole over medium heat. Add 1 tablespoon of the oil. Put half of the beef into the pan, tapping away the excess flour from each piece before it goes in. Fry for 10 minutes, turning a couple of times, until dark golden brown and crusted. Transfer to a bowl, then add a splash of water to the pan and scrape up any meaty bits. Pour this liquid into the bowl. Wipe out the pan with paper towels, then repeat with the second batch of beef.

DEGLAZING

The little crusty bits that form on the bottom of the pan are full of flavor. Adding liquid to the pan and scraping up the tasty bits is known as deglazing, and it's a great technique for making tasty sauces.

3

Meanwhile, roughly chop the onions and celery and cut the carrots into chunky pieces.

4

Transfer the second batch of beef to the bowl and wipe out the pan. Add 1 tablespoon of the butter and he final tablespoon of oil, then cook the onion, carrot, celery, a few sprigs of thyme, and the bay leaf for 10 minutes, until starting to turn golden.

5

Preheat the oven to 325°F. Return the meat and any juices to the pan, then stir in the tomato paste and pour in the wine and broth. The top pieces of meat should be just poking out of the liquid. This will depend on the size of your pan, so add a splash more wine or broth, or water, if you need to. Bring the pan to a simmer over low heat, then cover with a lid and put the pan in the oven for 2 hours.

6

Start preparing the dumplings. Grate the cheese and set aside. Cut the remaining butter into cubes and put it in a bowl with the rest of the flour and the baking powder. Rub the ingredients together, using both hands to lift the butter and flour from the bowl, then gently passing them between your fingers and thumbs. It should look like rough bread crumbs.

7

Before finishing the dumplings, check the stew. The meat should be tender enough to cut easily with a spoon. If it's ready, or nearly so, spoon off any excess fat from the top and season with salt and pepper. If not, give it another 30 minutes and test it again. When the stew is ready, finish the dumplings. Stir the milk, remaining thyme leaves, cheese, and salt and pepper into the flour mixture, then divide into 12 pieces and shape into balls.

8

Set the dumplings on top of the stew. Return the pan to the oven, uncovered, for 30 minutes.

9

The dumplings will swell and turn golden and the stew will be rich and brown. Serve with vegetables, such as Buttered Green Vegetables (page 330), and potatoes.

Crab Cakes with Herb Vinaigrette

Preparation time: 30 minutes,
plus 30 minutes for chilling
Cooking time: 12 minutes,
Serves 4–6 (makes 12 crab cakes)

Rather than serving your crab cakes
with a heavy mayonnaise, try spooning
over some citrus and herb dressing—it
brings every flavor to the fore. Serve
three crab cakes per person as a main
course for four, perhaps with some
boiled new potatoes, or two per person
as a starter for six.

7 oz good-quality white bread

1 large green chile

1 organic lemon

1 small bunch fresh flat-leaf parsley

2 tbsp crème fraîche or sour cream

2 tsp Worcestershire sauce

1 tsp cayenne pepper

1 large egg

1 lb 2 oz lump crabmeat, picked over
   for shell

2 tsp capers

1 small bunch fresh tarragon

1 small bunch fresh dill

3 tbsp sunflower or vegetable oil

¼ cup extra-virgin olive oil

1 lime

1 tbsp butter

3½ oz watercress

salt and pepper

1
Tear the bread into the bowl of a food processor, discarding the crusts, then process to fine crumbs.

2
Seed and finely chop the chile. Finely grate the zest from the lemon, then squeeze the juice into a small bowl. Roughly chop the parsley leaves. Put the bread crumbs, crème fraîche, lemon zest and 1 tablespoon of the juice, the chile, parsley, Worcestershire sauce, cayenne and egg into a large bowl.

3
Mix well until everything is evenly combined.

4
Now add the crabmeat and mix in gently, so that small clumps of crab are left intact.

5

Shape the crab mixture into 12 equal-size patties. Put them onto a plate or tray in a single layer, then chill for 30 minutes in the refrigerator to let the mixture firm up.

GETTING AHEAD
The crab cakes can be covered with plastic wrap and chilled for up to 24 hours, if you like.

6

While the crab cakes chill, make the vinaigrette. Roughly chop the capers and leaves from the tarragon and dill. Put them into a bowl, then add 2 tablespoons of the sunflower oil, the extra-virgin olive oil, and the remaining lemon juice. Squeeze the juice from the lime and add it to the bowl. Season with salt and pepper.

7

Preheat the oven to 275°F. Place a large frying pan over medium heat, then add ½ tablespoon each of butter and sunflower oil. When the butter foams, add 6 of the crab cakes. Cook for 3 minutes, or until crisp and golden underneath. Use a spatula to carefully turn the patties, then cook for another 3 minutes. Transfer to a plate covered with paper towels, then keep warm in the oven. Wipe out the pan with a paper towel, add the remaining butter and oil, then cook the second batch.

8

Serve the crab cakes with the herbed vinaigrette and a handful of watercress to garnish.

Roast Pork with Caramelized Apples

Preparation time: 30 minutes
Cooking time: 5 hours
Serves 6

Pork shoulder is a good-value cut that needs to be cooked slowly, until the meat is meltingly tender. The skin and the fat below it crackle up to a wonderful crunch. Perfect cracklings start with good quality free-range pork, with its skin well scored and rubbed with plenty of salt. Ask the butcher to score the skin for you, if possible.

---

1 tbsp light olive oil

4½ lb pork shoulder, fat and skin
   well scored

1 tsp fennel seeds

1 tsp kosher salt

1 onion

4 apples

½ lemon

several sprigs thyme

3 bay leaves

2 tbsp butter

scant 1 cup dry or medium
   hard cider

2½ cups chicken or pork broth

salt and pepper

1

Preheat the oven to 425°F. Rub most of the oil into the pork skin, then push the fennel seeds and salt into the slashes in the skin as evenly as you can. Put the pork into a roasting pan, then roast for 45 minutes.

2

Meanwhile, cut the onion into chunky slices. Quarter and remove the cores from the apples, but leave the skins on. Toss the apples with a squeeze of the lemon juice to prevent them from turning brown.

3

When the pork has roasted for 45 minutes, the skin will be starting to puff and crackle. Turn the oven down to 325°F, then cook for another 4 hours, scattering the onions, most of the thyme and the bay leaves around the pork when there's 1 hour of cooking time left.

4

When the pork is nearly ready, put the apples into a frying pan with the remaining oil and the butter. Place over medium heat and cook gently for about 15 minutes, turning regularly, until tender.

5

Transfer the pork to a cutting board and let it rest, uncovered, while you make the gravy. Spoon any excess fat from the pan, then place the roasting pan over low heat. Pour in the hard cider, let it bubble and reduce for 5 minutes, then add the broth. Reduce the broth and cider mixture for another 5 minutes, or until the liquid looks a little syrupy and has a good meaty flavor. Season with salt and pepper and strain into a gravy boat.

6

Finish the apples. Turn up the heat under the apples, sprinkle a few thyme leaves over them, then fry for 2 more minutes, or until glossy and golden.

7

When ready to serve, use a large sharp knife to carve the pork into thick slices. If the crackling is hard to cut through, cut it away from the meat in one piece, then snap it into shards before carving the meat. Serve the pork with the apples and gravy, plus vegetables such as Maple-Roast Winter Vegetables (page 328).

Vegetable Tagine with Chermoula and Couscous

Preparation time: 1 hour,
plus overnight soaking
Cooking time: 1¼ hours
Serves 6

A rich and tasty tagine is perfect for vegetarians or as a side dish to serve with roast lamb. Dried lima beans are worth the effort of pre-soaking, but you can use three large cans of lima beans, drained, instead, or defrosted frozen ones. Start from step 3, then add the beans to the pan with the rest of the vegetables in step 6.

2 cups dried lima beans

2 onions

4 large cloves garlic

½ cup olive oil

5 tsp ras el hanout spice mix
  (see note)

1 (14½-oz) can chopped tomatoes

2 tbsp tomato paste

generous 2 cups vegetable or
  chicken broth, plus 1¼ cups

1 lb 2 oz squash, such as butternut

3 zucchini

¾ cup dried prunes or apricots

2 tsp honey

1 large bunch fresh cilantro

1 large red chile

1 tbsp toasted sesame seeds

1 organic lemon

2⅓ cups couscous

1 tbsp butter

salt and pepper

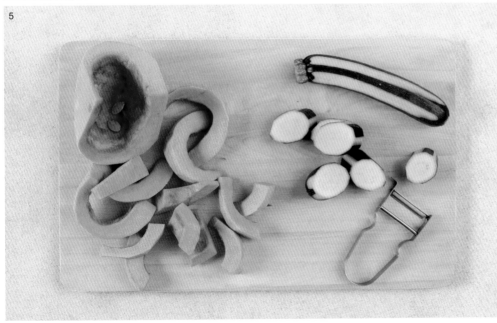

1
Put the lima beans into a large bowl of water and leave them to soak overnight. The beans will swell to about twice their original size.

2
Drain the soaked beans, put them in a large pan, cover with clean water and bring to a boil. Cook for 40–50 minutes, or until tender but not soft, occasionally removing any froth from the surface of the water if necessary. Drain well.

3
Meanwhile, roughly chop the onions and 3½ garlic cloves. Heat 3 tablespoons of oil in a large pan, then add the onions and garlic and fry over a gentle heat for 10 minutes, until soft.

4
Stir the ras el hanout into the pan, then cook for 2 minutes until the spices smell fragrant.

WHAT IS RAS EL HANOUT?
A classic Moroccan spice mixture, ras el hanout contains many aromatic spices including cinnamon, cumin, coriander, cloves, pepper, ginger, and even dried rose petals. If you can't find it, use a combination of these spices instead.

5
Add the tomatoes, then add the tomato paste, 2 cups of the broth and the drained beans. Cover, ring to a boil, then simmer for 30 minutes. The beans will be very nearly cooked by now. Meanwhile, peel and seed the squash and chop into large chunks. Peel some of the skin from the zucchini to make stripes, if you like, then thickly slice them. It's not essential to peel zucchini—the stripes are just for decoration.

6

Add the zucchini, squash, and dried fruit to the pan, then simmer again for 20 minutes, or until the vegetables are tender and the tagine is thick and saucy. Stir in the honey.

7

While you wait, make the chermoula dressing and prepare the couscous. Roughly chop the cilantro leaves and put them into a bowl. Finely chop the chile and crush the remaining garlic, then add to the bowl with the rest of the olive oil, and most of the sesame seeds. Grate in the lemon zest and squeeze in half of the juice. Season with salt and pepper.

WHAT IS CHERMOULA?
Classically used as a marinade, chermoula consists of chopped fresh herbs, chile, garlic, oil and lemon. Here these flavors are used in a chermoula-inspired dressing to finish the dish.

8

For the couscous, mix the couscous and the rest of the lemon juice in a large bowl. Dot the butter over the top in small pieces. Bring the remaining broth to a boil, then pour it over the couscous. Cover tightly with plastic wrap, then set aside for 10 minutes.

9

When the 10 minutes is over, remove the plastic wrap and fluff up the couscous with a fork. Season generously with salt and pepper and serve with the tagine, with spoonfuls of the chermoula swirled on top. Sprinkle with the remaining sesame seeds.

Roast Potatoes

Preparation time: 30 minutes
Cooking time: 40–50 minutes
Serves 6 generously

No Sunday dinner is complete without a pile of crunchy-on-the-outside, fluffy-in-the-middle roasted potatoes. Always start with a baking variety of potato, such as russets. Goose fat is great because it adds a rich, luxurious flavor of its own. Of course, you can use oil instead—try a light, flavorless oil such as vegetable, sunflower or peanut.

4½ lb medium-size baking potatoes,
  such as russets
½ cup goose or duck fat
  or scant ½ cup vegetable,
  sunflower, or peanut oil
1½ tsp kosher salt

1
Preheat the oven to 425°F. Peel the potatoes, then cut them into quarters, or pieces about the size of a small egg. Put the potatoes into a large pan and cover with cold water. Place over high heat, bring to a boil (which will take about 10 minutes from cold), add ½ teaspoon of the salt, then, when the pan is bubbling fiercely, turn the heat down a little and boil the potatoes for 2 minutes.

2
While the potatoes cook, spoon the fat or pour the oil into a large roasting pan. Put it into the oven to heat up.

3
Transfer the potatoes to a colander and let them drain thoroughly. Let them stand for 5 minutes. As the steam rises, they will dry out a little. Put the potatoes back into the pan, cover with a lid, then shake the pan briefly, holding the lid firmly, letting the potatoes rumble around inside. This will fluff them up, resulting in a crispier finish.

4
Very carefully, remove the roasting pan from the oven, then carefully spoon the potatoes into the fat. Toss them in the fat a little to coat, then season with the remaining salt.

5
Roast the potatoes for 40 minutes, or until very crisp and golden, turning once during cooking. The exact timing of the potatoes will depend on the size of the chunks and the variety of potato, so give them 10 minutes more if you think they need it. Serve immediately.

Green Salad
with Vinaigrette

Preparation time: 5 minutes
Serves 4–6 (easily doubled or more)

Transform even the most humble
lettuce into a salad with plenty
of flavor. Once you've started
making your own vinaigrette, you'll
never use store-bought again.

1 clove garlic
2 tbsp light olive oil
1 tbsp extra-virgin olive oil
1 tbsp red- or white-wine vinegar
1 tsp Dijon mustard
1 head leaf lettuce of your choice
salt and pepper

1
Crush the garlic. Put the garlic, oils, vinegar, and mustard into a small screw-top jar.

2
Screw the lid on tightly, then shake the ingredients together until thickened and smooth. Season to taste with salt and pepper.

STORING THE DRESSING
You can multiply the quantities and keep the dressing in a jar in the refrigerator for up to 2 weeks. Give it a good shake before use.

3
Tear the lettuce leaves into a large serving bowl. Just before serving, pour on the dressing. Use salad servers to toss the lettuce in the dressing several times. Make sure all the leaves are well coated, then serve immediately.

PREPARING LETTUCE
To wash and dry lettuce, fill a bowl with cold water and add the leaves. Swish them around a little, then drain. Either spin the leaves dry in a salad spinner or dab gently with a clean dish towel or paper towels.

Ratatouille

Preparation time: 15 minutes
Cooking time: 1 hour 10 minutes
Serves 4–6

Ratatouille makes a great vegetarian main dish or a side dish for roast lamb or other grilled meats. It can be served hot, warm, or at room temperature. It's usually cooked in a pan on the stovetop, but this oven-roasting method requires minimum effort, intensifying the vegetables' flavor while you do something else.

1 red bell pepper

1 yellow bell pepper

2 zucchini, about 11 oz total

2 small or 1 large eggplant

3 tbsp light olive oil

1 onion

2 cloves garlic

1 lb 5 oz canned chopped tomatoes

1 handful fresh basil leaves

salt and pepper

1
Preheat the oven to 400°F. Seed the peppers, then cut the flesh into large squares. Slice the zucchini thickly and cut the eggplant into large cubes. Put the vegetables into a large roasting pan, then drizzle with the oil and season with salt and pepper. Toss well, then roast for 20 minutes.

Meanwhile, thinly slice the onion and garlic. Stir the onion and garlic into the oily vegetables after the initial 20 minutes' cooking, then return to the pan. Roast for another 20 minutes, until the onions have softened and the vegetables are golden.

2
Add the tomatoes to the vegetables, then return to the oven for 10 more minutes, until sizzling at the edges.

3
Tear the basil leaves over the ratatouille, season with salt and pepper, then serve warm or hot, or let cool to room temperature.

Chunky Oven Fries

Preparation time: 10 minutes
Cooking time: 40 minutes
Serves 4 (easily halved or doubled)

Rather than reaching for a bag
of frozen oven fries, grab some
potatoes and make your own;
they're healthier, tastier and so
economical to make.

4 large potatoes, such as Yukon
   Gold, about 7 oz each
2 tbsp sunflower or vegetable oil
½ tsp kosher salt, or more to taste

1
Preheat the oven to 425°F. Keep the skins on the potatoes. Cut each potato in half along its length, then cut each half into 4 wedge-shaped fries. Put these into a nonstick roasting pan.

2
Drizzle the oil over the potatoes, then toss to coat using your hands. Bake for 40 minutes, turning them halfway through cooking. The easiest way to do this is with a spatula.

3
When the fries are golden all over and the skins crisp, sprinkle with the salt. Serve immediately.

VARIATION
For spicy fries, sprinkle a little paprika and chili powder over the potatoes when you add the oil.

Glazed Carrots

Preparation time: 10 minutes
Cooking time: 15 minutes
Serves 4–6

This method of cooking really concentrates the flavor of carrots and makes them look that little bit more impressive than just plain old boiled. Use whole baby carrots when they're available, but remember they'll probably need less cooking time during step 2.

1¾ lb carrots
2 tbsp butter
2 tsp sugar
1 handful fresh flat-leaf parsley
salt and pepper

1
Cut the carrots into ½-inch rounds. Put them into a medium pan with the butter, sugar, and 4 tablespoons water. Place the pan over high heat, then bring it to a boil. Once boiling, turn the heat to medium, cover the pan with a tight-fitting lid, then let the carrots cook for 10 minutes. Uncover the pan; the carrots will be almost tender.

2
Cook for 5 minutes more, uncovered, until all of the liquid has evaporated and the carrots are coated in a shiny glaze. Stir now and then as they cook. Season with salt and pepper.

3
Roughly chop the parsley leaves, then stir through the carrots. Spoon into a serving dish.

CHANGE THE HERBS
If you're planning to serve the carrots with chicken, try adding a little chopped tarragon instead of the parsley. Chopped mint will go particularly well with lamb.

Coleslaw

Preparation time: 15 minutes
Serves 4–6

The dressing for this coleslaw is
made with mayonnaise lightened
with yogurt. Although creamy
and full of flavor, it won't weigh the
vegetables down. See opposite
page for variations.

1 small white cabbage, about 14 oz

1 carrot

1 red onion

5 tbsp good-quality mayonnaise

5 tbsp natural yogurt, low-fat
   or regular

1 tsp Dijon mustard

1 tsp red-wine vinegar

1 handful fresh chives

salt and pepper

1
Cut the cabbage in half through the core, then into quarters. Peel away and discard the first few outer leaves. Cut the tough core away from each piece. Finely slice the cabbage.

2
Peel and coarsely grate the carrot. Cut the onion in half, then into quarters through the root, then thinly slice. Put the carrot and onion into a bowl with the cabbage and mix well.

3
Mix the mayonnaise, yogurt, mustard and vinegar in a small bowl until smooth. Now snip in the chives using kitchen scissors. Stir and season with salt and pepper.

4
Toss the dressing and vegetables together until the vegetables are evenly coated. Serve immediately or chill in the refrigerator for up to 24 hours.

VARIATIONS
For a cheesy coleslaw, grate 3½ oz Cheddar and stir into the mix.

For fennel coleslaw, substitute 2 fennel bulbs for the cabbage.

For Waldorf slaw, add a chopped apple and a handful each of walnut pieces and halved grapes. Add a few chopped celery stalks too, if you have them.

Garlic Bread

Preparation time: 20 minutes
Cooking time: 20 minutes
Serves 6

This slightly retro garlic bread is not quite Italian, not quite French, but it's delicious all the same, especially with a big dish of Lasagne (page 248) or Tagliatelle with Bolognese Sauce (page 262).

---

1 large clove garlic, or 2 if you like
    things garlicky
1 small bunch fresh flat-leaf parsley
1 small bunch fresh basil
¾ stick (6 tbsp) unsalted butter,
    softened
1 large baguette, or 2 smaller ones
salt and pepper

1

Preheat the oven to 400°F. Crush the garlic and finely chop the parsley and basil leaves. Put the butter into a small bowl, then mash in the garlic, parsley, and basil, season with salt and pepper, then mix well.

2

If using a long baguette, cut it in half so that it will fit into the oven later. Using a serrated knife, cut deep slashes in the bread at 1-inch intervals. Be careful not to cut all the way through the bread.

3

Using a table knife, spread a generous amount of the garlic butter into each gap in the bread. If you have any left over, spread it over the top of the loaves.

4

Put each loaf onto a large sheet of foil. Scrunch the foil around the loaves so they are completely enclosed.

5

Put the bread on a baking sheet and bake for 15 minutes. Open up each parcel a little to expose the top of the bread, then return to the oven for 5 minutes. The top crusts will now be crisp and golden, and the butter melted. Take the bread to the table as it is, or cut it into 3-slice portions before serving.

Dauphinoise Potatoes

Preparation time: 25 minutes
Cooking time: 1–1¼ hours
Serves 6

Simplicity itself, yet so delicious,
a dish of dauphinoise potatoes
makes a wonderful accompaniment
to roast meat or steaks, and can
be prepared well in advance if you're
entertaining. This recipe is rich
without being over the top, but if
you like you could add more cream
and less milk.

1¼ cups heavy cream

1¼ cups whole milk

1 clove garlic

1 whole nutmeg, for grating
    (or ¼ tsp ground)

3¼ lb medium-size baking
    potatoes, such as russets

1 tbsp butter

3 oz Gruyère or Cheddar cheese

salt and pepper

1
Put the cream and milk into a medium pan. Crush the garlic clove, add to the pan, then bring to a boil. As soon as small bubbles start to pop around the edge of the pan, take it off the heat. Finely grate ¼ teaspoon nutmeg, stir it into the pan, then let stand to infuse for at least 10 minutes.

2
Meanwhile, peel the potatoes, then slice them thinly, to less than ¼ inch thick. If the potatoes rock around too much on the board, cut them in half. Rest the potatoes on their flat edge, then slice them.

3

Preheat the oven to 350°F. Spread the butter around the inside of a large baking dish. Arrange a layer of potatoes in the bottom of the dish, then season with salt and pepper. Repeat until all of the potatoes have been used up.

4

Pour the infused cream over the potatoes. Only the very top of the potatoes should stick out of the liquid, but this can depend on the depth and width of your baking dish. Add a splash more cream if needed. Grate the cheese, then sprinkle it over the top of the potatoes.

5

Bake the potatoes for 1 hour, or until the top is golden and bubbling and the potatoes are tender. Check this by inserting a knife into the middle of the dish. The knife should slide easily through to the bottom. If the potatoes need longer but the top is already golden, cover the dish with foil and bake for 15 minutes more. Let the dish settle for a few minutes before serving.

Dressed Green Beans

Preparation time: 10 minutes
Cooking time: 10 minutes
Serves 4–6

If boiled or steamed beans seem
a little bit boring, try this easy way
to transform the humble green bean
into a special side dish, perfect
with roast chicken. Serve just warm
or at room temperature.

---

4 strips bacon

1 tsp light olive oil

1 lb 2 oz thin green beans

½ tsp salt

2 shallots or ½ small red onion

2 tsp wholegrain mustard

2 tbsp red- or white-wine vinegar,
   or cider vinegar

salt and pepper

1
Cut the bacon into small pieces with a knife or snip with kitchen scissors. Place a frying pan over medium heat, then add the oil. After 30 seconds, add the bacon.

2
Fry the bacon gently for 10 minutes until crisp and golden and surrounded with the melted bacon fat.

3

While the bacon cooks, bring a medium pan of water to a boil. Trim the stem ends from the beans, leaving the slender tops. Put the beans and salt into the boiling water. Bring the pan back to a boil, then cook the beans for 5 minutes, or until they are just tender.

4

Meanwhile, peel, then finely chop or slice the shallots or onion.

5

Taste one of the beans to check that they're cooked to your liking. Drain them in a colander. Stir the shallots or onion, mustard, and vinegar into the bacon pan, then season with pepper and a little salt. Add the beans to the pan.

6

Turn the beans over in the dressing until well coated, then serve.

Maple-Roast Winter Vegetables

Preparation time: 15 minutes
Cooking time: 50 minutes
Serves 4–6

Boiling winter root vegetables can mean they lose their flavor and goodness, but roasting intensifies their flavor, and the skins crisp up, too. Celery root, sweet potatoes, butternut squash, and Jerusalem artichokes could all be substituted if you prefer. This is a great side dish with any of the roasts in this book.

1 medium rutabaga, about
   1 lb 5 oz in total
4 medium parsnips, about
   1 lb 5 oz in total
5 medium carrots, about
   1 lb 5 oz in total
¼ cup light olive oil
6 cloves garlic
2 sprigs fresh rosemary
1 tbsp maple syrup or honey,
   or more if you like
salt and pepper

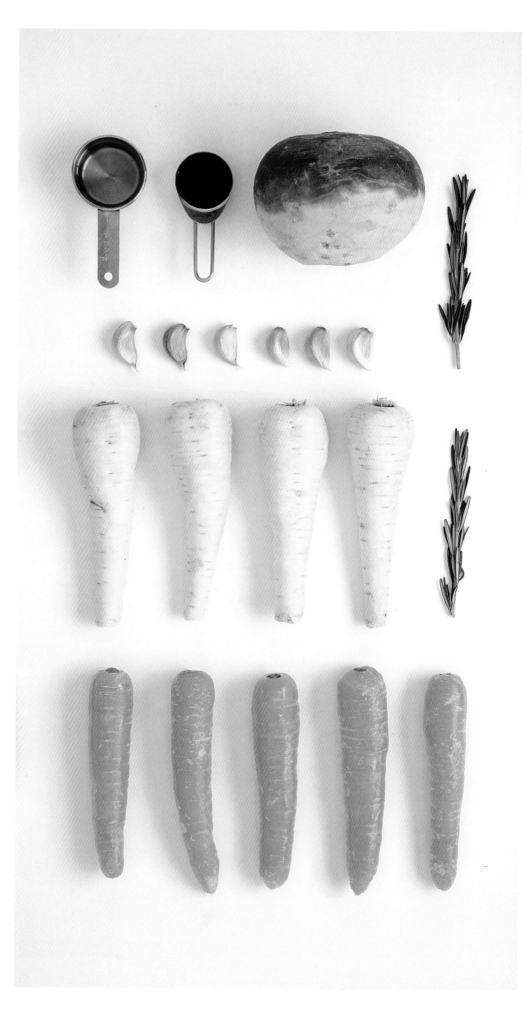

1

Preheat the oven to 425°F. Peel the rutabaga, but simply scrub the parsnips and carrots, leaving the skins on. Cut all of the root vegetables into large pieces, all about 1¼ inches across. Put into a large (ideally nonstick) roasting pan. It looks like a lot of vegetables, but they will shrink considerably in the oven as they roast. Spoon the olive oil over the top, then rub the oil all over the vegetables with your hands. Season with plenty of salt and pepper. Roast the vegetables for 30 minutes, until starting to soften.

2

Meanwhile, pick the needles from the rosemary sprigs, then chop them finely. Stir the garlic cloves (still in their skins) and rosemary into the vegetables. Return the pan to the oven, then roast for 20 more minutes, or until the vegetables are tender and golden around the edges. The garlic cloves will be tender within their papery skins.

3

While the vegetables are still sizzling hot, drizzle the maple syrup or honey over them. Serve the vegetables immediately, making sure everyone gets a garlic clove, ready to squeeze.

Buttered Green Vegetables

Preparation time: 5 minutes
Cooking time: 8–10 minutes
Serves 6

When you're completely new to
cooking, even the simplest of
vegetable dishes can be a mystery.
This handy recipe will go with almost
anything, and can easily be adapted
to include other green vegetables.

---

1 head broccoli

3 leeks

2 tbsp butter, plus more
   to serve if desired

1 tsp olive oil

2¼ cups frozen baby peas
   (petits pois)

salt and pepper

1

2

1
Bring a pan of water to a boil, then season with salt. Meanwhile, pull or chop the broccoli into florets, cutting any larger ones in half. Slice the leeks into rings about ¼ inch thick, and rinse them well.

2
Heat the butter and oil in a frying pan, then add the leeks. Cook for 5 minutes over medium heat, stirring occasionally, until just softened.

3
Meanwhile, put the broccoli into the boiling water. Return to a boil, then cook for 2 minutes. Add the peas, then return to a boil again. The broccoli will be just tender and the peas sweet and bright. Drain well in a colander. Add the peas and broccoli to the frying pan, then toss well with the softened leeks. Season with salt and pepper, then add another pat of butter to serve, if you like.

3

Apple Pie

Preparation time: 35 minutes, plus
45 minutes for chilling and standing
Cooking time: 40 minutes
Serves 8

Nothing says America like a big,
beautiful apple pie. Add a handful
of blackberries to the filling if you
like, and be sure to enjoy it with big
scoops of ice cream or dollops of
whipped cream.

1 tbsp flour, plus extra for rolling out
2 quantities basic pie crust (see
    page 242), or 12 (14-oz) packages
    store-bought pie dough
1 organic lemon
3¼ lb apples, such as Granny Smith,
    Rome, Jonagold or Golden
    Delicious
⅓ cup fine sugar, plus 1 tbsp
1 tsp ground cinnamon
1 large egg
ice cream or whipped cream (see
    page 338), to serve (optional)

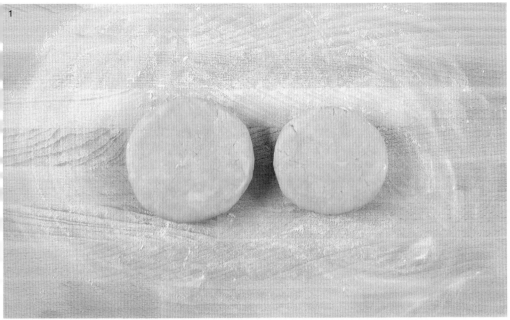

1
Working on a floured surface, shape the dough into 2 discs, one slightly larger than the other. Wrap them in plastic wrap, then chill in the refrigerator for 30 minutes, or until firm but not hard. If using ready-made pastry, leave the blocks as they are.

2
Meanwhile, squeeze the juice from the lemon into a large pan. Peel and core the apples, then cut into very chunky slices, around 1 inch thick. As you chop each apple, put the pieces into the pan and toss with the lemon juice. The lemon juice will keep the apple from turning brown.

3

Cook the apples gently in the pan over low heat for 5 minutes, or until the slices are just starting to soften and looking juicy at the bottom of the pan. Drain the apples, if necessary, in a colander, discarding the liquid, then put them in a bowl and gently stir in 1/3 cup sugar, 1 tablespoon flour, and the cinnamon. Let cool.

4

Flour the work surface and a rolling pin. Using the rolling pin, press shallow ridges evenly across the larger piece of dough, then rotate it by a quarter turn. Repeat this until the dough is about 1/2 inch thick. This will help the dough to stretch without becoming tough.

5

Have ready a 9-inch pie pan. It should have a lip so that the dough has something to stick to. Now roll out the dough. Push the rolling pin in one direction only, turning the dough by a quarter turn every few rolls, until it is less than 1/4 inch thick. Using the rolling pin to help, lift the dough over the plate.

6

If you have made your own
dough, use the leftover white from
the egg that you separated earlier.
If you have used store-bought
pie crusts, separate the egg now
(see page 243) and reserve the
white. Beat the white a little with
a fork. Dip a pastry brush into the
egg white, then brush lightly around
the lip of the pie crust. It will help
the top and bottom pieces stick
together.

7

Put the apples in the dough-lined
dish, forming a small mound.

8

Roll out the second piece of dough
as described in steps 4 and 5, until
it is large enough to cover the top
of the pie. Gently drape the dough
over the top of the apples, then
press it down at the edges to seal.

9

Trim the edges using a pair of scissors or a sharp knife, then slash the pastry over the apples a few times, so that steam can escape while the apples cook.

10

If you're feeling creative, press the edges of the pastry together with your thumbs to make a ridged pattern. Cut a few leaves from the excess dough. Stick them onto the pie with a little of the egg white.

11

Brush the top of the pie evenly with a thin layer of egg white, then sprinkle with the remaining 1 tablespoon sugar. Chill for 15 minutes (or up to 1 day). Preheat the oven to 375°F.

12

Place the pie on a baking sheet, then place in the oven to bake for 40 minutes, or until the pastry is deep golden all over. Let stand for at least 30 minutes before slicing, to allow the juices and apples to settle and the crust to firm a little. Serve warm or cold with whipped cream or ice cream.

HOW TO WHIP CREAM
Choose heavy or whipping cream and make sure that both the cream and the bowl are cold. Start whipping with hand-held electric beaters on medium-low speed, adding a little confectioners' sugar if you like. Whip until the cream just starts to hold its shape in soft peaks, then turn off the beaters immediately—it's important not to over-whip it.

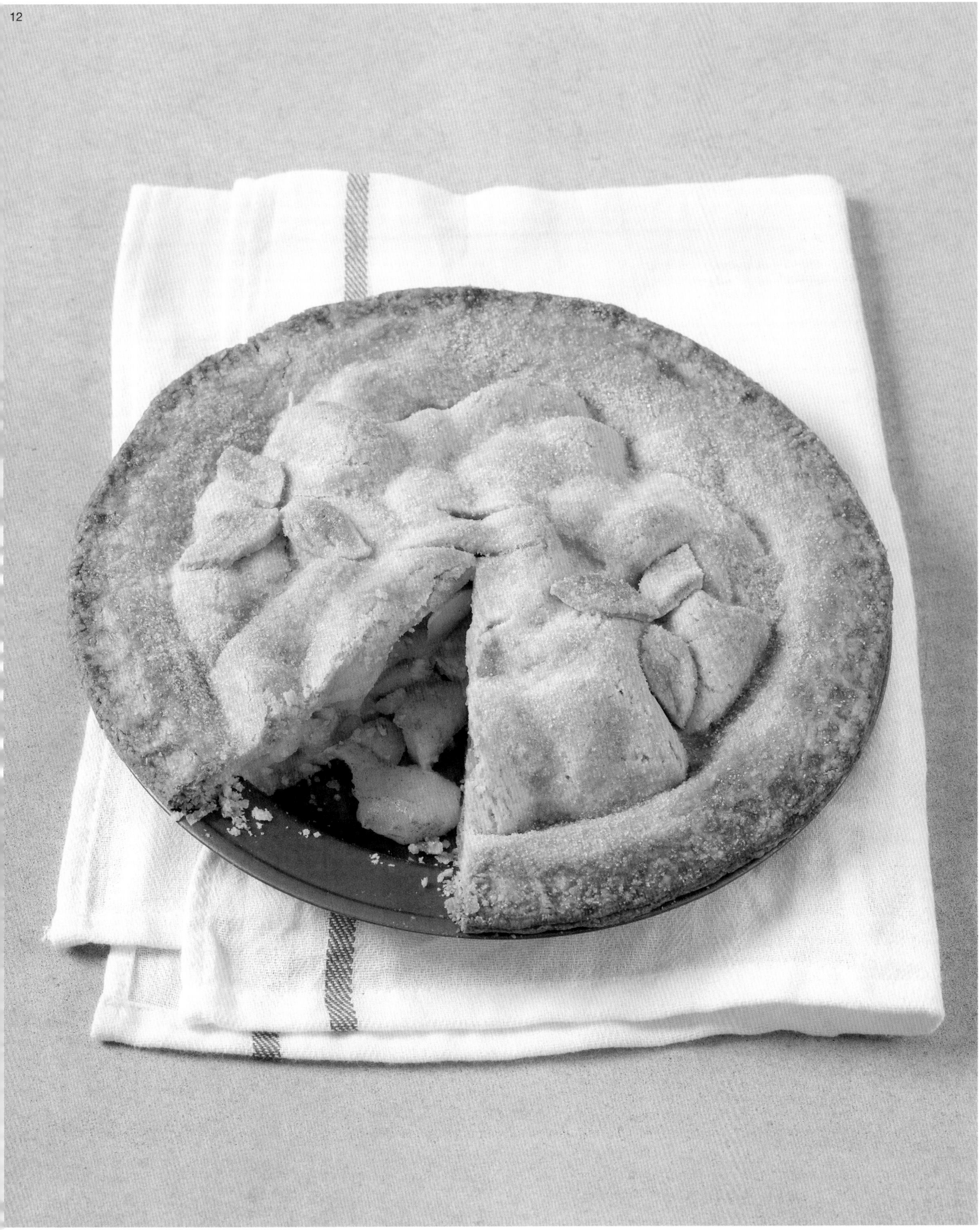

Chocolate Pots

Preparation time: 10 minutes,
plus 10 minutes for standing
and 3 hours for chilling
Cooking time: 5 minutes
Serves 6

These silky-smooth custards are
great for entertaining and they're
quick to make too. For a bitter-sweet
edge, make sure that the chocolate
is a good-quality bar containing
70 percent cocoa solids. They're
delicious served with sweet biscotti.

---

7 oz dark chocolate, preferably
  70% cocoa
2 tbsp unsalted butter
3 tbsp freshly made very strong
  coffee (or 1 heaping tsp coffee
  granules mixed with 3 tbsp
  boiling water)
1¼ cups heavy cream,
  plus extra to serve (optional)
2 large eggs
biscotti, to serve (optional)

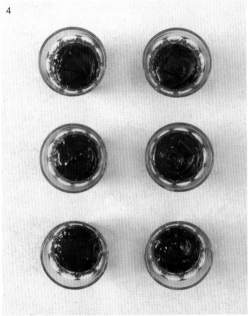

1

Break the chocolate into pieces, then put it into a large heatproof bowl. Dot the butter over the chocolate and add the coffee.

2

Pour the cream into a small pan, then put it over medium heat until small bubbles appear around the edge of the pan and it is starting to steam. Watch the pan carefully, as cream can quickly boil over. Pour the hot cream over the chocolate, then let stand for 10 minutes. Meanwhile, separate the eggs and beat the yolks together with a fork.

SEPARATING EGGS
Gently crack the shell of one egg against the side of a small bowl, then slowly pull the shell apart as cleanly as you can along the crack, pouring the yolk into one side. Gently transfer the yolk from one half of the shell to the other until all of the white has drained away into the bowl. Place the yolk into a separate bowl.

3

Stir the cream and chocolate together until smooth and even. Beat the yolks into the chocolate mixture.

4

Use a large spoon to spoon the mixture into 6 small cups or glasses. Chill in the refrigerator for at least 3 hours, or until chilled and just set. The pots can be made 1 day ahead and kept in the refrigerator. Remove 1 hour before serving to let them soften a little.

5

Pour a little cream over the chocolate pots, if desired, then serve, accompanied by biscotti, if desired.

Key Lime Pie

Preparation time: 30 minutes,
plus at least 4 hours for chilling
Cooking time: 20 minutes
Serves 8–10

With its delicious citrus bite, sweet
cream topping, and irresistibly
crumbly ginger crust, one slice of
this pie just isn't going to be enough.
It's a perfect pudding for a dinner
party—it seems impressive but it's
actually very simple.

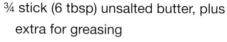

¾ stick (6 tbsp) unsalted butter, plus
   extra for greasing
11 oz ginger snaps
8 limes or 14–16 key limes (you'll
   need enough to yield ½ cup juice)
2 large eggs
1 (14-oz) can sweetened
   condensed milk
2 cups whipping cream
1 tbsp confectioners' sugar

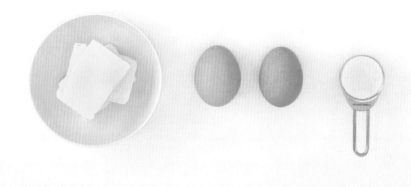

1

Use a little butter to grease the base and sides of a fluted 9-inch loose-bottom tart pan or pie dish, then line it with a circle of parchment paper. Preheat the oven to 350°F. Heat a small pan over medium heat. Add the butter and let it melt. Break the ginger snaps into the bowl of a food processor, then process them to fine crumbs. Alternatively, put them into a large plastic food-storage bag, squeeze out the air, then seal the top. Use a rolling pin to crush the ginger snaps into fine crumbs.

2

Turn the processor on, then drizzle the butter onto the crumbs. If you crushed the ginger snaps in a bag, transfer them to a bowl and stir in the melted butter. When ready, the crumbs will look like wet sand.

3

Transfer the buttery crumbs into the pan and smooth them out over the base and up the sides of the pan using the back of a spoon, pressing them down firmly in an even layer.

4

Put the pan onto a baking sheet, then bake for 10–15 minutes, or until the crust has turned a dark, golden brown.

5

Meanwhile, make the filling. Finely grate the zest from the limes, saving a little for decoration later if you like. Then squeeze their juice: you'll need about ½ cup for a really tangy pie. Beat the juice, zest, eggs, condensed milk, and 1 cup of the cream together.

6

Pour the filling into the prepared shell. Bake the pie for 20 minutes, or until the filling is set around the outside, but still jiggles in the middle. Cool completely, then chill for at least 4 hours, or ideally overnight. If wrapped well, the pie will keep chilled for up to 2 days at this point. Simply top with cream when ready to serve.

7

Using a balloon whisk or a hand-held electric mixer, whip the rest of the cream with the confectioners' sugar until it just holds its shape in loose folds.

8

Remove the pie from the pan, if you like. Transfer the pie onto a serving plate, then spread the whipped cream over the filling, swirling it a little as you go.

9

Sprinkle with the rest of the lime zest, then serve.

Lemon & Poppy Seed Drizzle Cake

Preparation time: 20 minutes
Cooking time: 45 minutes
Cuts into 8 slices

If you haven't baked a cake before, start here. Zingy and light, this delicious loaf cake will be better than anything you can buy and it takes no time to put together. A drenching of lemon syrup gives the cake its characteristic crust, and will keep it moist for several days if stored in an airtight container.

1½ sticks (¾ cup) soft unsalted
   butter, plus extra for greasing
2 organic lemons
scant 1 cup fine sugar, plus
   4 tbsp for the glaze
3 large eggs
1 tsp vanilla extract
scant 2 cups self-rising flour
1 tsp baking powder
¼ tsp kosher salt
3 tbsp milk
2 tsp poppy seeds

1
Preheat oven to 350°F. Rub a
little butter over the inside of 9 x 5
x 3-inch nonstick loaf pan, then
line it with a strip of parchment
paper, leaving some overhang at
either end.

2
Finely grate the zest from the
lemons, then squeeze the juice. Set
the zest and juice aside separately.

3

Put the butter, sugar, eggs, vanilla, flour, baking powder, salt, and milk into a large mixing bowl. Use a hand-held electric mixer or a stand mixer to beat the ingredients to a thick, creamy batter. This should only take about 30 seconds. It's important not to let the mixture stand around too long once the wet ingredients have been mixed with the dry.

4

Add the poppy seeds and half the lemon zest to the batter, then stir. Pour the mixture into the lined pan, using a spatula to scrape the bowl clean. Lightly smooth the surface of the batter a little.

5

Bake for 45 minutes, or until golden, risen, and springy to the touch. To test if the loaf is cooked, insert a skewer or toothpick into the middle. It should come out dry. If there are traces of batter on the skewer, return the loaf to the oven for another 10 minutes and test it again. Let the loaf cool in its pan.

While the loaf is still just warm, combine the lemon juice, leftover zest and remaining sugar, then spoon this evenly over the loaf. Leave to cool completely. The lemon and sugar will harden to a zingy, crystallized crust.

6

Cut into slices to serve.

Lemon Tart

Preparation time: 50 minutes
plus 40 minutes for chilling,
plus cooling
Cooking time: 45 minutes
Serves 12

A homemade lemon tart, with its
zingy citrus custard and crisp, sweet
pastry, is the ultimate dessert
to follow any meal. If you'd rather
use store-bought dough, follow the
recipe from step 5.

For the basic sweet pie dough
1 large egg
1¼ cups all-purpose flour, plus
    extra for rolling
¼ tsp kosher salt
¾ stick (6 tbsp) cold unsalted butter
2 tbsp fine sugar

For the filling
4 organic lemons
1¼ cups heavy cream
6 large eggs
1 cup fine sugar
confectioners' sugar, for dusting
    (optional)

1

First, make the dough. Separate the egg yolk and white. Add 2 tablespoons ice-cold water to the yolk, then beat together with a fork. Put the flour into the bowl of a food processor and add the salt. Cut the butter into cubes, then scatter them over the flour.

SEPARATING AN EGG
Gently crack the shell against the side of a small bowl. Gently pull the shell apart as cleanly as possible along the crack, pouring the yolk into one half of the shell. Gently transfer the yolk from one half of the shell to the other until all of the white drains away into a bowl below. Drop the yolk into another small bowl.

2

Process the butter and flour for about 10 seconds until the mixture resembles very fine bread crumbs and no flecks of butter remain. Now pulse in the sugar.

3

Add the yolk mixture to the processor, then pulse in one-second bursts until the dough comes together in big clumps.

DON'T HAVE A FOOD PROCESSOR?
It will take a little longer, but you can make the pastry by hand by rubbing the butter into the flour with your fingertips and thumbs, until the mixture looks like fine bread crumbs. If the mixture starts to feel warm, chill it for 5 minutes, then continue. Pour the egg over the flour and butter mixture as evenly as you can, then use a round-bladed knife to mix to a dough. The key to tender, crumbly pastry is not to overwork it and to keep it cool.

4

Place the dough on a work surface, then shape it into a flat disc. Wrap in plastic wrap, then chill for at least 30 minutes, until firm but not rock hard.

5

Dust the work surface and a rolling pin with flour. Have ready a 9-inch round, loose-bottom tart pan. Using the rolling pin, press shallow ridges evenly across the pastry, then rotate it by a quarter turn. Repeat this until the pastry is about ½ inch thick. This will help the pastry to stretch without becoming tough.

6

Now roll out the pastry. Push the rolling pin in one direction only, turning the pastry by a quarter turn every few rolls, until it is less than ¼ inch thick. Using the rolling pin to help, lift the pastry over the pan.

7
Ease the pastry gently into the pan, then press it in gently into the edge of the pan using your knuckles.

8
Trim the top of the pastry with a pair of scissors so that it overhangs the pan by ½ inch. Place the pan on a baking sheet, then chill in the freezer for 10 minutes (or longer in the refrigerator if you have time), until the pastry feels firm. Set a rack in the middle of the oven, then preheat it to 350°F.

9
Tear a sheet of parchment paper large enough to completely cover the pan and overhanging pastry. Crumple the paper, then unfold it to cover the pastry. Cover the paper with a layer of pie weights, mounding them up a little at the edges. Bake the pastry shell, still on its baking sheet, for 20 minutes.

ANY HOLES?
If your pastry has ripped or small holes have appeared, don't panic. Dampen a little of the leftover pastry and stick it down well to seal the gap.

PIE WEIGHTS
Pie weights are actually small ceramic balls used to weigh down the pastry as it cooks, which helps it to keep its shape. Ceramic weights are the most effective, but dried chickpeas or rice can be used instead. Cool and reuse them for baking only.

10

Remove the paper and the weights. The pastry should be pale but dry and turning gold at the edges. Return it to the oven and bake for another 15 minutes, or until the base is starting to brown. Remove from the oven. Turn the oven down to 300°F.

11

While the pastry is baking, make the filling. Finely grate the zest from the lemons and set aside. Squeeze the juice from the lemons into a bowl. Using a fork, beat the cream, eggs and sugar into the juice. Strain the mixture through a fine-mesh sieve into a large measuring cup. Stir in the lemon zest.

12

Pull the oven rack out a little and put the tart onto it, still on its baking sheet. Pour the lemon filling into the pastry shell, then gently slide the rack and tart back into the oven. Bake for 45 minutes, or until the filling is set and barely jiggles in the center when the baking sheet is shaken.

13

Let the tart cool completely. Trim any overhanging edges now, using a serrated knife, if desired. To remove the tart from the pan, set it on a can or mug, and press down gently on the edge of the pan until it slips down, leaving the tart on its base. Ease the tart onto a plate or board and serve, dusted with confectioners' sugar if you like.

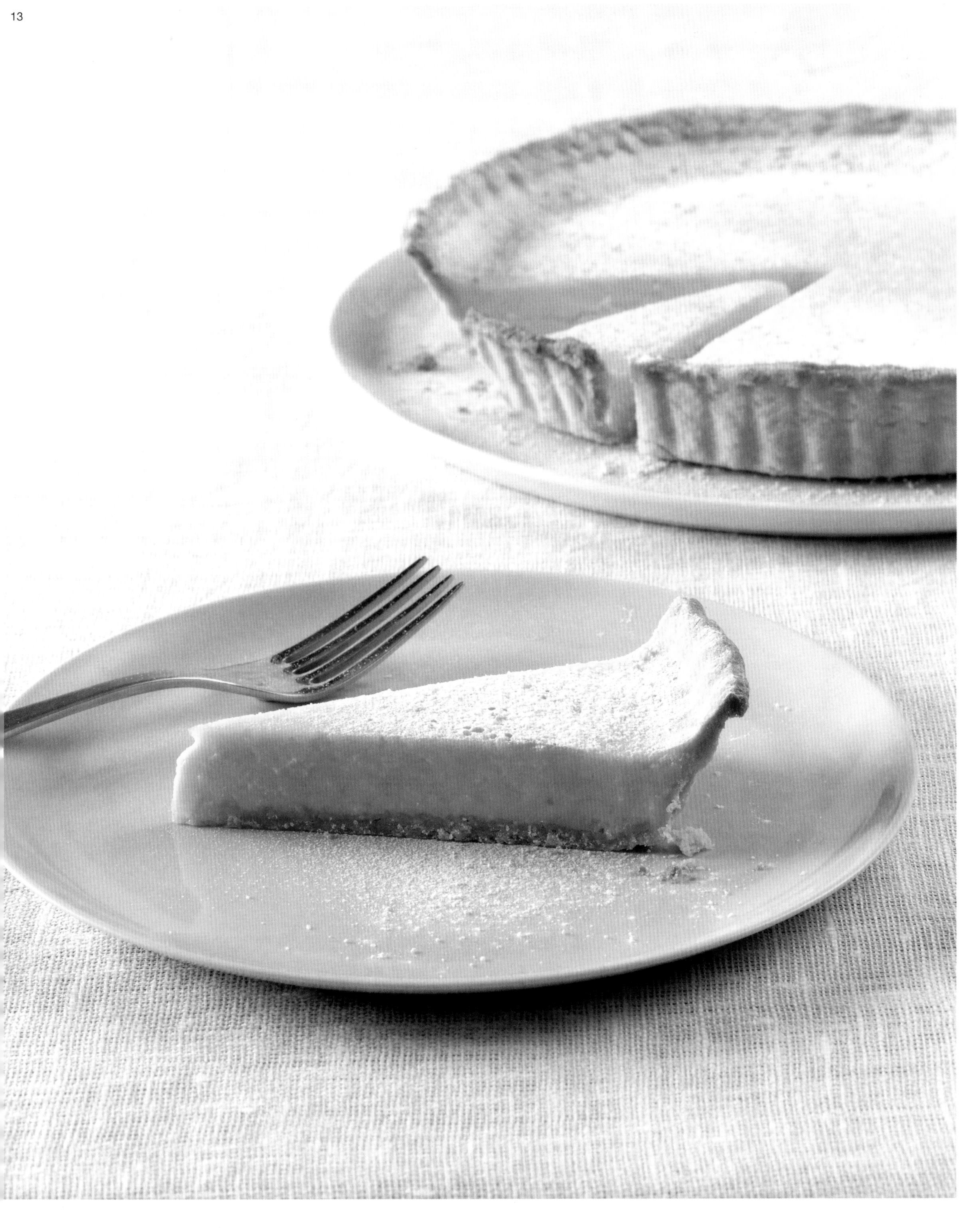

Sticky Toffee Pudding

Preparation time: 20 minutes
Cooking time: about 30 minutes
Serves 6–8

Dates are the magic ingredient in this classic British pudding, adding moisture and sweetness from within. In the US, this would be called a cake, but in Britain the term "pudding" rules. The sticky sauce is devilishly good over simple vanilla ice cream, too.

---

5 oz pitted dates

2¾ sticks (1⅓ cups) softened
    unsalted butter, plus a little extra
    for greasing

1½ cups light brown sugar

4 large eggs

1 tsp vanilla extract

¾ tsp pumpkin pie spice (or a
    combination of ground cinnamon,
    cloves and nutmeg)

1¼ cups self-rising flour

¼ tsp kosher salt

⅔ cup heavy cream

heavy cream or ice cream,
    to serve (optional)

1

Put the dates into a small saucepan, then pour in enough water to just cover them. Place the pan over a medium heat, then bring to a boil. Cook for 5 minutes, or until the dates are very soft.

2

Drain the dates, discarding the cooking liquid. Put them into the bowl of a food processor, then process until smooth. Cool for a few minutes. Meanwhile, preheat the oven to 350°F and rub a little butter around the inside of a 8 × 12-inch baking pan or small roasting pan, then line it with parchment paper.

TO LINE THE PAN
Cut a rectangle of parchment paper a little larger than the pan, then make a 4-inch cut in each corner toward the center. Press the parchment into the pan, letting the paper from the snipped corners overlap and seal together.

3

Add 1¾ sticks butter and a scant 1 cup brown sugar to the food processor with the dates. Process until smooth.

4

Add the eggs, vanilla, pumpkin pie spices, flour, and salt, then process everything together to a smooth batter. Spoon the batter into the prepared pan. Bake the pudding for 30 minutes, until golden and well risen.

5

Meanwhile, make the sticky toffee sauce. Put the remaining sugar and butter into a pan. Add the ⅔ cup cream, then cook very gently for 5 minutes, or until the grains of sugar have dissolved.

6

Turn up the heat and simmer for 10 minutes, until it has thickened and darkened to a silky toffee sauce.

7

When the pudding has baked for 30 minutes, insert a skewer into the middle. If the skewer comes out dry, it is ready. If there are any traces of batter on the skewer, bake 5 minutes longer before checking again.

8

Cut the cake into squares then transfer to plates. Spoon some of the sauce over the top and serve, with a little more cream or ice cream if desired (see page 360).

TO MAKE INDIVIDUAL PUDDINGS
Butter 8 small molds, then fill with the pudding batter. Sit the molds in a roasting pan, then bake for 20 minutes, or until risen and golden. Check with a skewer, as in step 7.

8

Vanilla Ice Cream with Chocolate Sauce

Preparation time: 20 minutes,
plus 10 hours for freezing
Cooking time: 5 minutes
Serves 6

Making your own ice cream is so
satisfying, especially when the result
is as creamy and delicious as
this. There's no need for any special
equipment, but if you do have an
ice cream machine that needs to
be frozen before use, make sure it's
in the freezer for at least 12 hours
before you start.

1 vanilla bean

6 large eggs

½ cup fine sugar

1 tsp cornstarch

1 cup heavy cream

1 cup whole milk

1 tsp instant coffee granules

3½ oz dark chocolate, preferably
   70% cocoa

4 tbsp unsalted butter

1 tbsp corn syrup

1

Scrape the seeds from the vanilla bean. To do this, slit the vanilla bean along its length with a small sharp knife. Run the knife along the length of the halved pod. The seeds will mound up along the edge of the knife. Repeat with the other half.

2

Separate the eggs (see page 243), then put the yolks, sugar, vanilla seeds, and cornstarch together in a large bowl.

3

Using a balloon whisk or hand-held electric mixer, whisk the ingredients together until pale and creamy.

4

Put the cream and milk into a medium pan and bring just to a boil.

5

Pour the hot cream and milk over the egg mixture in a thin and steady stream, whisking as you go, to make a custard.

6

Give the pan a quick wash, then put the custard back into the pan and set it over very low heat. Heat the custard slowly, whisking all the time, until it starts to steam and has thickened slightly. It's ready when you can draw a line through the custard on the back of a wooden spoon.

LUMPS IN THE CUSTARD?
Don't worry, this just means that the egg has overcooked a little. Pass the mixture quickly through a fine-mesh sieve and into a cold bowl. This will stop it cooking immediately. Move on to step 7.

7

Pour the custard into a large freezerproof container, such as an old ice cream tub or a baking dish, ideally sitting inside another dish filled with ice, and let it cool completely.

8

Once the custard has cooled, freeze the mixture for 4 hours. Whisk the custard at least once an hour to break up any crystals that form at the side of the container. Once the custard looks thick and smooth and more like ice cream, freeze it, without stirring, for at least another 6 hours, or ideally overnight. Well wrapped, the ice cream will last for up to 2 weeks in the freezer.

IF YOU HAVE AN ICE CREAM MACHINE
Start the machine churning, then pour in the cooled custard. Let it churn until thick and smooth (normally about 30 minutes), then spoon into a freezerproof container and freeze completely.

9

To make the chocolate sauce, first half-fill a pan with water and bring it to a simmer. Dissolve the coffee in 5 tablespoons boiling water. Break the chocolate into squares, then put them into a large heatproof bowl. Add the coffee, butter, and corn syrup.

10

Set the bowl over the pan, making sure that the bottom of the bowl doesn't touch the water, then heat for 5 minutes, stirring occasionally, until melted and smooth.

11

Let the ice cream soften at room temperature for 10 minutes before scooping into balls and serving with the warm chocolate sauce.

Butterscotch
Banana Bread

Preparation time: 20 minutes,
plus cooling time
Cooking time: 1 hour 10 minutes
Makes 8 slices

This moist, filling quick bread is the
perfect use for overripe bananas
in the fruit bowl. The frosting isn't
essential, as the bread is also
delicious sliced and buttered, but
its smooth toffee taste is worth
trying at least once.

3 medium-size very ripe bananas,
　total peeled weight about 11 oz
1½ sticks (¾ cup) softened unsalted
　butter, plus extra for greasing
¾ cup light brown sugar
½ tsp kosher salt
3 large eggs
1 tsp vanilla extract
¾ cup all-purpose flour
1 cup whole wheat flour
2 tsp baking powder
½ cup chopped walnuts,
　plus extra to decorate, if you like
½ cup cream cheese

1
Rub a little butter over the inside of a 9 × 5-inch (2-pound) loaf pan, then line it with a strip of parchment paper, leaving some overhang at either end. Preheat oven to 325°F.

2
Peel the bananas and put them in a bowl. Use a fork to mash the fruit to a lumpy pulp.

3
Put the bananas, 1 stick of the butter, ½ cup of the sugar, the salt, eggs, vanilla, flours, and baking powder into a large bowl, then use a hand-held electric mixer or a stand mixer to beat the ingredients until smooth.

WHOLE WHEAT FLOUR
This will add a little extra nuttiness and texture to your loaf. If you'd rather use all white flour, that's fine.

4
Stir in the walnuts, then pour the mixture into the prepared pan.

5

Bake the loaf for 1 hour 10 minutes, or until risen, golden, and springy to the touch. Test if the cake is done by inserting a skewer or toothpick into the middle of the thickest part. If it comes out clean, the cake is ready. If there are traces of batter on the skewer, bake for 10 minutes longer, then check again. Cool in the pan for 10 minutes, then transfer the loaf to a cooling rack and leave to cool completely.

6

While it cools, make the frosting. Put the remaining butter and sugar into a pan with 1 tablespoon water. Place it over very gentle heat, then wait until the sugar has dissolved. Let the mixture simmer for 3 minutes, until it looks like a silky caramel. Remove from the heat and let cool.

7

Put the cream cheese into a bowl, then add the caramel, gradually beating or whisking them together to make a smooth, coffee-colored frosting.

8

Spread the frosting over the cake, then top with a few more nuts to decorate, if you like.

Chocolate Brownies

Preparation time: 30 minutes,
plus cooling time
Cooking time: 20–25 minutes
Makes about 20 pieces

There isn't a time or occasion
when a brownie doesn't do the job.
Coffee time? Brownie. Dessert?
Warm brownie with ice cream.
Birthday? A stack of brownies!
These are just how you want them:
very, very chocolaty and with
a slight crust that gives way to a
deliciously dense filling.

1½ sticks (¾ cup) unsalted butter

7 oz dark chocolate, preferably
   70% cocoa

½ cup macadamia nuts (optional)

4 large eggs

1⅓ cups fine sugar

1 tsp vanilla extract

1 cup all-purpose flour

⅓ cup unsweetened cocoa powder

½ tsp kosher salt

1

2

4

1
Rub a little butter all over the inside of a 9 × 13-inch baking pan, then line the pan with parchment paper. Heat the oven to 350°F.

TO LINE THE PAN
Cut a rectangle of parchment paper a little larger than the pan, then make a 4-inch cut in each corner toward the center. Press the parchment into the pan, letting the paper from the snipped corners overlap and seal together.

2
Melt the remaining butter in a small pan over medium heat. Break the chocolate into squares, then put them into the hot butter and take the pan off the heat. Let the chocolate melt for 5 minutes, then stir until smooth. Let cool for 10 minutes.

3
Meanwhile, roughly chop the macadamia nuts, if using. Put the eggs, sugar, and vanilla into a large bowl, then beat with a hand-held electric mixer or a stand mixer for 1 minute, until thick and pale.

4
Pour the cooled chocolate mixture into the eggs, then stir until thoroughly combined. A spatula is useful here, as it will get right into the edge of the pan.

5

Sift in the flour and cocoa powder and add the salt.

ADDING SALT TO CHOCOLATE
Salt and chocolate is a match made in heaven, as each one emphasizes the flavor of the other. Only add a little, though.

6

Using a spatula or large spoon, fold the dry ingredients into the egg and chocolate mixture until no dry flour remains. Pour the mixture into the prepared pan, then scatter the macadamias over the top.

HOW TO FOLD
Using a large spoon or spatula and a figure-eight movement, cut through the flour and chocolate, lifting the mixture up and over. Repeat until the mixture is thoroughly combined. This helps preserve the air in the mixture.

7

Bake for 20–25 minutes, until just risen around the edge and with a papery crust. You should be able to detect a slight wobble in the center beneath the crust—check after 18 minutes by gently shaking the pan. Let cool completely in the pan.

8

To remove from the pan, hold diagonally opposite corners of the paper lining, then lift the brownie out and onto a cutting board. Use a large knife to cut the brownie into squares, making them as big or as small as you like.

CHANGE THE FLAVOR
Instead of finishing the brownies with crunchy macadamia nuts, you could try using chopped white chocolate, walnuts, or even mini marshmallows.

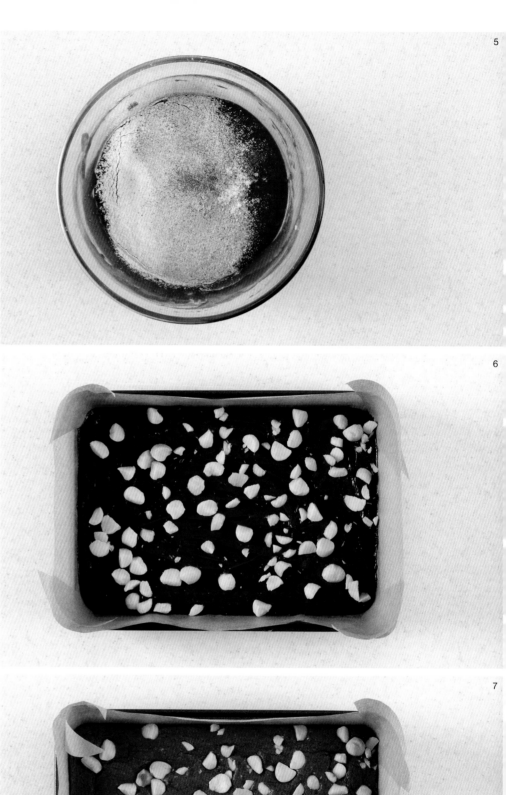

Panna Cotta with Raspberries

Preparation time: 30 minutes,
plus 30 minutes for cooling and
6 hours for chilling
Serves 6

Italian for "cooked cream,"
a panna cotta with fresh vanilla and
raspberries makes for an impressive
but simple dinner party dessert.

---

5 sheets leaf gelatin

1 vanilla bean

1¾ cups heavy cream

1¾ cups whole milk

⅓ cup fine sugar

1¼ cups (7 oz) raspberries

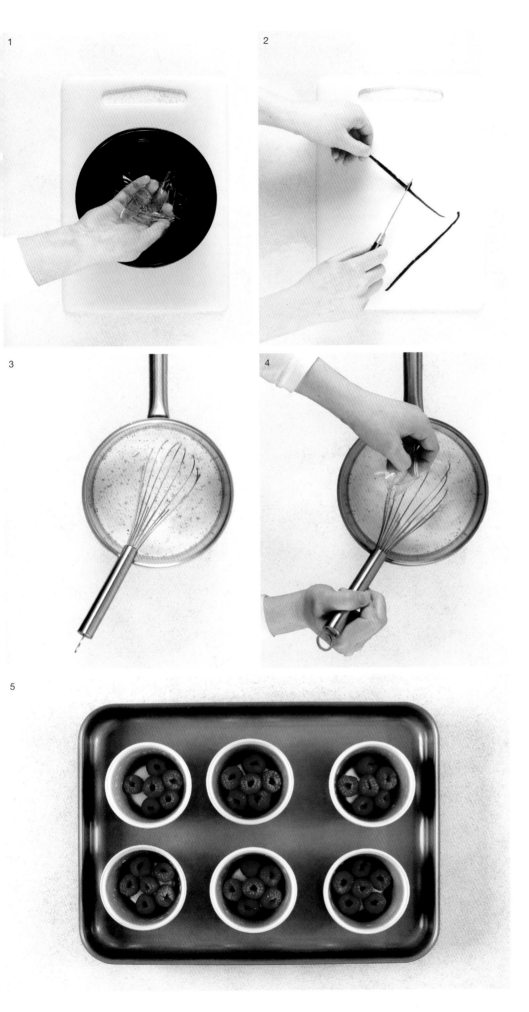

1
Fill a small bowl with cold water, then add the gelatin sheets. After a couple of minutes' soaking, they will have softened and feel like jelly.

GRANULATED GELATIN
If you can't find leaf gelatin, use a ¼-ounce packet or 3 teaspoons unflavored granulated gelatin instead. Follow the package instructions, or sprinkle it evenly over 2 tablespoons cold water in a heatproof bowl. Let stand until the gelatin has swollen and absorbed the liquid. Heat a shallow pan of water, then sit the bowl with the gelatin over the pan, keeping the heat low. The gelatin will melt. Don't overheat it, as this can impair the flavor of the dish. Once melted, stir into the warm cream in step 4.

2
Scrape the seeds from the vanilla bean. To do this, slit the vanilla bean along its length with a small sharp knife to make 2 halves. Run the knife along the cut edge of the bean halves to remove the seeds.

3
Put the vanilla seeds, cream, and milk into a pan, then whisk to separate any clumps of vanilla. Put the pan over medium heat and bring to a boil. Remove from the heat. Stir the sugar into the mixture, then let it dissolve for 2 minutes.

4
Remove the gelatin from the water and squeeze it out. Stir the gelatin into the still-warm cream until it has completely dissolved.

5
Set 6 (½-cup) molds, ramekins, or tea cups on a baking sheet or in a roasting pan. Wet the insides of the molds with cold water, then shake out the excess. Put 6 raspberries in the bottom of each mold.

6

Transfer the cream mixture to a small pitcher or pourable measuring cup, then pour it carefully into the molds. Let cool for 30 minutes.

7

Cover the surface of each panna cotta with a piece of plastic wrap— this will prevent a skin forming on the top—then chill them in the refrigerator for at least 6 hours, or ideally overnight.

8

When ready to eat, remove the plastic wrap. If you have used molds, loosen the edge of each panna cotta and turn them on to plates. If you have used ramekins or teacups, serve as they are. Scatter a few raspberries around the panna cotta to decorate.

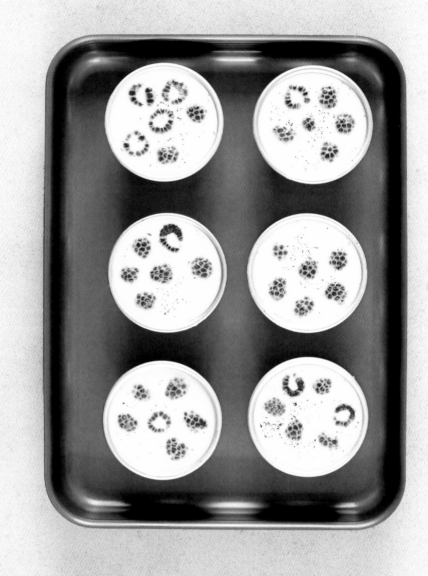

Frosted Cupcakes

Preparation time: 25 minutes,
plus cooling time
Cooking time: 20 minutes
Makes 12 deep cupcakes

Friends will think you've been to
a bakery when you bring out a
plate of these. Adding yogurt and
ground almonds to a simple vanilla
cake batter makes for light-yet-moist
cupcakes that keep really well.
If you're cooking them for children
and want to avoid nuts altogether,
substitute the same amount of
all-purpose flour for the almonds.

2½ sticks (1¼ cups) unsalted butter

⅔ cup plain yogurt (yogurt with
   live cultures is best, as it has a
   milder flavor)

4 large eggs

1½ tsp vanilla extract

scant 1 cup fine sugar

1¼ cups self-rising flour

1 tsp baking powder

1 cup almond meal

¼ tsp kosher salt

2¼ cups confectioners' sugar

1 tbsp milk

a few drops food coloring

sprinkles, to decorate

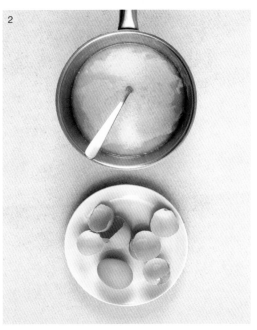

1
Line a 12-cup muffin pan with large paper cases. Preheat the oven to 375°F. Melt 1½ sticks of the butter in a medium pan, then remove from the heat and let cool for 5 minutes.

2
Stir the yogurt into the butter, then crack in the eggs. Add 1 teaspoon vanilla, then beat everything with a fork until smooth.

3
Put the fine sugar, flour, baking powder, almond meal, and salt into a large bowl, then mix them together. Make a well in the middle of the mixture, ready to add the liquid ingredients.

4
Have a spatula ready. Pour the yogurt and butter mixture into the dry ingredients, then quickly mix together with the spatula until you have a soft batter with no lumps of dry flour or almond meal left. Don't over-stir the mixture, however.

5
Spoon the batter into the cases until they are quite full. The simplest way to get the batter from the bowl is to hold the bowl over the pan while you spoon it in, as the batter is quite runny.

6
Bake the cupcakes for 18–20 minutes, until they are evenly risen, golden brown, and smell sweet. Let them cool for 5 minutes in the pan.

7

Transfer the cupcakes from the pan to a wire cooling rack and let them cool completely. Make the frosting while the cupcakes cool. Sift the confectioners' sugar. Put the remaining butter into a large mixing bowl. Using hand-held electric beaters, beat it until very smooth and soft. Add the confectioners' sugar, remaining vanilla, and a little of the milk. Stir the sugar slowly into the butter at first to prevent it from puffing up in a cloud. Once the sugar is mostly mixed into the butter, start the mixer and beat for a minute or two, until the frosting is very light and fluffy. Add a drop more milk if the mixture seems stiff, but be sparing, as a little goes a long way.

8

Color the frosting, if desired. Use a tiny drop of the color at first, stir well, then add more if needed.

9

Spoon some of the frosting onto each cupcake, then swirl and spread it out with either the back of the teaspoon or a small frosting spatula.

10

Decorate the cupcakes with sprinkles to serve, if you like.

GETTING AHEAD
If you're making the cupcakes ahead, the unfrosted cakes will keep well in an airtight container for 3 days, or freeze for up to a month. The frosting can be made up to 3 days ahead and kept covered in the refrigerator. Bring it back to room temperature and beat it until creamy before frosting the cupcakes.

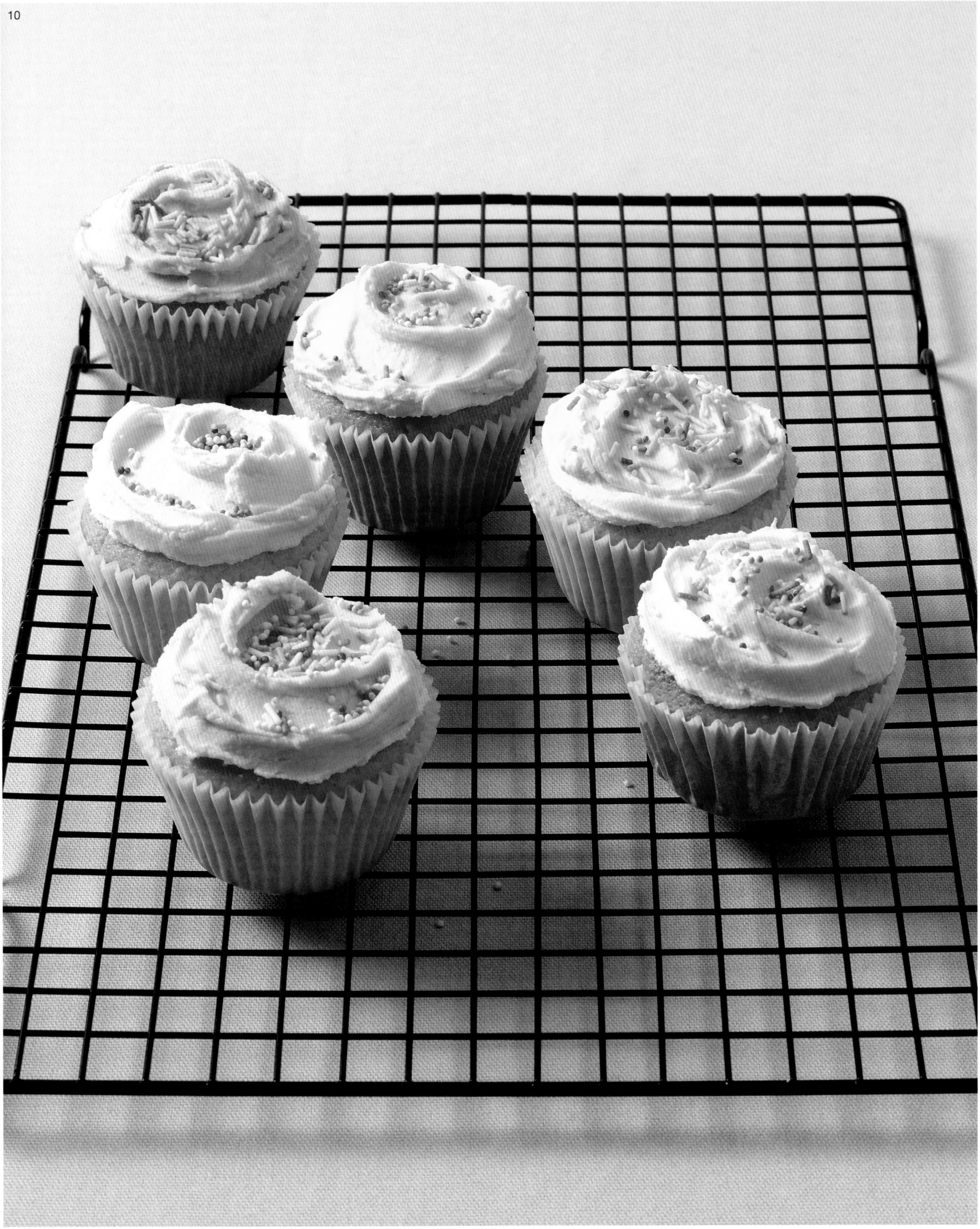

Pecan Cranberry Pie

Preparation time: 50 minutes, plus
chilling and cooling time
Cooking time: 30–35 minutes
Cuts into 10 slices

Studded with jewel-like cranberries,
this is a pecan pie fit for any
celebration. The cranberries offer a
welcome tanginess to contrast with
the sticky maple and sugar filling.

2 cups pecans

all-purpose flour, for dusting

1 quantity basic pie dough (see
    page 350), or 1 (14-oz) package
    store-bought pie dough

4 tbsp unsalted butter

½ cup maple syrup

1 cup dark brown sugar

1 tbsp brandy (optional)

¾ cup dried cranberries

salt

1 tsp vanilla extract

2 large eggs

crème fraîche or whipped cream
    (see page 338), to serve (optional)

1
Preheat the oven to 350°F. Put the pecans onto a baking sheet and roast them for 10 minutes, until golden and fragrant. Let cool.

2
Dust the work surface and a rolling pin with flour. Have ready a 9-inch round, loose-bottom tart pan. Using the rolling pin, press shallow ridges evenly across the dough, then rotate it by a quarter turn. Repeat this until the dough is about ½ inch thick. This will help the dough to stretch without becoming tough.

3
Now roll out the dough. Push the rolling pin in one direction only, turning the dough by a quarter turn every few rolls, until it's less than ¼ inch thick. Using the rolling pin to help, lift the dough over the pan.

4
Ease the dough into the pan, then press it gently into the edge of the pan, using your knuckles.

5
Trim the edges of the dough with a pair of scissors so that it just overhangs the pan. Set on a baking sheet, then chill in the freezer for 10 minutes (or longer in the refrigerator if you have time), until the pastry feels firm. Make sure there's a rack set in the middle of the oven.

6

Tear a sheet of parchment paper large enough to completely cover the pan and overhanging dough. Crumple the paper, then unfold it to cover the pastry. Cover the paper with a layer of pie weights (see page 246), mounding them up a little at the edges.

7

Bake the pie crust, still on its baking sheet, for 15 minutes. Remove the paper and the weights. The crust should be pale but feel dry and be turning gold at the edges. Return to the oven and cook for another 10 minutes, or until the base is starting to brown. Remove from the oven.

8

While the crust cooks, make the filling. Reserve 12 of the pecans, then chop the rest fairly finely.

9

Melt the butter in a pan, then remove from the heat and stir in the maple syrup, brown sugar, brandy (if using), cranberries, a pinch of salt, the vanilla extract and eggs. Beat with a fork until evenly combined. Stir in the chopped pecans.

10

Pour the mixture into the baked pastry shell, then scatter the remaining whole pecans over the top. Carefully transfer the pie, still on its sheet, to the oven.

11

Bake for 30–35 minutes, or until the filling is set around the outside and has just the slightest wobble in the middle. If the pastry seems to be going too brown, simply cover with foil. Cool the pie completely before taking it out of the pan (see page 354). Serve in thin slices, with crème fraîche or whipped cream, if you like.

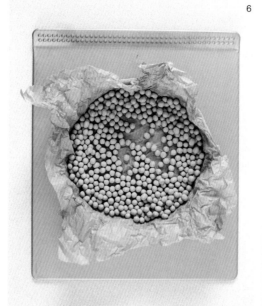

Peach & Raspberry Cobbler

Preparation time: 25 minutes
Cooking time: 40 minutes
Serves 6

Adding almond meal and a handful of raspberries to a classic cobbler lifts the flavor of the peaches and lightens the topping. Choose yellow-fleshed peaches if you can, for the best color. The peaches can be replaced by nectarines, then by plums a little later in the year.

6 just-ripe peaches

1 cup (6 oz) fresh or defrosted
   frozen raspberries

2 tbsp cornstarch

scant ½ cup fine sugar, plus 3 tbsp

¾ stick (6 tbsp) cold unsalted butter,
   plus 1 tbsp

1 cup self-rising flour

½ cup almond meal

½ tsp baking powder

¼ tsp kosher salt

⅔ cup buttermilk or milk

1 tsp vanilla extract

1 handful sliced almonds

whipped cream (see page 338) or
   ice cream, to serve (optional)

1

Preheat the oven to 375°F. Cut the peaches in half, then remove the pits with the tip of the knife. Cut each half into 3 or 4 slices. If they cling to the pit, just cut the flesh into chunks around it. Put the peaches and half of the raspberries into a large baking dish or shallow casserole. Sprinkle the cornstarch and 3 tablespoons sugar over the top, then splash on 6 tablespoons water. Stir well. Cut the 1 tablespoon butter into small pieces, then dot it over the fruit.

2

Make the cobbler topping. Put the flour into a large bowl, then stir in the almond meal, baking powder, and salt. Sometimes the almonds can be a little clumpy, so break them up with your fingers if necessary. Cut the butter into cubes and add to the dry ingredients.

3

Rub the ingredients together. To do this, use both hands to lift the butter and flour from the bowl, then gently pass them between your fingers and thumbs as they drop back into the bowl. As you repeat the action, the butter will gradually work its way into the flour. Lift the mixture as you go, to keep it cool and aerated.

4

The mixture should resemble fine bread crumbs.

5

Stir in the scant ½ cup sugar, then the buttermilk or milk, and the vanilla. Stop stirring as soon as a lumpy batter comes together. Gently mix in the remaining raspberries, being careful not to squash them too much.

6

Spoon the cobbler topping over the peaches, then sprinkle the sliced almonds over the top. The topping will spread out as it cooks, so don't worry about smoothing the surface.

7

Place the cobbler on a baking sheet and bake for 40–50 minutes, or until the topping is golden brown and well risen, and the fruit is saucy and bubbling beneath.

8

Serve hot, warm, or cold with whipped cream or ice cream.

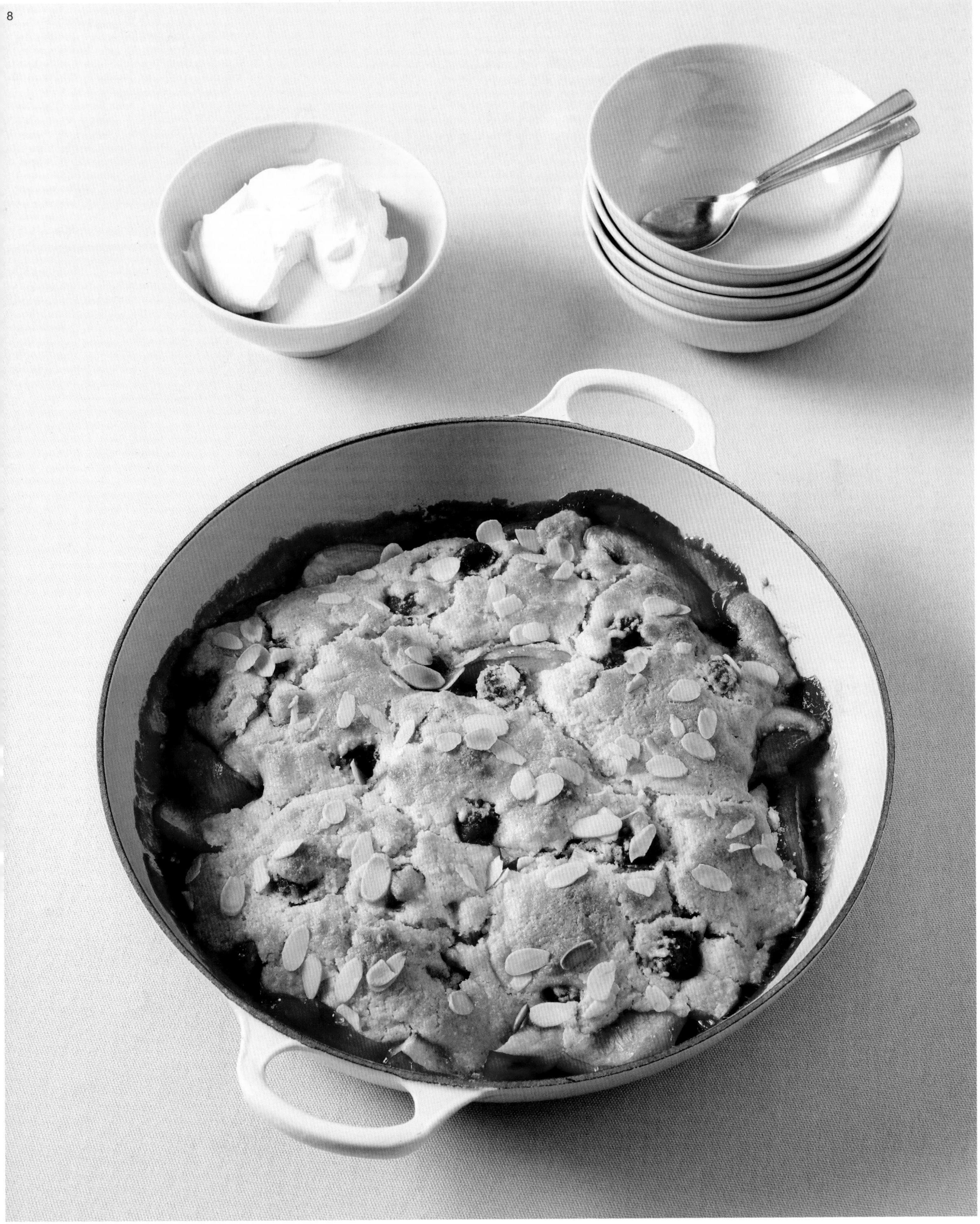

Chocolate Truffle Cake

Preparation time: 30 minutes,
plus cooling time
Cooking time: 35–40 minutes
Cuts into 12 slices

Dark and rich, this cake makes
a show-stopping birthday cake.
It's perfect for dessert too. As with
most baked goods, this dessert
is best eaten the day it's made, but
the sponge cakes can be made
up to two days ahead and kept in
an airtight container if needed.

---

2 sticks (1 cup) unsalted butter,
   softened, plus extra for greasing

11 oz dark chocolate, preferably
   70% cocoa

1½ cups fine sugar (organic,
   if you can find it)

4 large eggs

1¼ cups buttermilk or mild plain
   yogurt

1 tsp vanilla extract

1¼ cups self-rising flour

½ tsp kosher salt

½ tsp baking powder

¼ cup unsweetened cocoa powder

½ cup confectioners' sugar

⅔ cup sour cream or heavy cream

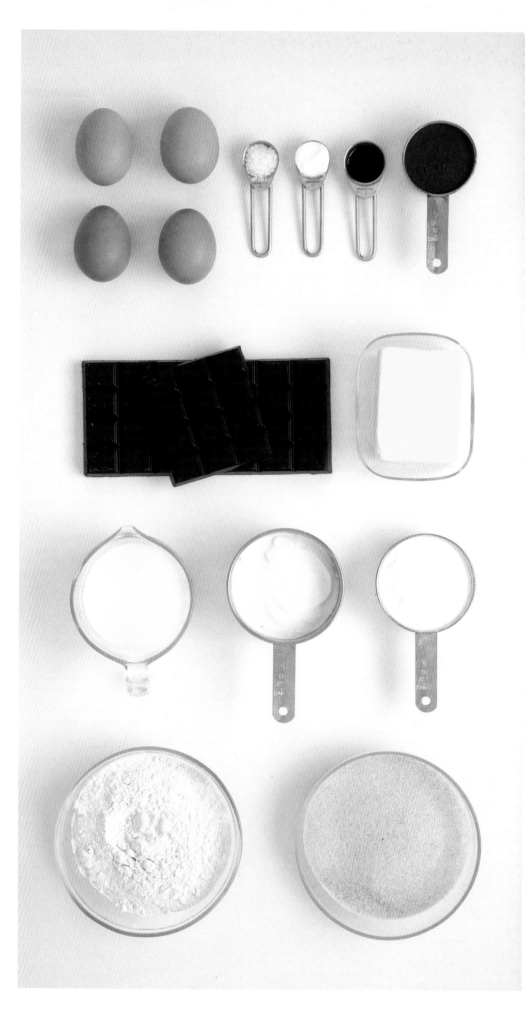

1
Rub a little butter around the insides of two 8-inch cake pans, then line the bases with circles of parchment paper. Preheat the oven to 325°F.

2
Break the chocolate into squares and put 7 ounces of it into a heatproof bowl. Place the bowl over a pan of barely simmering water, making sure that the bowl doesn't touch the water, then let the chocolate melt for about 5 minutes, stirring once or twice, until smooth throughout. Alternatively, microwave on high for 1½ minutes.

3
Put 1¾ sticks of the butter into a large bowl, then add the fine sugar, eggs, buttermilk or yogurt, vanilla, flour, salt, and baking powder. Sift in the cocoa powder.

4
Using a hand-held electric mixer or a stand mixer, beat everything together until smooth and creamy. Don't worry if you have any lumps of butter—they'll melt when the warm chocolate goes in next.

5
Pour in the melted chocolate and beat again briefly until the mixture is smooth throughout.

6

Divide the batter equally between the prepared cake pans. Keep the chocolaty bowl—you'll need it to make the frosting later.

7

Bake the cakes, both on the same rack, for 35–40 minutes, or until risen, and a skewer or toothpick inserted into the middle of the cake comes out clean. Cool the cakes in their pans for 10 minutes, then turn them out onto a wire cooling rack to cool completely. The tops of the cakes are quite delicate, so take care as you do this.

8

While the cakes cool, make the frosting. Put the rest of the chocolate and butter into the chocolaty bowl and melt together over a pan of simmering water, as in step 2.

FROSTING THE SIDES?
If you'd like to frost the sides as well as the tops of the cakes, you'll need to increase the frosting quantities to 5 oz chocolate, 3 tablespoons butter, ¾ cup confectioners' sugar and 1 cup sour or heavy cream.

9

Remove the bowl from the heat, sift in the confectioners' sugar and pour in the cream. Stir to a smooth liquid mixture. It will thicken up to a spreading consistency as it cools. Do not chill it.

10

Use a frosting spatula to spread half of the chocolate frosting over one of the sponge cakes.

11

Transfer to a serving plate. Top with the second cake, then spread the rest of the frosting over the top. Cut into slices to serve.

Apple & Blackberry Crumble with Custard

Preparation time: 30 minutes
Cooking time: 45–50 minutes
Serves 6

A comforting crumble is the
perfect dessert to have up your
sleeve for autumn and winter nights.
The custard recipe will give you
a smooth, slightly thickened custard,
which would be wonderful with
the Apple Pie (page 334) too.

2½ lb apples, such as Granny Smith,
  Rome, Jonagold or Golden
  Delicious
1 cup blackberries
¾ cup plus 2 tbsp fine sugar
½ lemon
1¼ cups plus 2 tbsp all-purpose
  flour
¼ tsp kosher salt
1¼ sticks (⅔ cup) cold unsalted
  butter
1 whole nutmeg, for grating
½ cup rolled oats
2 tsp cornstarch
1¼ cups milk
1¼ cups heavy cream
1 vanilla bean or 1 tsp vanilla extract
4 large eggs

1
Preheat the oven to 375°F. Peel and core the apples, then cut them into thick slices. Spread out the apples and blackberries in a large baking dish, then stir in 1 tablespoon of the sugar and the juice from the lemon half.

2
Next, make the crumble topping. Put the flour and salt into a large bowl. Cut the butter into cubes and add it to the bowl.

3
Rub the ingredients together. To do this, use both hands to lift the butter and flour from the bowl, then gently pass them between your fingers and thumbs as they drop back into the bowl. As you repeat the action, the butter will gradually work its way into the flour. Lift the mixture up as you go, to keep it cool and aerated.

4
The mixture should resemble fine bread crumbs. Finely grate 1 teaspoon nutmeg, then stir this, ½ cup of the remaining sugar and the oats into the crumble mixture.

5
Spread the crumble mixture over the fruit in an even layer. Bake the crumble for 45–50 minutes, until the topping is dark golden and crisp and the fruit is bubbling underneath.

6

Meanwhile, make the custard. Mix the cornstarch with 2 tablespoons of the milk in a small bowl, stirring until smooth. Pour this mixture into a medium nonstick saucepan along with the rest of the milk, the heavy cream, the remaining 1½ oz sugar, and the seeds from the vanilla bean (see page 361), or the vanilla extract. Separate the eggs (see page 243) and add the yolks to the pan.

7

Whisk together, then put the pan over low-to-medium heat. Bring the custard just to the boil, whisking all the time, until it thickens. It's ready when you can draw a line through the custard on the back of a wooden spoon.

LUMPS IN THE CUSTARD?
Adding a little cornstarch stabilizes and thickens the custard, making it much more difficult to overcook the egg in the mix. If the custard does look lumpy at any point, don't worry, just pass it through a fine-mesh sieve.

8

Serve the crumble warm, with the custard passed separately for each guest to pour over the crumble.

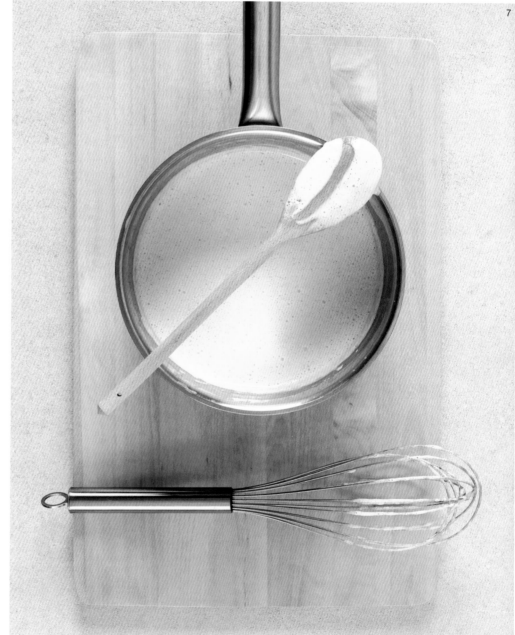

Baked Vanilla Cheesecake with Berries

Preparation time: 40 minutes, plus chilling time
Cooking time: 50 minutes
Serves 10

This smooth, light, and creamy cheesecake is a great crowd-pleaser. The berries can easily be swapped for your favorite fresh fruit, or poached plums (see page 32) would also work well. It's important that the ingredients are at room temperature, not chilled, before you start mixing.

1 stick (½ cup) unsalted butter, plus a little extra for greasing

9 oz tea biscuits or graham crackers

1 vanilla bean, or 1 tsp vanilla extract

1¾ lb cream cheese, at room temperature

1⅓ cups fine sugar

2 tbsp all-purpose flour

1 cup sour cream

4 large eggs

14 oz frozen berries, defrosted

1

Preheat the oven to 350°F. Rub a little butter all around the inside of a 9-inch round loose-bottom spring-form cake pan, then line the bottom with a circle of parchment paper cut to the same size as the base.

2

Put a small pan over medium heat. Add the butter and let it melt. Break the crackers into the bowl of a food processor, then process to fine crumbs. If you don't have a food processor, put the crackers into a large plastic food-storage bag, squeeze out the air, then seal the top. Use a rolling pin to crush the crackers into fine crumbs.

3

With the food processor on, drizzle the butter onto the crumbs until you have a damp, sandy-looking mix. If you crushed the crackers by hand, put them in a bowl and stir in the melted butter.

4

Transfer the buttery crumbs into the prepared pan. Smooth them out with the back of a spoon, pressing them down firmly in an even layer.

5

Put the pan on a baking sheet, then bake for 15–20 minutes, until the base has turned dark golden brown.

6

If using a vanilla bean, slit it along its length with a small sharp knife and scrape out the seeds from both halves. Put the cream cheese, 1 cup of the sugar, vanilla seeds or extract, flour, and half of the sour cream into a large bowl. Using a hand-held electric mixer or a stand mixer, beat until creamy and smooth.

7

Add the eggs one at a time, beating well after adding each egg, until smooth. Pour the mixture into the pan, then smooth the top with a spatula. Tap the pan once to bring any bubbles to the surface.

8

Bake for 10 minutes, then turn the oven temperature down to 275°F and cook for another 40 minutes. The cheesecake should be set, with a slight wobble in the center. Turn off the oven, then open the door a little and leave the cheesecake to cool on the oven rack. As it cools, the surface may crack across the middle, but this doesn't matter, as the top will be covered with sour cream later on.

9

For the berry topping, put the fruit into a saucepan with the remaining sugar. Heat gently for 3 minutes, or until the sugar has dissolved and the berries have collapsed slightly and released their juices.

10

Use a slotted spoon to scoop the fruit into a bowl, then turn up the heat under the pan and boil the juices for 2 minutes, or until slightly thickened and syrupy. Pour the sauce over the berries and let cool completely.

11

When the cheesecake is cool, chill it for at least 4 hours, or ideally overnight. To serve, run a frosting spatula around the edge of the pan, then unclip the sides and ease it off the base and onto a plate. You might find sliding a frosting spatula between the parchment paper and the base helpful. Otherwise, simply serve it straight from the base of the pan. Spread the remaining sour cream over the top. Slice and serve with the syrupy berries.

Chocolate Chip Cookies

Preparation time: 20 minutes
Cooking time: 12 minutes
Makes 18 cookies

If you like your cookies melt-in-the-mouth, slightly chewy, and full of chocolate bits, then this recipe is for you. The basic cookie dough is a good all-around one that you can adapt with lemon zest, raisins, chopped nuts, or whatever you like. For salty-sweet peanut butter cookies and a sustaining chewy oatmeal version, see the variations on the main recipe (see page 402).

5 oz chocolate (made up of
    milk, dark, or white, or a mixture
    of all three), or good-quality
    chocolate chips
1¾ sticks (scant 1 cup) unsalted
    butter, softened
¾ cup fine sugar
1 large egg
1 tsp vanilla extract
2 cups self-rising flour
¼ tsp kosher salt

1
Roughly chop the chocolate on a cutting board.

2
Line 2 baking sheets with parchment paper and preheat the oven to 400°F. Put the butter and sugar into a large bowl. Use a hand-held electric mixer or stand mixer to beat the butter and sugar together until pale and creamy. Separate the egg (see page 243), then add the yolk and the vanilla extract to the bowl.

3
Beat the contents of the bowl together for a few seconds until combined. Add the flour and salt, then stir in with a spatula or wooden spoon. The mixture will seem quite stiff, but that's fine.

4

Using a spatula, fold in the chopped chocolate. Be careful not to overwork the mixture.

BAKE THEM RIGHT AWAY
Once you've added the flour to the creamed mixture, bake the cookies sooner rather than later. The same applies to making cakes or pancakes that contain self-rising flour, baking powder, or baking soda.

5

Roll the cookie dough into 18 or 20 rough walnut-sized balls and put them onto the prepared baking sheets. The dough spreads a lot as it cooks, so make sure the cookies will have enough room. Save some for another batch if necessary.

6

Bake the cookies for 10–12 minutes, or until golden at the edges and pale in the middle. The cookies will rise in the oven, but then fall as they cool. Leave the cookies on their baking sheets until firm, then transfer to wire racks to cool completely, using a spatula. If you couldn't fit all the cookies onto the 2 baking sheets, finish baking the rest of the batch now. Keep the cookies in an airtight container for up to 3 days.

PEANUT BUTTER COOKIES
Stir 2 tablespoons crunchy peanut butter and ½ cup roasted peanuts into the dough instead of the chocolate.

GINGER OATMEAL COOKIES
Stir in 2 teaspoons ground ginger, 2 finely chopped balls of preserved ginger from a jar and a generous ½ cup rolled oats, instead of the chocolate.

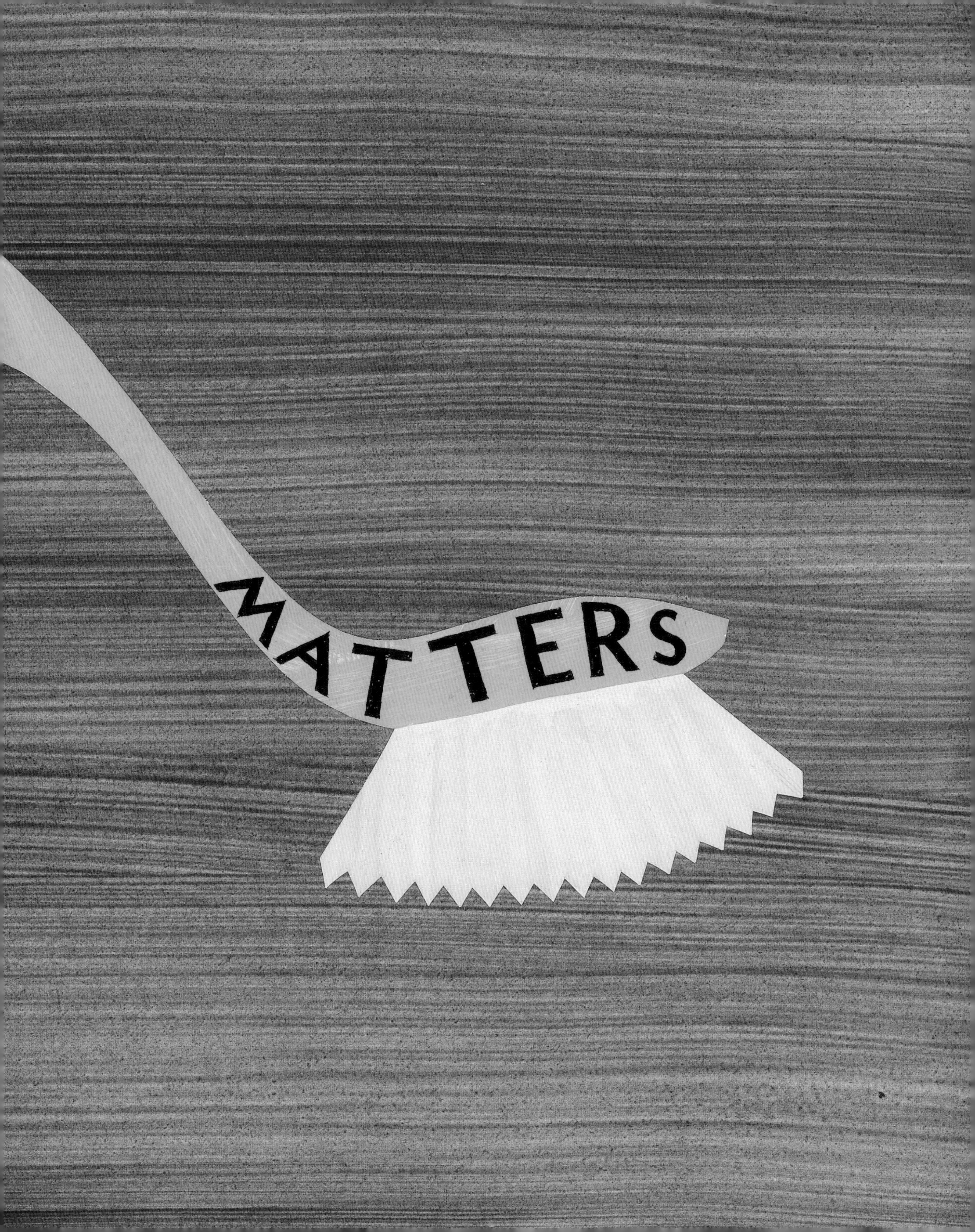
MATTERS

Planning a Menu

Although most of the dishes in this book were conceived as stand-alone favorites, many of them go together to make delicious meals. Planning a good menu is all about getting a balance between courses and, for a stress-free experience, keeping the meal as simple and straightforward as possible, bearing in mind the amount of time you have available. Here you'll find menu ideas for all sorts of occasions, designed to help you take the dilemma out of dinner.

There's no need to stick to the formal format of starter, main course, and dessert—the way we eat has changed, and for a casual get-together, your friends and family will be more than impressed if you bring out something homemade to share. Plating up in the kitchen suits some recipes and can be nice at dinner parties, but bringing food to the table in its cooking dish is by far my favorite way to serve. That way, everyone can dig in and the conversation can flow.

Bistro dinner
Coq au Vin (Chicken with Red Wine) (page 230)
Dauphinoise Potatoes (page 320)
Lemon Tart (page 350)

Beginners' Christmas or Thanksgiving dinner
Crab Cakes with Herb Vinaigrette (page 292)
Roast Chicken (or Turkey) with Lemon & Leek Stuffing (page 252)
Maple-Roast Winter Vegetables (page 328)
Buttered Green Vegetables (page 330)
Pecan Cranberry Pie (page 380)

Brunch party
Berry Smoothie (page 18)
Fruit-Filled Morning Muffins (page 40)
Scrambled Egg & Smoked Salmon Bagels (page 28)
Butterscotch Banana Bread (page 364)

Chinese made easy
Crispy Duck Pancakes (page 196)
Chicken Stir-Fry (page 112)
Serve Jasmine tea & fortune cookies for dessert

Comforting winter dinner
Beef Stew with Herb Dumplings (page 288)
Mashed Potatoes (page 136)
Buttered Green Vegetables (page 330)
Apple Pie (page 334)

Curry night
Chicken Tikka & Raita Lettuce Cups (page 204)
Butternut Curry with Spinach & Cashews (page 104)
Lamb & Potato Curry with Fragrant Rice (page 238)
Vanilla Ice Cream (page 360) *with fresh mangoes*

Diner dinner
Cheeseburgers (page 108)
Chunky Oven Fries (page 312)
Coleslaw (page 316)
Vanilla Ice Cream with Chocolate Sauce (page 360)

Halloween party
Sticky Barbecue Ribs (page 174)
Chicken Noodle Soup (page 72) or Tomato & Thyme Soup (page 76)
Shepherd's Pie (page 258) or Macaroni & Cheese (page 128)
Chocolate Brownies (page 368)

Kids' birthday party
Pizza Margherita (page 188)
Frosted Cupcakes (page 376)

Lunch al fresco
Lamb Chops with Tomato & Mint Salad (page 132)
Ratatouille (page 310)
Baked Vanilla Cheesecake with Berries (page 396)

Make-ahead Italian dinner
Antipasti with Tapenade & Tomato
 Bruschetta (page 180)
Lasagne (page 248)
Garlic Bread (page 318)
Green Salad with Vinaigrette (page 308)

Mediterranean dinner party
Antipasti with Tapenade & Tomato
 Bruschetta (page 180)
Mediterranean Fish Stew (page 270)
Green Salad with Vinaigrette (page 308)

Roast dinners
Roast Pork with Caramelized Apples
 (page 296)
Maple-Roast Winter Vegetables
 (page 328)
Buttered Green Vegetables (page 330)
Sticky Toffee Pudding (page 356)

Roast Lamb & Rosemary Potatoes
 (page 266)
Glazed Carrots (page 314)
Baked Vanilla Cheesecake with Berries
 (page 396)

Roast Beef & Yorkshire Puddings
 (page 274)
Roast Potatoes (page 306)
Buttered Green Vegetables (page 330)
Apple & Blackberry Crumble with
 Custard (page 392)

Roast Chicken with Lemon & Leek
 Stuffing (page 252)
Dauphinoise Potatoes (page 320)
Dressed Green Beans (page 324)
Peach & Raspberry Cobbler (page 384)

Quick weeknight supper
Stuffed Chicken with Tomatoes &
 Arugula (page 154)
Chocolate Brownies (page 368)

Steak dinner
Steak with Garlic Butter (page 158)
Chunky Oven Fries (page 312)
Green Salad with Vinaigrette (page 308)

Vanilla Ice Cream with Chocolate
 Sauce (page 360)

Spanish dinner
Patatas Bravas (Spicy Potatoes) with
 Chorizo (page 208)
Paella (page 280)
Vanilla Ice Cream (page 360) *with a rich,
sweet sherry such as Pedro Ximenez*

Dinner with friends
Pan-Fried Fish with Salsa Verde
 (page 222)
Panna Cotta with Raspberries (page 372)

Tex-Mex dinner
Cheese Nachos with Guacamole
 (page 184)
Chilli Con Carne with Baked
 Potatoes (page 218)
Key Lime Pie (page 342)

Thai-style banquet
Chicken Satay with Peanut Sauce
 (page 200)
Thai Curry with Beef (page 168)
Shrimp Pad Thai (page 164)
*Serve mango sorbet or fresh
 pineapple for dessert*

Vegetarian Moroccan-style banquet
Hummus with Marinated Olives
 & Pitas (page 192)
Vegetable Tagine with Chermoula
 and Couscous (page 300)
Lemon & Poppy Seed Drizzle Cake
 (page 346) *with fresh figs & yogurt*

Vegetarian supper
Mushroom Risotto (page 116)
Green Salad with Vinaigrette (page 308)
Chocolate Pots (page 340)

Watching the game
Chicken Wings & Blue Cheese
 Dip (page 176)
Stuffed Potato Skins with Sour Cream
 Dip (page 212)
Cheese Nachos with Guacamole
 (page 184)

Al dente
The point during cooking at which pasta or vegetables are tender, but retain some bite.

Baking potatoes
General term used for non-waxy potatoes. Also known as starchy potatoes. Used widely for roasting, mashing, and making fries. Always bring these to a boil from cold, rather than adding them to boiling water as with a new potato.

Balsamic vinegar
A dark, slightly sweet-tasting vinegar. The traditional and most expensive is produced from the grape juice of either Modena or Reggio Emilia in Italy, then aged and mellowed in a series of wooden casks.

Batter
A mixture of flour, beaten egg, and a liquid, such as milk or water, that is used to make pancakes and to coat food for deep-frying. Raw cake mixture is called cake batter.

Braise
To cook gently in a sealed pan with stock or thickened sauce.

Brown
To pan-fry ingredients in very hot fat in order to color the surface.

Casserole
A metal, ovenproof glass, or ceramic cooking dish with a lid. It is also the term for a dish prepared in such a container.

Caramelize
To cook until golden and a little sticky—the point at which the natural sugars in the food start to caramelize.

Chargrill
To cook in grill pan with ridges.

Coat
To cover a dish with a substance, such as a sauce.

Couscous
Fine semolina that has been rolled and coated with wheat flour. It is steamed and served with meat and fish stews on the North African coast and elsewhere in the Mediterranean.

Cream
To beat eggs or butter and sugar together with a whisk or wooden spoon until they become thick and pale in color.

Deglaze
To pour a liquid, such as wine, stock, or water, into the pan in which meat or vegetables have been fried or roasted to incorporate the sediment on the base of the pan into the sauce.

Drain
To remove the liquid from a food, usually completely, by tipping the food into a colander or sieve and letting all of the liquid pour away. Sometimes you will need to keep the cooking liquid; always check first.

Drizzle
To pour a little liquid over a surface.

Emulsify
To mix two substances together vigorously to form an even suspension. Whisking or shaking oil and vinegar together for a salad dressing, or adding butter to egg yolks for hollandaise sauce are good examples.

Fluff up
To loosen and separate the grains of rice or couscous once cooked, using the tines of a fork.

Fold
To mix food gently from the bottom of the bowl to the top, in an under-over motion that distributes ingredients without knocking out the air.

Glaze
To brush pastry or dough evenly with either milk, egg, or a mix of both, to give a shiny, golden appearance once baked. Can also apply to meats and vegetables coated in a shiny sauce.

Knead
To work a dough against a work surface with the palm of the hand until smooth.

Marinate
To place raw meat or other foods in an aromatic or acidic liquid to tenderize it before cooking, or to add extra flavor. Take care not to marinate for too long, as marinades can almost "cook" food, over-tenderizing it and affecting your end result. Marinate delicate fish for no more than a few hours. Meat and chicken can be left for up to 24 hours.

Overcrowd a pan
To leave very little space between pieces of food in a pan, whether frying or roasting. This will lead to the food sweating rather than browning or crisping up, giving an inferior result. If in doubt, spread it out.

Partially cover a pan
To leave the lid of a pan slightly askew, so as to let some steam escape. This helps a sauce to reduce, but not too much.

Poach
To cook gently in a liquid such as stock, water, milk, or sugar syrup.

Preheat
To set the oven or broiler to the desired temperature, and then leave it to become hot. Preheating times can vary drastically from oven to oven, so get to know yours.

Pulse in a food processor
To turn a food processor on and off in short sharp bursts of a second or so (many have pulse buttons for this purpose), to chop ingredients together without blending completely.

Purée
To reduce ingredients to a smooth paste in a food processor or blender. Also the name given to the paste itself.

Reduce
To boil or simmer a liquid to evaporate the water it contains, thereby concentrating the flavor and thickening it.

Resting
Allowing meat to sit out of the oven after roasting and before carving. As meat roasts, the muscle fibers contract, squeezing the juices towards the outer edges. During resting, the fibers relax, letting the juices redistribute within the meat, giving a more succulent result. Meat continues to cook during resting time, so always err on the side of caution with meat timings.

Return to a boil
To let a liquid come back to a full bubble once an ingredient has been added to it. Most timings start from this point.

Ricer
A potato ricer is rather like a giant garlic press – the potatoes are pressed through fine holes and only need a quick stir to come together as creamy mashed potatoes.

Rising
The process of increasing the volume of baked goods by adding rising agents such as yeast, baking powder, or baking soda.

Sauté
To cook food in a high-sided skillet or sauté pan with very little fat over high heat.

Seed
To remove the seeds from a fruit or vegetable, first cutting it in half then scraping out the seeds with a spoon or the tip of a knife.

Simmer
To cook slowly over gentle heat. A simmer is the point at which a liquid is about to boil, with just a few bubbles breaking the surface.

Slash
To make a diagonal cut in a piece of fish to prevent it from curling up during cooking, and to help it cook evenly.

Steam
To cook in a perforated container set over boiling water with a tight-fitting lid.

Stock
A flavored cooking liquid obtained by simmering beef, veal, or poultry bones with vegetables and herbs for 2–3 hours. Skim off the fat before use. For speed, a bouillon cube can be dissolved in hot water, and good liquid broth is also available in stores.

Stuff
To fill the inside of a piece of meat or a vegetable with stuffing.

Sustainably caught fish
Or "eco-friendly" fish, from stocks that are not under pressure from over-fishing. Caught by methods that do not negatively impact on the environment.

Syrupy
A term used in reference to sauces, whereby the sauce is thickened down by reduction, to a slightly thicker, and often shiny consistency.

Thicken
To add ingredients, such as flour or egg yolks, to make a sauce or soup thicker.

Well
A hole hollowed out of a mound of flour, into which liquids are added.

Whisk
To beat rapidly with a flexible tool to increase the volume and aerate ingredients such as egg whites and mayonnaise.

Zest
The thin outer layer of a citrus fruit, on top of the white pith. Usually finely grated.

Basic Preparations

These photographs show you what to aim for when you're doing the most common types of vegetable preparation.

Finely chopped carrot

Crushed garlic

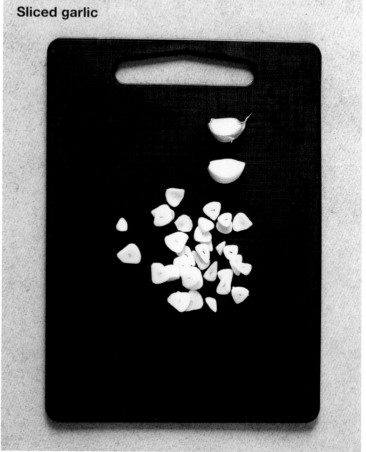

Sliced garlic

Finely chopped onion

Sliced onion

Roughly chopped onion (1)

Roughly chopped onion (2)

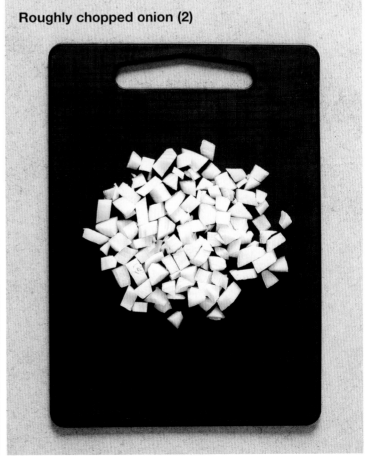

Seeded and finely sliced chile

Seeded and finely chopped chile

Roughly chopped herbs

Finely chopped herbs

Index

Author's Acknowledgements

This book has been a team effort, and I owe many people great thanks for their skill, love, support, hope, and vision. First up, Emilia Terragni, Laura Gladwin, Beth Underdown and the rest of the Phaidon team — you are a dedicated lot. Laura, thank you for opening the door. I'm full of admiration for your endless patience, encouragement, and determination to make this book what it is.

Huge thanks also to Angela Moore, for the beautiful photographs and for sharing your home with us for such a long time during the shoot. Together with Jennifer Wagner, Nico Schweizer, and Jeffrey Fisher, you have created something more lovely than I had ever imagined.

To my assistant food stylist Marisa Viola; you were a true wonder. I really valued your input, fantastic organization, and zen-like calm. (Marisa, together with Angela's assistants Pete, Julian and Bruce, created the ingredients shots, which look simple, but were a devil to achieve. Thank you all.)

A special note to Katy Greenwood, Susan Spaull, and Michelle Bolton King for recipe testing, plus Gem and Stu McBride for their enthusiastic tasting. Also thanks to Barney Desmazery, Sara Buenfeld, and the team past and present at *BBC Good Food* magazine, from whom I've learned so much.

Mum, Dad, family, and friends, thank you for your unerring belief and encouragement. And finally, most importantly, thank you to Ross. For everything.

Phaidon Press Inc
180 Varick Street
New York, NY 10014

www.phaidon.com

First published in 2010
© 2010 Phaidon Press Limited

ISBN 9 780 7148 5958 3
(US edition)

A CIP catalogue record for this book is available from the British Library.

Photographs by Angela Moore
Illustrations by Jeffrey Fisher
Designed by SML Office
Printed in China

NOTE ON THE RECIPES
Some recipes include raw or very lightly cooked eggs. These should be avoided by the elderly, infants, pregnant women, convalescents, and anyone with an impaired immune system.